France, Germany and the Western Alliance

FRANCE, GERMANY and the WESTERN ALLIANCE

A Study of Elite Attitudes on European Integration and World Politics

- **KARL W. DEUTSCH**
  Yale University

- **LEWIS J. EDINGER**
  Washington University

- **ROY C. MACRIDIS**
  Brandeis University

- **RICHARD L. MERRITT**
  Yale University

Charles Scribner's Sons NEW YORK

CONTENTS

v

PART III
A COMPARISON OF FRENCH AND GERMAN ELITES
IN THE EUROPEAN POLITICAL ENVIRONMENT
  Karl W. Deutsch

Preface

In early 1964 we undertook a study of foreign policy problems in the Western European political environment. The substance of this research dealt primarily with three problems:

1. Are nation-states and national policies in Western Europe, and particularly in France and West Germany, being superseded by supranational loyalties, interests and institutions? If so, in what respects and to what extent?

2. What are the implications of recent nationalistic and/or supranational currents in European politics, and again particularly in France and West Germany, on the acceptability of various proposals for arms control or disarmament which are relevant to the interests and policies of the United States?

3. What are the most important trends in the domestic politics of France and West Germany, especially with respect to the continued stability of these governments? How do these trends impinge upon French and West German foreign policy?

The principal investigators, including political scientists from ten American universities, interviewed members of elite groupings in France and West Germany during the summer of 1964, analyzed data from Western European public opinion surveys conducted between 1954 and 1963 and initiated systematic content analyses of the postwar press in four countries.

This volume presents our findings on the attitudes of French and West German elites toward such issues as European integration and arms control. It consists of four major parts: (1) the presentation of our plan for research and some of the theoretical and practical issues we encountered in interviewing members of European elites; (2) a discussion of the attitudes of French elites, including the sources of consensus and dissensus in the de Gaulle Republic, the balance and interplay of elites and the prospects for change after de Gaulle, as well as an analysis of French elite views on European political developments and the prospects for arms control; (3) a discussion of the attitudes of West German elites toward the major issues of Europe's future and the bearing of such peculiarly German problems as the creation of a new defense establishment, relations with the East and reunification upon Western European politics; and (4) a concluding section comprising an analytical comparison of elite attitudes in France and West Germany, the integration of other findings emerging from our overall study and the implications of our general findings in terms of both the future of European politics and American foreign policy formulation.[1]

The elite interviews and other data reported here point to underlying trends in Western European politics. That changes affecting the Western Alliance have occurred in the two years since we completed our research and wrote the draft of this book is clear. They range from increased American involvement in Vietnam to the emergence of Communist China (still outside the United Nations) as a power with nuclear capabilities and a rudimentary delivery system, to French withdrawal from military aspects of NATO, to a virtual burial of the multilateral

---

[1] Specific questions of arms control and of the elite attitudes relevant to them, are dealt with in greater detail in a separate book by Karl W. Deutsch, *Arms Control and the Atlantic Alliance: Europe Faces Coming Policy Decisions* (New York: John Wiley & Sons, 1967). In thus separating the subject matter of our single large research undertaking into two volumes, this one focussed on the general elite politics of France and Germany, and the other centered specifically upon arms control, we have endeavored to keep the overlap of information to the minimum necessary to ensure continuity in each case; and we are grateful to both publishers for their cooperation.

nuclear force idea, to a cabinet crisis and change of government in West Germany in late 1966. With but a few exceptions, our interviews in the summer of 1964 focussed less on specific developments than on the orientations of leaders toward basic questions. It is, then, not particularly surprising to find many of the most recent developments in French and German policies and politics a reflection of these basic orientations. That the MLF, for instance, met with considerable opposition from our leaders was indicative of a set of conditions that led American policy-makers ultimately to abandon the project. That President de Gaulle's demand for a greater French share in the formulation of Atlantic policy was shared by the bulk of French leaders doubtless strengthened the firmness of his moves away from military integration in NATO. It is in this sense— basic orientations toward politics rather than attitudes toward specific events—that the data analyzed in this book must be viewed.

In the preparation of this volume we relied upon many people for assistance. Our deepest debt of gratitude goes to those who assisted in conducting the elite interviews: Gerard Braunthal of the University of Massachusetts, Bernard E. Brown of Brooklyn College, Robert Burton of Columbia University, Henry C. Galant of Skidmore College, Eugene C. McCreary of the Carnegie Institute of Technology and Peter Merkl of the University of California at Santa Barbara. Colleagues who participated in other parts of the project of which this study forms a part are J. Zvi Namenwirth and Bruce M. Russett of Yale University and Donald J. Puchala of Columbia University. Several consultants provided valuable services at vital points in the project: Henry W. Ehrmann of Dartmouth College, Morton Gorden of the University of Pennsylvania, Stanley Hoffmann of Harvard University, Daniel Lerner of the Massachusetts Institute of Technology, Erwin K. Scheuch of the University of Cologne and Adolf Sturmthal of the University of Illinois.

The initial list of French respondents was established by detailed suggestions from our colleagues in the Institute of Political Science of the University of Paris: Professors Jacques Chapsal, François Goguel, Georges Lavau, Serge Hurtig, Alfred Grosser, Jean-Baptiste Duroselle, René Remond, Jean Touchard, Henri Gréard and Messieurs Lancelot, Bodin, Hassner, and Thoma. Professors Ehrmann, Hoffmann and Sturmthal also contributed substantially in the preparation of our panel of potential French respondents.

Specialists who identified reputed leaders in West Germany included: Professor Karl D. Bracher of the University of Bonn; Dr. Rupert

Breitling of the University of Heidelberg; Professor Dr. Fritz Burgbacher of the University of Cologne, Treasurer of the Christian Democratic Union and CDU Member of the Bundestag; Herr Fritz Erler, Chairman of the Social Democratic Bundestags' *Fraktion;* Dr. Erwin Faul of the University of Heidelberg; Professor Carl J. Friedrich of Harvard University and the University of Heidelberg; Dr. Wolfgang Hirsch-Weber of the Free University of Berlin; Professor Otto Kirchheimer of Columbia University; Dr. Kurt Nemitz of the *Deutscher Gewerkschaftsbund;* Dr. Uwe Nerlich of the *Deutsche Gesellschaft für auswärtige Politik;* Herr Günter Triesch of the *Deutsches Industrieinstitut;* and Professor Rudolf Wildenmann of the *Wirtschaftshochschule Mannheim.* To all these men we are deeply grateful.

Many others assisted us in a variety of ways. Professor Jean Stoetzel and Mlle. Helene Riffault of the *Institut Français d'Opinion Publique* (IFOP) opened to us their files on French public opinion; Frau Professor Elisabeth Noelle-Neumann, Wolfgang Hartenstein, Klaus Liepelt and Viggo Graf Bluecher gave us access to their files on West German public opinion. Professor Rudolf Wildenmann and Heribert Schatz allowed us the use of data collected for a study of Bundestag deputies by the *Wirtschaftshochschule Mannheim.* Professors Daniel Lerner and Morton Gorden permitted us to use their data on Western European elites gathered under the auspices of the Massachusetts Institute of Technology. Professor Ferdinand A. Hermens permitted us to use his *Forschungsinstitut für politische Wissenschaft und europäische Fragen* (Cologne University) as a clearinghouse for our correspondence from May through September 1964. Claire Merat coordinated aspects of the project in Paris; as did Lutz and Gerlinde Erbring in Cologne. Research assistance was provided at Yale University by Fred Bamber, Henning Eikenberg, James Kerr, Anna Merritt, Thomas Moseley, Ellen Pirro and Helga Voss-Eckermann; and at the State University of New York at Buffalo by Margaret Cox and Ellen Ginsberg. Patricia Stannard provided secretarial assistance; Edna Marcarelli typed the original manuscript; and Susan Flores prepared the index.

In acknowledging our indebtedness to these many individuals and institutions, we should like to stress that the ultimate responsibility for any conclusions or errors in this book remains ours alone. Overall editor of the volume was Richard L. Merritt.

We should also like to take this opportunity to express our appreciation to the administration of Yale University, which sheltered the project from the outset; to the administrations of Yale University, the State University of New York at Buffalo and Washington University, which permitted us to take time off from our teaching duties to conduct the research and which in many other ways facilitated the project; to George deForest Lord, Master of Trumbull College of Yale University, who graciously provided accommodations for our many conferences; and to the Yale Political Science Research Library, which provided too many services to be detailed here. Without this tremendous institutional support, the project could not have been carried through to completion.

Above all we wish to thank our panel of 320 French and West German leaders who allowed us to bombard them with questions. It is the perspectives of these leaders, who must remain unnamed, that form the heart of this study.

This volume is based, in part, on a study prepared under a contract with the United States Arms Control and Disarmament Agency. The judgments expressed in this volume are those of the authors and do not necessarily reflect the views of the United States Arms Control and Disarmament Agency or any other department or agency of the United States Government.

K.W.D.
L.J.E.
R.C.M.
R.L.M.

CHAPTER 1

Interviewing French and
West German Elites

The mid-1960's find Western Europe in a critical state of flux. The prospects for any form of political integration—prospects that had seemed so bright at the outset of the decade—appear to be fading rapidly, as the Common Market encounters major obstacles, the Franco-German love affair of earlier years cools off and the French begin to withdraw from the North Atlantic Treaty Organization. Meanwhile, the likelihood of nuclear diffusion, both in Europe and elsewhere, seems to be growing year by year; and heavy American military involvement in Southeast Asia causes many Western Europeans to wonder aloud whether the United States can fulfill its commitment to defend Western Europe against Communist aggression. In Europe, as throughout the world, small steps toward decreased international tension often appear overshadowed by mounting conflict.

But what are the underlying currents of Western European politics? Is the general sentiment toward unification so great among Europeans that it can outlast disagreements over individual problems such as agriculture? Or have past trends toward unity been make-believe—loudly proclaimed in the press and generally accepted by the masses, but not fully accepted by the emerging national decision-makers of the new France and West Germany? Or have they been forced upon an unwilling population by a few idealists who base their hopes more upon wishful thinking than upon the facts of Western European politics? Does de Gaulle's current effort to build up a *force de frappe* find general support among younger French leaders who will remain long after de Gaulle has passed from the European scene? Or are the hopefuls—aspirants to the highest offices of the land after the General's departure—firmly convinced that the future of France lies with a North Atlantic defense system and a solid alliance with America? What echo does the sometimes-heard demand for nuclear weapons find among German leaders and citizens?

In an effort to find the answers to such questions as these about the course of Western European politics, we undertook in the summer of 1964 an extensive survey of the attitudes of French and West German leaders in the fields of politics, civil service, business, communications, military life and other professions. All told, we talked with 147 members of French elites and 173 West German leaders in structured interviews averaging one and a half hours in length.

THE FOCUS OF THE STUDY

In our interviews with these French and West German leaders, our main focus was on foreign policy—most specifically Western European integration and arms control. The importance of domestic political considerations in the formation of foreign policy, however, demanded that we direct some of our attention to these issues. Thus we concentrated on four aspects of the politics of Western Europe.

Domestic Affairs

a) The respondent's evaluation of the current governmental system in his country; his feelings concerning the permanency of the current form of government; personnel changes that he thinks either likely or unlikely in the near future.

b) His evaluation of the structure of the political system in his country; who has the power; how the distribution of political influence among social groups has changed since World War II; how it is likely to change again in coming years.

c) His impression of the political process in his country; where the great domestic political cleavages and conflicts are.

d) His evaluation of the internal cohesiveness and stability of his society.

Foreign Policy and International Relations

a) The respondent's perception of the structure of international politics; whether it is becoming increasingly bipolar or multipolar; his evaluation of changes in the international system.

b) His definition of his country's national interest; how it may best be pursued and protected.

c) His evaluation of the foreign policy of the current government; what changes in foreign policy are likely; what features of the current foreign policy are likely to continue over time.

d) His feelings about German and East European questions and his suggestions for ways to ease tension in Central Europe.

European Integration and Alliances

a) The respondent's impression of the desirability of a European union; his feelings about the feasibility of such a union at present and in the next several years.

b) His impression of the possible nature and extent of European union; whether he thinks united Europe will take the form of a confederation, a federation or something else; which countries he feels should and would be included in such a European union.

c) His evaluation of the purpose and importance of a European union.

d) His feelings about his country's membership in NATO and other regional and international organizations.

Arms, Arms Control and Disarmament

a) Whether or not the respondent feels the security of his country threatened; what he perceives to be the nature of the threat; what defense may be taken against the threat.

b) His evaluation of a national nuclear deterrent for his country; what its purpose might be; whether he sees a purpose in a national

3

nuclear deterrent for any country that does not now possess nuclear weapons; his general views on nuclear proliferation outside Western Europe.

c) What (if any) form of arms control or disarmament arrangement he thinks will be most effective in reducing the threat of war; what form of arms control or disarmament arrangement he feels might be feasible for both East and West at the present time as well as ultimately.

d) His evaluation of whether arms control is a military or political question; his perception of whether the substance of the agreement (i.e., "reach the agreement in any way as long as the military threat is reduced") or the procedure by which the agreement is reached (i.e., "we will respect an agreement reached only after our country has been consulted in the negotiation and given its approval") is most crucial.

This book discusses in some detail the attitudes of French and West German leaders on such issues as these. Before going into the specific responses, however, it seems necessary to elaborate upon the value of elite analysis and to describe how we went about our survey: drafting questionnaires; selecting samples of French and West German elites; meeting with and interviewing them; and preparing their responses for analysis.

ELITE ANALYSIS

The term "elites" means many things to many people. As we use the term, it refers to both formal and informal decision-makers at a society's national level; and, of course, we are interested in decisions important for the politics of that society. The elite structure of a society may be pluralistic or tightly integrated. In the former case, which is true of most countries molded in the Western tradition of liberalism, various elites may be competing for such scarce resources as wealth or access to political power. If there is interaction among these elites, or if their membership overlaps, it is generally of only marginal importance for the national decision-making process: The interaction is usually of short duration and covers a narrow range of issues. But it is not difficult to think of societies in which a small group of like-minded men have controlled all or most politically relevant aspects of life. We can also differentiate between special and general elites. Special (or "functional") elites comprise those who represent their own individual spheres of public life: decision-makers in politics, government, business, the military, communications, religion and so forth. General elites are those who dominate the life of the society as a whole. Thus in a highly politicized society the political elites may be of chief importance; in a theocracy religious elites may dominate; and in a society that adheres to an entrepreneurial way of life business elites may be predominant. The elite structure of both France and West Germany in the postwar years has been pluralistic. Political decision-making is more often a case of bargaining among special elites (and between them and the public at large) than one in which a single elite imposes its will on the others. It is in this sense that we focus on the various elites of the two countries in our study of trends in Western European politics.

Interviewing highly placed persons in public and private life has a long and honorable tradition. Only recently, however, have social scientists sought to do this on a systematic basis cross-nationally, using more careful sampling techniques to decide who their respondents should be, using schedules of questions to ensure that all respondents are asked the same set of questions in roughly the same way and using questions that can be scaled in such a way as to give us additional clues about the underlying attitudes of the respondents.[1] Any such undertaking raises immediately a number of important questions.

The most important of these are: What is the value of elite interviews anyway? What can they tell you about political processes and foreign policy-making in a country? Of the several answers to such questions, one refers to the level of conscious behavior: Elites play a crucial role in a state's policy process. Elite groupings are in some cases directly responsible for policy through initiation, legislation and administration. If we are interested in, let us say, French foreign policy, then it simply makes good sense to talk with the people at the Quai d'Orsay who for-

---

[1] Some of the major systematic elite studies of recent years include Harold D. Lasswell and Daniel Lerner, eds., *World Revolutionary Elites: Studies in Coercive Ideological Movements* (Cambridge, Mass.: MIT Press, 1965); Karl W. Deutsch and Lewis J. Edinger, *Germany Rejoins the Powers: Mass Opinion, Interest Groups, and Elites in Contemporary German Foreign Policy* (Stanford, Calif.: Stanford University Press, 1959); Lloyd A. Free, *Six Allies and a Neutral: A Study of the International Outlooks of Political Leaders in the United States, Britain, France, West Germany, Italy, Japan and India* (Glencoe, Ill.: Free Press, 1950); Wendell Bell, *Jamaican Leaders: Political Attitudes in a New Nation* (Berkeley and Los Angeles, Calif.: University of California Press, 1964); Marshall R. Singer, *The Emerging Elite: A Study of Political Leadership in Ceylon* (Cambridge, Mass.: MIT Press, 1964); Frederick W. Frey, *The Turkish Political Elite* (Cambridge, Mass.: MIT Press, 1965).

mulate it, with the first secretaries who transmit information, with the parliamentarians who enact the necessary legislation and pass on the budget. Other elite groupings—business or labor leaders, for instance, or the communication media—may play a less direct role in policy-making. Sometimes they act as interest groups lobbying to secure certain goals; at other times they act as veto groups who must be placated before a given policy can be implemented. To understand why a particular policy is adopted, it is usually necessary to know what pressures were put on decision-makers by such interest groups—how important they perceived their stake in the proposed measure to be, what steps they took to make their interests known, their access to the corridors of power and their influence relative to that of competing interest groups.

Another answer refers to less manifest sources of policy: The values, beliefs and attitudes of the broad stratum of elites are indicative of those that go into the making of policy. If the elites comprise a reasonably homogeneous group—bound by ties of class, possibly, or educated at a mere handful of schools—then we may expect the perspectives of individual members to be similar in important respects. If, however, the elite groupings are of diverse social backgrounds, then we might expect greater conflict in their perspectives. Even in this case it often happens that men of diverse backgrounds are socialized to a common way of thinking as they move up the ladder of politics, business and other key aspects of social life. When this is the case, talking with representative officials at the Quai d'Orsay (to carry our earlier example a bit further) would tell us much about the environmental framework of a particular policy even if we are unable to talk with the people who actually formulated it. It is also possible to infer—although with considerably less confidence about the accuracy of the inference—the values, beliefs and attitudes that went into that foreign policy measure if we merely have access to the broader stratum of individuals from whom Quai d'Orsay officials were recruited or with whom they consort in their hours of leisure.

Besides the significance of these conscious and less manifest sources of policy formation, we must note the fact that today's elites are largely responsible for recruiting and promoting tomorrow's elites into positions of power, and that men tend to put their trust in their own kind. In a stable society, we can fairly safely predict that the basic values, beliefs and attitudes of the leaders of the 1960's will be carried over to the leaders of the 1970's, albeit with some modifications. (The volatile politics of a state in which elites have provided education for the lower classes without commensurate opportunities for social mobility might, by way of contrast, pave the way for the sudden overthrow of established elites by an alignment of counter-elite leaders.) Despite political shifts, postwar society in France and West Germany has been fairly stable: The phenomenon of the self-perpetuation of elites together with the fact that today's younger leaders will spend long years being socialized to positions of power suggest that we may expect a reasonable degree of stability in elite perspectives during the years to come.

But, it may be countered, of what value is it to know about elite perspectives in a polity where a single man determines alone what will and what will not be done? Even the most monocratic ruler reflects the perspectives of those elite members who advise and influence him. In a modern society, it is impossible for a single man, whether he be Charles de Gaulle, Franklin D. Roosevelt, Konrad Adenauer, or Adolf Hitler, to initiate and implement single-handedly measures to keep an entire state functioning or in bondage. He must rely upon associates who tell him what the major problems are, offer information and advice, suggest solutions, assist in carrying out the decisions. And, in the modern society, his base of support must be large. If this supportive base of elite groupings surrounding the leader does not mirror completely the perspectives of the leader, it is nonetheless important to recognize the likelihood that from the subalterns of today will emerge the leaders of tomorrow—men who will be charged with the responsibility of retaining or revising or even rejecting the policies of the present-day leader. Hence elite perspectives are of especial significance for gauging long-run trends in policy formulation.

Another important question pertains to the truthfulness of elite respondents in an interview situation: Do they tell the interviewer what they really believe? Whether or not the respondent accurately indicates his attitudes to the interviewer is, of course, impossible to answer with certainty in each individual case. By explaining fully the scholarly nature of our inquiry and by guaranteeing the confidential nature of the interview, we felt that we enhanced the likelihood that the respondent would express his true feelings. As will be clearer in a later section of this chapter and elsewhere in this book, our interviewers felt that, for the most part, the elite members with whom we talked were open in their responses, judging by the mannerisms of the respondent, the logical consistency of his responses and the relationship between his responses

7

in the interview and his remarks published elsewhere. In the last analysis only a close watch on the future behavior of our elite respondents will give us clues about the extent to which their expressed attitudes represented their real attitudes; but, even then, since a man may change his mind, future behavior may be misleading about that man's current views.

Assuming the validity of elite interviews for learning about political processes, why did we limit our study to only two countries? Are not Great Britain and the other countries of the European community just as important as France and West Germany in the study of the politics of Western Europe? Our reasons for limiting the study were two in number, the one of theoretical import and the other of a practical nature. First, we felt that it would be most efficient to concentrate upon the two countries that we felt are of crucial importance in determining the present and future course of European politics. If French and West German leaders can agree upon some form of political integration for Western Europe or upon some kind of arms limitation arrangement, then it seems extremely likely to us that other Western European states—particularly Italy and the Benelux countries—will go along with the Franco-German decision. This is, of course, not true with respect to all political decisions, as the role of the Netherlands in some EEC agricultural disputes testifies. What is more important is the fact that no agreement between any other pair of European countries would be so acceptable to the rest as one between France and West Germany. Without these two countries in basic agreement, wider cooperation in Western Europe is unlikely. Second, limitations in the amount of time and research resources available to us necessitated narrowing the scope of the study to only two countries. Given world enough and time (and sufficient foundation support) we would have been delighted to carry out our project in Italy, for example, or in Great Britain; and we hope that at some future time we shall be able to gather comparable data.

THE QUESTIONNAIRES

Our initial task was to prepare a set of questionnaires that would enable us to secure a maximum amount of information on the manifest and underlying attitudes of the respondents and at the same time be manageable in interviews with busy men. After a series of preliminary discussions among Bernard E. Brown, Karl W. Deutsch, Roy C. Macridis and Richard L. Merritt to delineate the major areas of concentration, and a conference in late January 1964 at which we presented our ideas and discussed them with the consultants to the project, a conference to draft the final questionnaires was held at Trumbull College of Yale University on 25-26 April 1964. This conference was attended by the four mentioned previously as well as by Gerard Braunthal, Lewis J. Edinger, Peter Merkl, Donald J. Puchala and Erwin K. Scheuch.

At this conference we prepared three types of questionnaires. The first was a list of 20 questions designed to elicit the manifest attitudes of the respondents on the four key sets of issues discussed above. (The list of questions may be found in the appendix.) Since the interviews were designed to be open-ended, the interviewers were free to pursue any single question on which the respondents seemed particularly knowledgeable or in which they were interested. Our stipulation, however, was that, regardless of which questions were treated more intensively, the interviewer should strive to get the respondent's attitudes on all the major questions.

Immediately after the conference at Trumbull College, Puchala analyzed the list of questions in terms of the types of responses most likely to be received and recast them in the form of a precoded Manifest Attitude Questionnaire. The field procedure called for the interviewer to carry into each interview a list of the 20 major questions, to take notes on the responses of the interviewee, and then, after the completion of the interview, to code the respondent's answers according to the precoded Manifest Attitude Questionnaire. Points that the respondent talked about, but which were not covered by the questionnaire, were to be noted by the interviewer by means of a portable tape recorder. The taped supplementary statements also enabled the interviewer to comment on the respondent's attitude toward the interview itself, the points on which the respondent laid particular stress and other relevant items of information.

Second, we thought that it would be useful to evaluate systematically the latent attitude structure of the respondent's responses, that is, the implicit patterns of orientation that might shed some light on the avowed attitudes of the respondents. After considerable discussion at the conference itself, Edinger and Scheuch prepared a Latent Attitude Questionnaire designed to permit the interviewer to rate the respondents along a number of perceptual dimensions. These dimensions were:

9

1. *Information:* Familiarity with the issues raised; extent of information; ability to see specific issues as parts of a larger picture (ability to structure events); sense of competence to render an opinion.

2. *Involvement:* Perception of the general significance of the issues raised (saliency); emotional involvement (affect); firmness of opinion, that is, degree of unreceptiveness to new information (cloture); insensitivity to the opinions of other political actors relative to the issues raised; tough-mindedness on the issues raised.

3. *Influence:* Sense of actual influence, that is, any feeling of participation in policy-making relative to the issues raised; sense of potential influence, or a self-assessment of any latent ability to influence policy-making.

Interviewers were to rate respondents on an overall basis and on the basis of each of the four major categories of issues (domestic policy, foreign policy, European integration, and arms control and disarmament).

Third, since it was imperative to have some idea about the social background of the respondents, we prepared a Biographical Data Questionnaire. The basis of the questionnaire was that used by Edinger in his previous analyses of West German elites. Puchala and Edinger, in collaboration with Macridis, drafted a new questionnaire suitable for a cross-national survey of French and German elites. Among the items of information we sought were the age of the respondents, their occupational development and social class, religion, party affiliation, participation in the world wars of our century, length of service in government or business and so forth. Biographical Data Questionnaires were filled out for French respondents by a clerical staff in Paris under the direction of Macridis, relying primarily upon such printed sources as the *Bottin Administratif,* the *Annuaire du Conseil National de Patronat Français,* the *Who is Who in France,* and various publications of the *Assemblée Nationale* and the Senate. In West Germany, Lutz and Gerlinde Erbring gathered what data were available in public records, and the individual interviewers sought to fill in the gaps in their sessions with respondents.

THE SAMPLE OF ELITES

The selection of French and West German leaders to be interviewed proved a thorny problem. There were several possible ways to do this. One way would have been to draw a random sample of the notables appearing in recent editions of *Who is Who in France* and the West German *Wer ist Wer* (*Who is Who*). Such a procedure avoids some biases in the selection of respondents (except those biases due to the processes by which prominent individuals are selected for inclusion in such publications). Had we been interested in general elite perspectives on life and politics, or had we been able to interview several times more elite members than was possible, then this might have proved to be the most reasonable procedure. (It must be added, however, that, due to obvious methodological difficulties, this has never been done in any cross-national elite analysis.) Given our interest in specific political attitudes and our expectation that we could interview only between 150 and 175 individuals in each country, this approach did not seem to be appropriate. We feared it extremely likely that, in a random sample of names listed in registers of the prominent, we would encounter large numbers of society matrons, fashion experts, professors of art history or archeology, entertainers and others who often neither know nor care much about politics and are not politically influential. Also, we thought it unlikely that such registers would list bright young men on their way up in the foreign office, or second-level officials who are important in policy-making processes. Thus we chose deliberately to sacrifice randomness to our hope of compiling a sample of potentially knowledgeable and influential leaders.

Such a decision implies a new question: On which groups within the politically relevant stratum of French and West German society should we concentrate? The dilemma is clear. Ideally we would like to have included as many groups as possible: legislative, political party, civil service, judicial, military, mass media, academic and intellectual, farm, labor, business, commercial, financial, export-import, war veterans, refugee, religious and other groupings. All these, potentially at least, play roles in the policy-making processes of the two countries. To include in our sample representatives of all of them, however, would have meant that if we were to remain within our limit of 150 to 175 respondents per country we could interview only a handful of leaders from each grouping. Such a sampling procedure would not give us sufficient information to differentiate among the groups as to their positions on foreign policy issues. Moreover, it would have compounded the difficulty of decisions about which individuals to interview as representatives of groups.

We therefore decided to concentrate upon five groups—political, military, mass media and intellectual, civil service and business elites—

and to have a sixth category of "other professional groups," including labor, professional association, church and other leaders. This decision seemed justified by the precedents set by other elite studies, such as the Lerner and Lasswell studies, Bell's study of Jamaican leaders and the analysis of postwar West German elites by Deutsch and Edinger cited earlier. We regretted the fact that we were unable to interview a more extensive sample of elite groups; but nonetheless felt confident that, of all the groups in French and West German society, these were the ones most likely to be important for the political process. Limiting the number of groups also meant that we could try to interview more than just a handful of representatives of these groups.

The next task was to identify which leaders we should interview. We wrote to established scholars and experts on French and West German politics, asking them to suggest names of important individuals who were at once representative of the six occupational categories and knowledgeable about the politics of their own country and Europe as a whole. We particularly asked our informants for recommendations in their own fields of specialization. Simultaneously we carefully searched governmental and other handbooks listing elite positions, noting which positions were most important for the policy-making process and who filled these positions. Thus the sample rested on both the reputational and positional characteristics of the potential respondents. On the whole, the final list of 441 French and 650 West German leaders is a panel of unusually well-informed and influential men and women who are representative of the various groups that interested us.

Obviously it must be borne in mind that we were dealing with elites and not with stratified random samples of the entire population. Our elite groups, therefore, do not mirror overall population characteristics such as sex, education, social background, age or region of origin. Our elites quite clearly do not correspond to the profile of the gainfully employed population in France and West Germany. In both countries the rulers differ in many respects from the ruled. They tend to be older than average, better educated, higher in terms of socio-economic status, male rather than female and to come from larger towns. Our sample was not designed to be representative of the mass of French and West German voters, but rather of the leadership community in the two countries.

An important element shaping the panel of respondents whom we actually were able to interview was self-selection. We wrote letters to all potential respondents, asking them to grant us a strictly confidential interview of about one hour and requesting a specific appointment. The letters informed the recipients that they had been identified as "prominent" French or German leaders whom we, as American scholars, should consult in connection with our endeavor to ascertain the views of leading personalities in the countries of the Atlantic Community regarding common problems for the purpose of comparative analysis. Before 5 June 1964, when our interviewers reached Paris, we had received 203 favorable answers from the 441 French leaders to whom we had written; another 20—mostly political, military and civil service leaders—answered saying explicitly that they did not wish to be interviewed. Of the 650 Germans we had contacted, 111 did not reply at all, 58 declined to be interviewed or replied evasively (including two who denied being prominent or influential) and 481 agreed to be interviewed. Thus our task was to decide, given our limitations of time, which of the respondents willing to be interviewed we could in fact visit.

In France the matter was complicated by the fact that most of the respondents preferred to be interviewed during the month of June and the first week of July. The need to fill the minimum quota in each of the leadership categories and the problem of bringing respondents and interviewers together at a mutually convenient time and place forced us to make some hard decisions. In Germany, after completion of the first wave of 47 interviews in May and June 1964, we found it necessary to institute a rough system of ranking our prospective respondents for the second wave, using as criteria their reputed prominence in the eyes of our informants, their positions and their accessibility. In a number of instances individuals who had initially declared themselves willing to be interviewed turned out to be inaccessible or cancelled their interviews; in large part this was due to the great dispersion of elites among West German cities and the impossibility for interviewers to conduct interviews on the same morning in, let us say, both West Berlin and Bonn. Where possible we substituted other respondents, but the dropout rate led to some minor imbalances in distribution among the various categories which were not originally intended.

CHARACTERISTICS OF THE SAMPLE

Occupational Categories

We ultimately interviewed 147 French and 173 West German leaders, broken down as shown in Table 1.1. Two notes must be appended to this categorization. In the case of the French military elite, we were

Table 1.1

RESPONDENTS ACCORDING TO OCCUPATIONAL CATEGORIES

Category	France	West Germany
1. Political (30 intended)	32	38
2. Military (15)	7	14
3. Opinion leaders (30)	29	42
4. Civil servants (30)	32	16
5. Business (30)	19	36
6. Other prof. groups (30)	28*	27
Total (165-175)	147	173

* Including 2 respondents who were unclassifiable according to occupational categories.

unable to secure enough names of responsible persons to interview. There was great reticence on the part of our French colleagues in giving us names of military leaders; in addition, certain officers were in such sensitive positions that from the outset it seemed highly unlikely that they would consent to be interviewed. This was later borne out in an interview held on the very first day of interviewing with a key parliamentarian whom the interviewer had known over a period of years. When we asked him to give us additional names of officers, he responded that the military would *not* answer. He was willing to provide us with his good offices but, since he was clearly not very anxious to do so, we dropped the matter. (When we told him that this was unfortunate since German generals would consent to the same set of interviews being conducted on the other side of the Rhine, he answered that this was proof that West Germany does not have a national army!)

Second, in the case of German civil servants, the number of interviewees is apparently smaller than it actually is, since some of the opinion leaders are technically employed as civil servants.

Age Cohorts

To determine the effect of age on foreign policy attitudes, we divided those of our respondents whose birth date we know (88% in

France and 94% in West Germany) into age cohorts. Our assumption here is that different age groups have distinct historical experiences which they bring to the policy-making process. A group of men who had personally experienced two bitterly fought wars between France and Germany might react differently to proposals for Franco-German unity, for instance, than might a group of youthful leaders who had been too young during World War II to understand what the fighting was all about.

As it turned out, our expectation that the age of the respondents makes a significant difference regarding their political attitudes was borne out by the data from the interviews only in regard to some issues—a finding that is itself significant. The breakdown of the various elites by age category (shown in Table 1.2) is nonetheless useful for understanding the structure of our sample of respondents.

The older members of the generation of French and West German leaders responsible for the establishment of the postwar polity were represented by a small group of respondents seventy years or older (3% in France, 4% in West Germany) and by a much larger group of respondents in their sixties (18% and 30% respectively). Old enough to have known four different political systems in each country and the collapse of three of them, these respondents were also old enough to have become politically identified with political parties in the 1920's and, in the case of West German respondents, to have become politically involved with the Hitler regime (at least a third had been either Nazis or anti-Nazis). And they were men who apparently had played leading parts in postwar political and socio-economic reconstruction. It must be added, however, that the influence of these leaders is likely to diminish rapidly in coming years as death and retirement lead to the withdrawal of most of them from present positions of reputed prominence. Where in this study opinions associated with Retiring and Senior Elites vary significantly from those of other groups, it should be borne in mind that they represent views of comparatively limited importance for an analysis of *future* trends in leadership opinion.

The Middle Elite—men in their fifties—represents the younger members of the founding generation of postwar politics. Too young to remember much about European politics before World War I or to have fought in that war, most respondents in this age group were still students during the 1920's or had just entered an occupation. Of the West Germans in our sample, at least 43 per cent had been politically involved in

Table 1.2
AGE COHORTS

FRANCE

Elite Categories	Number of Respondents	Per cent of Respondents Whose Ages Were Ascertained	Per cent by Groups of Percentage of Respondents of Known Age		
			Retiring and Senior Elite 60-77	Middle Elite 50-59	Junior and Ascending Elite 26-49
Political	32	100%	32%	26%	42%
Military	7	100	57	29	14
Opinion Leaders	29	92	18	22	52
Civil Service	32	88	12	15	62
Business	19	89	21	32	37
Others	28	66	10	24	31
Total	147				

Number of Respondents of Known Age (129):

    a. in each age group: 30, 34, 65

    b. as a percentage (88%)* of total respondents: 21%, 23%, 45%

WEST GERMANY

Elite Categories	Number of Respondents	Per cent of Respondents Whose Ages Were Ascertained	Per cent by Groups of Percentage of Respondents of Known Age		
			Retiring and Senior Elite 60-77	Middle Elite 50-59	Junior and Ascending Elite 26-49
Political	38	100%	27%	34%	39%
Military	14	57	7	43	7
Opinion Leaders	42	98	36	33	29
Civil Service	16	100	50	38	12
Business	36	98	39	50	9
Others	27	93	40	30	22
Total	173				

Number of Respondents of Known Age (163):

a. in each age group | | | | 59 | 65 | 39

b. as a percentage (94%)* of total respondents | | | | 34% | 38% | 22%

* Each of these percentages does not total 100% because in some cases information was incomplete.

17

the Hitler era, either as members of Nazi organizations (15%) or as opponents (28%). Unlike the Retiring and Senior Elites, the members of the Middle Elite are due to remain active in positions of prominence for at least another decade and indeed to reach the top level of seniority during that period. They are likely, therefore, to have a correspondingly greater influence not only on public policy-making but on the recruitment and promotion of new elite members as well. Hence, the opinions associated with members of this group are of considerable significance in terms of both the present and future attitudes of French and West German leaders. Their agreement or disagreement with the views of other age groups is a factor to be watched for in the discussion to follow.

The new men of power who have been moving into leadership positions were represented among our respondents by individuals between forty and fifty years of age (29% in France, 15% in West Germany) and those under forty (16% and 8%, respectively). In comparing the responses of French and West German leaders to the questions we posed, it must be remembered that the share of Junior and Ascending Elites in our French sample is about twice as great as that in our West German sample. It may very well be, however, that this differential reflects the relevant status of these age groups in current French and West German society. In either country a man under fifty is still considered young when it comes to filling positions of leadership, particularly in business and academic life, but also in the civil service and the military as well.

Particularly prominent in politics and the mass media, occupations that today permit relatively rapid ascent, the older members of this under-50 group may still remember the Briand-Stresemann era of good feeling, the fall of the Weimar Republic and the rise of Hitler and the formation of the Popular Front. They were old enough to have practiced an occupation, served in the Second World War or in the Resistance and have become politically involved in the politics of the Nazi and Vichy governments. Members of the Ascending Elite grew up during the unstable 1930's and, although most of the West Germans (62%) had served with the *Wehrmacht,* few got involved in politics until the postwar period. Since members of the Ascending and Junior Elites will be gradually replacing those of the founding generation in positions of power in public life, their influence is likely to increase significantly over the next decade relative to the older groups. Insofar as markedly different attitude patterns between this and other age groups may emerge in our findings, these differences may indicate potential changes in French and West German leadership as these younger men take over. The absence of such differences, however, would suggest that, at least among the present leadership represented by our respondents, membership in this youngest age group does not carry with it a different outlook toward national and international issues and that there may be a higher degree of intergenerational stability in the trend of French and West German elite opinion.

THE INTERVIEWS

The interviews themselves were conducted in France between 8 June and 14 July 1964, by Roy C. Macridis, Bernard E. Brown, Henry C. Galant, and Robert Burton; and in West Germany between 26 May and 13 October 1964, by Lewis J. Edinger, Gerard Braunthal, Peter Merkl, and Eugene C. McCreary.

To obtain answers to most, if not all, the questions in our schedule required about ninety minutes, leaving even in the best of circumstances little time for elaboration or freewheeling discussions. Some respondents clearly resented this limitation and sought to ignore it; others tended to restrict themselves to excessively brief answers. At times, when a respondent indicated that he had little time to spare for the interview and/or seemed particularly knowledgeable on or interested in certain issues, the interviewers deliberately omitted questions on others. In most interviews we sought to cover the principal topics first, returning, if time permitted, to a discussion of details and secondary issues.

Most of the interviews lasted more than the hour we had requested. About half took from sixty to ninety minutes of the respondent's time and most of the others lasted up to two hours and more. Interviewers usually sought to extend the interview beyond an hour and, while some respondents explicitly or implicitly agreed to continue or to have a second visit, most were unwilling to go much beyond the appointed time. A tenacious interviewer might persist, but the payoff seemed in such cases of diminishing value as respondents grew restless, telephones rang, secretaries and assistants intruded and indications multiplied that the interview was expected to end. In a number of instances the interviewer had to terminate the interview prematurely to meet another appointment or to catch a train. In both France and West Germany interviewers generally went to the office or home of the respondent; in France, several additional interviews were conducted in the ameliorating atmosphere accompanying French cuisine.

Interviewing in France

Interviewers in France found that the respondents were generally frank in their answers. Except in a few cases, we did not detect any effort to please us or give answers that would satisfy the "American" observer. To be sure we were repeatedly told that the United States was a "friend," that the Atlantic Alliance could not be destroyed, that present frictions were temporary and often exaggerated—but we felt that this was an expression of sincere attitudes rather than words designed to please the interviewer, especially since the same people who expressed their friendship for the United States also expressed their fears and criticisms. American investments in Europe were, for instance, considered by a number to be a danger; occasionally our policy in Latin America and Southeast Asia was bluntly termed "narrow-minded," "stupid," "colonial," "reactionary" and so forth; genuine fears were expressed about internal developments in the United States, often with serious concern about the fate of American democracy. If there was any feeling of anti-Americanism, we sensed only some of its undertones and in few cases saw its more vibrant aspects. These came chiefly from members of the Gaullist Union pour la Nouvelle République (UNR) and some retired generals, but also, significantly enough, from some of the young political leaders and intellectuals.

Further, we observed a general cynicism and also a relative lack of information among French elites on matters of disarmament and arms control. Lack of information, it must be pointed out, stems directly from certain basic assumptions they shared in the early summer of 1964: Disarmament is primarily a technical question; it will be "taken care of" only when political and national conflicts become attenuated; there is no sense in speculating too much about the future on this, for it depends on who is elected president in the United States and who would succeed Khrushchev; it depends on the turn that the Sino-Soviet dispute takes; and so forth. There is no panacea. There is no complete answer. To hope for disarmament is one thing, to expect it to materialize is another. The most we can expect in certain circumstances is that a gradual understanding will emerge which in turn might lead to some form of arms control and disarmament. Few believed, as we shall see, that the Geneva talks are "serious," though many deplored the fact that France is not present. Most felt, while applauding all efforts made, that we are "not yet ready" for disarmament. Because of this prevailing attitude, it was difficult to pin down French elites on disarmament questions and to glean their attitudes with the degree of accuracy that we had hoped for.

We ought also to point out our general impression—vague and imprecise, but nonetheless a strong impression—about virtually all French respondents. Though they differ fundamentally on many issues, as will be discussed in later chapters, they have a common set of reactions.

There is, first of all, a certain belief in the uniqueness of France, its humane civilization, its civilizing mission, its balance and tolerance. Even young political respondents, who take a hard and pragmatic attitude to politics and to the state of the world as it is, share this belief. This comes out clearly in a number of ways and with regard to a number of issues. France, for instance, will show the way to the underdeveloped societies and will increasingly assume an obligation to see them develop —an attitude shared by all but a handful of our respondents.

Second, France, despite the humiliation of World War II, speaks on behalf of Europe. The European vocation is unmistakable in most respondents, irrespective of whether or not they favor European unification.

Third, virtually all respondents, including the many who criticize it or do not lend much credence to it, take pride in France's nuclear accomplishment. The bomb may be interpreted in different ways, and some want to see it scrapped; but the very question of what to do with it is a source of pride even among those who do not believe that it adds to the nation's prestige.

Fourth, nearly all respondents, no matter how much they criticize the Limited Test-Ban Treaty of 1963, feel rather unhappy with de Gaulle's aloofness in the negotiations dealing with arms control and disarmament at Geneva. Most think that France should not have been absent nor should it remain so now. Indeed, according to these respondents, it should be the "genius" of the country to sponsor and promote negotiations that may avert war or nuclear disaster.

Fifth, the majority of respondents shares a latent fear of Germany. They are restive about German economic power and unwilling to consider German reunification. If a large majority believes that the Franco-German rapprochement is here to stay, an equally significant majority wishes to make sure that Germany will not again prove the stronger partner. But in the same connection the possibility of a war between Germany and France seems to be buried.

Finally, there is a growing belief, shared by a majority of respondents, that whatever the institutions after de Gaulle (and a majority accepts a "presidential system") France will never again return to the instability of the Fourth Republic.

These generalizations reflect moods more than specific attitudes. They are the thoughts and the hopes of spokesmen of a people badly shaken by defeat and diminution of status, a people led today by a man who, after experiencing the very depths of national humiliation and impotence, is now dedicated to the task of seeing to it that the same will never happen to France again.

In short, the mood of France's nationalism today is primarily self-assertive and compensatory. It has none of the broad ideological claims of nineteenth century liberal nationalism, none of the expansionistic and militant traits of earlier German nationalism. It dreams of no conquest or expansion, aspires to no imposition upon anything or anybody, claims no subservience of other peoples and nations to France—except perhaps in its claim to speak on behalf of Europe. It simply states, as de Gaulle has stated so many times in his inimitable way, that France is France and that her way of life has a place in the universe and must be respected. It is very much in the nature of a proclamation of freedom, dignity and respect after many years of servitude. The *capitis diminutio* is over and de Gaulle's life is a testament proclaiming the French to be independent. What they plan to do with their freedom and independence, however, is another matter.

Interviewing in West Germany

Turning to the West German respondents, in our letter asking for an interview we had endeavored to facilitate access and rapport by explaining that ours was strictly a scholarly enterprise, that the identity of our respondents would not be made public, and that their views were of great importance to us in our effort to learn how common problems of the Western Alliance were perceived by prominent leaders in various member countries. Frequently we found it necessary to elaborate on these points prior to, or during, an interview.

We learned that Germans who think of themselves as members of the elites (and who were approached by us as such) are sometimes inclined to resent the notion of a survey of opinions which they believe to be more or less unique. In one instance, a prominent university professor and political scientist told the interviewer in no uncertain terms that he disliked our allegedly "positivistic" approach; in two other instances leaders refused interviews since we would not pay a fee; in still another case the potential respondent turned down our request precisely because we intended to keep responses anonymous. These, however, were decidedly exceptions.

In general, rapport was almost invariably good: Three-fourths of our respondents seemed cooperative to the interviewers and most of the rest at least friendly (particularly mass media leaders). Only two per cent were considered hostile or suspicious and less than ten per cent evasive in their answers.

A few leaders, including over a third of the military leaders, tended to preach some special message. Such a "go-tell-your-leaders" attitude seemed to be based on the impression that we represented the United States government. More generally, the self-selection initiated by our original request for interviews may well have introduced a certain bias by eliminating potentially uncooperative respondents and giving us access mostly to those who more or less wanted to make their views as "prominent German leaders" known to Americans. In fact, a number of replies to our requests emphatically welcomed such an inquiry and an interview. Although the interviews were explicitly off-the-record, it seemed to us that most of our respondents, particularly those holding official and public offices, would not or could not voice opinions that were intended to be confidential. There were, however, significant exceptions to this pattern, and a few respondents really seemed to let their hair down.

Elite interviews, whether in France or West Germany or elsewhere, differ sharply from public opinion polls. It is hard to set down in quantitative terms (although we have tried to do so) the subtleties and the nuances of the responses. French and West German elites are extremely articulate and, in most cases, very well informed. One question is often answered in terms that connect it with others. Each question is put by the respondent in its general logical context before it is answered. It was not always easy to move from the general to the particular, nor was it possible to interrupt the respondent's thought, since in its generality it revealed much more than what specific answers alone might have shown. If these facts, which are at once the limitations and strengths of the interviewing procedures we followed, are borne in mind in reading the following chapters, the value of the study as a whole will be enhanced.

PREPARATION OF THE INTERVIEW DATA
FOR ANALYSIS

After the interviewers had returned their completed questionnaires, we turned to the final stage of data preparation. Without discussing in any detail the various technical decisions that we made, it should be noted that the steps included: a review of the coding categories on the questionnaires in light of the types of responses which we had not foreseen but which our interviewers had recorded; preparation of a codebook based on the questionnaires with expanded response categories; coding and putting the data on punch cards; and some simple pre-analytical manipulations of the data, such as the preparation of cross-tabulation by means of an IBM 7094 computer, which also gave us statistical measures of significance. At this stage we attempted no elaborate computer analysis (such as factor analysis of the responses). Using the recorded (and later transcribed) impressions of the interviewers themselves, the punch card data and the cross-tabulations and statistical summaries as a springboard, French and West German elite attitudes could then be systematically analyzed.

In the analysis that follows, we shall discuss first of all the attitudes of French leaders toward important aspects of internal and European politics. The second major portion of the study goes in some detail into the perspectives of our respondents in West Germany. Finally, we shall outline some of the cross-national facets of French and West German elite attitudes, putting them into a framework of other systematically gathered data on European and Atlantic politics, and focusing upon the implications of these findings for American foreign policy.

Part I

AN ANATOMY OF
FRENCH ELITE OPINION

CHAPTER 2

Profiles of French Political Elites

The years since de Gaulle's return and the establishment of the new Constitution have brought about a noticeable, but by no means definitive, restructuring of political orientations in France. It is very difficult to reconcile them or identify them with the traditional political parties. Professor Goguel's perceptive distinction between the "Party of Movement" and the "Party of Order" is no longer satisfactory.[1] The *Union pour la Nouvelle République* (UNR), for instance, is manifestly a party of both "Order" *and* "Movement," while the Communist Party may well be a party neither of "Order" nor of "Movement." Political parties are changing labels and programs. What is more, none of them, with the possible exception of the Communists, corresponds to a clearly identifiable pattern or cluster of policies and attitudes. Conversely, identical political attitudes are shared by members of different parties and quite frequently by persons who do not belong to any party. Party distinctions no longer do justice to the richness of the para-political or extra-party

[1] François Goguel, *La Politique des Partis sous la IIIᵉ République* (Paris: Editions du Seuil, 1948).

activity going on in France today. Similarly, the venerable distinction between Left and Right is virtually meaningless except in identifying residual ideological categories and attitudes.

Another possible approach that has the advantage of simplicity is to look at the present spectrum of political forces in terms of the existing two camps—Gaullists and anti-Gaullists—very much along the lines of the referendum of October 1962, the national election of November 1962 and the presidential election of December 1965. The serious flaw in this scheme, however, is that it provides us with no clues to the likely realignment of political forces in the years to come. With the disappearance of de Gaulle the two camps will lose their identity.

To accommodate the present fluidity of political labels and parties we constructed five basic political "profiles" [2] or "types" among contemporary French elites. These profiles relate to the traditional political parties but take into account attitudes and orientations that cannot be identified in terms of the parties. They make room for the para-political activity being conducted outside the political parties. Finally, they take into consideration the phenomenon of Gaullism and give it proper weight in assessing likely future trends. Our "profile-types" are the following: *Gaullists, Riders, Notables, Aspirants,* and *Unreconstructed.* To these five we should add the *Communists* who continue to represent a relatively stable political sub-culture expressed through a cohesive and well-organized party—perhaps the only instance where a set of overall political attitudes can be identified with a single political party.

Gaullists

The Gaullists accept virtually everything de Gaulle has done. From an institutional point of view, they see no system other than that of the present with the traits that de Gaulle has given to it. In domestic affairs Gaullists are highly satisfied with the regime; they consider as its positive features leadership and stability and see few, if any, conflicts in the society. Their expectation that the UNR and the Fifth Republic will survive de Gaulle is accompanied by their vehement rejection of any Popular Front against him. They not only approve retrospectively of de Gaulle and his policies, but also indicate a widespread tendency to give the same approbation for the future.

In international relations the Gaullists might best be described as

---

[2] The elite profiles and a number of the tables in this section were prepared in collaboration with Donald J. Puchala of Columbia University.

nationals. They believe that the disappearance of international domination by the Americans and the Soviet Union is giving rise to a new multipolarity in which individual nations are masters of their own foreign policy. They approve wholeheartedly of the regime's foreign policy but fear that de Gaulle's departure may bring about a radical change in French foreign policy. They consider the *force de frappe,* the unwillingness on the part of the United States to give France atomic secrets, the domination of the North Atlantic Treaty Organization (NATO) by the United States and often American "stupidity" and "lack of know-how" to be the major sources of friction between the United States and France. The Gaullists also argue that de Gaulle is working for "Europe." They favor the present arrangements—economic integration but only cooperation and coordination at the political and military levels.

Gaullists generally claim that France cannot rely upon NATO. They would favor NATO reforms toward equality among France, England and the United States in the joint development of a global strategy, but would prefer a national nuclear force or a Franco-British nuclear force or a European force. They reject the feasibility of a NATO-controlled or a nuclearized multilateral force (MLF). In sum, the Gaullists consider the national deterrent to be the best defense without, however, discounting the need of alliances and without rejecting the American deterrent.

Riders

The Riders support the General's politics, seem to acquiesce in the constitutional arrangements of the Fifth Republic, and advocate continuing its major institutional arrangements. There is, however, no deep conviction among them. Many of these men are apparently gambling—but not for very high stakes—on the continuation of the Fifth Republic, on an uneventful resolution of the problem of succession and on a continuing UNR majority. But at the same time, their eyes roam to different tables where different games are being played, where different institutional arrangements are being considered and where different expectations about the future are being entertained.

In domestic affairs Riders are in general satisfied with the regime despite some minor reservations. They consider the positive features to be stability, leadership and the Constitution. They see some ideological and party conflicts but do not consider them important. They doubt that the old parties are dead and *hope* that the UNR and the Fifth Republic will survive de Gaulle.

With regard to international affairs the Riders too might be called *nationals,* but *cautious nationals.* Along with the Gaullists they perceive a trend in international politics away from bipolarity with its American and Soviet dominance, and toward multipolarity wherein separate, sovereign nations shape their own foreign policies. Although they favor independent national action in international affairs, however, the Riders are more sensitive than the Gaullists to the need of alliances and even programs for integration.

The Riders approve of de Gaulle's foreign policy in general. Some nonetheless think (or expect) that de Gaulle's departure may bring about radical changes in French foreign policy. They are somewhat restive with the increasingly nationalistic flavor of French foreign policy. They hint that de Gaulle is contributing to it. Yet, they do not envisage reductions in national sovereignty and favor present arrangements with regard to Europe. They think that France can rely to a limited extent upon NATO. They would favor NATO reforms to provide greater equality among England, France and the United States in the development and implementation of global strategy.

The Riders have serious doubts about the feasibility of a NATO-controlled multilateral force. If it were to materialize, they say, each of the three major contributors—France, England and the United States— ought still to have nuclear weapons at its disposal to use unilaterally in the event of extreme threats to national interests. Ultimately, Riders believe that an independent national deterrent may be the best defense for France.

In general, the Riders seem somewhat more flexible and amenable to foreign policy alternatives than do the Gaullists, but few Riders outrightly contradict Gaullist stands.

Notables

The Notables are primarily leaders of the "old parties"—Radicals, Socialists, *Mouvement Républicain Populaire* (MRP), Independents. They are out of the political spotlight;[3] they feel more out of tune with the system than is in fact the case. This group shares the dubious distinction of having brought about de Gaulle's return to power only to be

---

[3] A former Prime Minister sat in his small office while his secretary was trying to communicate something to one of the secretaries of the presidency. Let us say his name is Nevel. His secretary was saying, "Monsieur le President du Conseil Nevel wishes . . . ." "Who?" was apparently the answer. "Nevel," repeated the secretary with a show of irritation. We can only infer what the next question was because the secretary proceeded in our presence to spell the name— "N-e-v-e-l"!

ruthlessly thrown out of the Fifth Republic. Since de Gaulle's ascendancy, they have continued interacting among themselves to form a large centrist group. But they have had no appreciable success. They deride the old ideologies and factionalisms that they continue to embody.

There is another and more positive side to the situation of the Notables: pride in the economic, European and even "atomic" accomplishments of the Fourth Republic. Associated with this there is a new firmness forged out of humiliation and political defeat, coupled with new demands for social and economic reforms—a combination of the old Socialist and Radical vision that never came to life. Notables are going through a period of honest soul-searching. Many of them are relatively young men who are beginning to realize that they will write the epilogue to the Gaullist adventure and the prologue to the future.

Generally speaking, the Notables are dissatisfied with the current governmental system. They do not think that the old parties are dead, or that party and ideological conflicts have disappeared. According to most Notables, the UNR will not survive de Gaulle. With regard to international affairs, most Notables might be generally classified as either "Atlantics" or "Europeans." They emphasize cooperation, alliances and integrative programs rather than independent national action. Their preferences for cooperation within alliances or integration stem largely from their feelings that the domination of the United States and the Soviet Union is "in the nature of things" and will continue. Most Notables agree that contemporary international politics is largely a politics of "camps" rather than states.

The Notables therefore disapprove of de Gaulle's foreign policy and believe that his departure will bring radical changes in this area. They not only favor closer links (federation or confederation) among the "Six" of the European Economic Community (EEC), but would also favor British membership to offset German strength. *Some consider England's entry a must.* Notables feel that a "coordinated" nuclear deterrent—first Atlantic, second European, preferably both—is the best defense. They do not believe that the French deterrent is credible. Rather, they view the motives underlying de Gaulle's *force de frappe* mainly as drives for prestige and political position.

Aspirants

The general intellectual and political "unrest" about the future of the Fifth Republic is best seen among a special group—the Aspirants. These men are extremely involved in political issues. They debate and deliberate in clubs and newspapers but shy away from political parties. They decry ideologies and ideological divisions and stress concrete issues, but scratch them and you will find each and every one an *ideologue* with a vision of the *pure et dure* republic committed to planning, socialism and equality.

Political Aspirants are, relatively speaking, young (between the ages of 35 and 45). Most of them were born in the early 1920's. The Popular Front and Hitler and World War II were experiences that shaped their thinking. The majority are university graduates; a good number are civil servants; some are professors and writers; others have been active in professional or trade union movements (especially those that came from the *Action Catholique de la Jeunesse Française* and who are now among the *Jeunes Agriculteurs*, the old *Confédération Française de Travailleurs Chrétiens*—now the *Confédération Démocratique du Travail*—and the *Jeunes Patrons*).

In domestic affairs the aspirants are generally dissatisfied with the current governmental system. They disapprove of the economic and social policies as well as the personal nature of the regime. They see few deep-seated conflicts in the society. The strength of the Communist Party and the pervasiveness of old parties are viewed as anomalies. Social policies and welfare measures, they say, should overcome divisions between static and dynamic France. By and large they believe that the institutions of the Fifth Republic, especially the presidential system, can be made to work in a "democratic" manner.

With regard to world politics, the Aspirants believe that domination by the United States and the Soviet Union is coming to an end. They see bipolarity currently fragmenting into multipolarity, but they are restive about this trend. Although they are not happy with independent national action in world politics, they nonetheless approve of some aspects of de Gaulle's foreign policy—his recognition of China, for example, or his policies toward underdeveloped countries, his attitude toward NATO and the United States—and accept, but with reservations, the Franco-German treaty. They are the most highly committed "Europeans" of any of the French elite groups. They outrightly favor reduction of national sovereignty. To them this means European federation or confederation including the "Six" plus Great Britain (to balance and offset German power).

In Atlantic affairs, the Aspirants believe that France can rely upon NATO to a limited extent. Most of them favor the reform of NATO to provide more equality among the United States, France and England in global strategy formulation and implementation and to provide for either the nuclear integration of the "Six" or the creation of an independent Franco-British deterrent. They have serious doubts about a NATO-controlled nuclear force or MLF. On balance, they are clearly more "European" rather than "Atlantic."

Concerning the *force de frappe,* the Aspirants see its *raison d'être* as mainly political. It is a device to secure NATO reforms. They do not think that the force is credible militarily, and most believe that after de Gaulle it will cease to be an independent French force and become "Europeanized."

Unreconstructed

The group we have called the "Unreconstructed" is a small segment of the French elite. The Unreconstructed are mostly Notables who reject virtually all reforms and policies undertaken by de Gaulle since 1958, whether institutional, economic, or in the realm of foreign policy. Some are military men who were either forced to resign or chose to resign because of de Gaulle's Algerian policy. Others are die-hard rightwingers. Some come from among the Independents. They tend generally to be fifty-five years of age or older. A handful of the Unreconstructed continues to be influential in the army, or among certain conservative and nationalist organizations or through the newspapers and periodicals they control.

The Unreconstructed are opposed to presidential government, favor a return to the Fourth Republic, wish to see the Senate returned to its former position and power, hope that the old parties (except the Communists) will regain their former strength and power in the National Assembly and disapprove of further economic and social reforms and welfare measures. They do not expect that the UNR or the Fifth Republic will survive de Gaulle. They will not grieve over its collapse.

In foreign affairs, the Unreconstructed think that domination by the United States and the Soviet Union is giving way to multipolarity and a broader range of independent national action. They disapprove of this trend, viewing it as inherently unstable and dangerous.

The Unreconstructed disapprove of every feature of de Gaulle's foreign policy and believe that virtually everything will be changed after de Gaulle. In European affairs the Unreconstructed pay lip service to the idea of reduced national sovereignty and favor closer cooperation and

33

Table 2.1

FIFTH REPUBLIC POLITICAL TYPES: CATEGORICAL SUMMARIES

	Gaullists	Riders	Notables	Aspirants	Unreconstructed
Attitude toward de Gaulle's leadership	Deference	Deference	Rejection	Rejection	Hostility
Enthusiasm about Fifth Republic	High	Qualified	Limited	Limited	Negative
Positive features of Fifth Republic	Many	Many	Some	Some	None
Feeling about future of Fifth Republic	Bright	Questionable	Dim	Dim	No future
Attitude toward French party system	Disdain	Disdain (perhaps superficial)	Respect	Qualified respect	Nostalgic respect
Attitude toward France in Europe	National decision-making must remain dominant	Nationals but confederation acceptable	Favor supra-nationality	Favor supra-nationality	Indeterminate

Table 2.2

GENERAL CHARACTERISTICS OF FIFTH REPUBLIC POLITICAL TYPES

	Gaullists	Riders	Notables	Aspirants	Unreconstructed
General	1. Extreme deference toward de Gaulle—stand for what de Gaulle stands for and would stand for	1. Verbally Gaullists—but skeptical about future; commitment to de Gaulle is conditional	1. Old political leaders —attachment to old parties and parliamentary system	1. Younger—look to a reformed Fifth Republic after de Gaulle	1. Unalterably opposed to de Gaulle and everything he stands for
Domestic affairs	1. Content with current regime 2. Current regime will last	1. Content with current regime 2. Not so sure it will last	1. Accept some features of current regime 2. Do not think it will last	1. Accept some features of Fifth Republic 2. Do not think Fifth Republic as now constituted will last 3. Look for party reform	1. Unalterably opposed to de Gaulle and everything he stands for
Foreign affairs	1. Favor regime's foreign policy 2. Approve force de frappe 3. Disapprove NATO in current form 4. Anti-MLF	1. Favor regime's foreign policy but not enthusiastically	1. Critical of regime's foreign policy	1. Critical of NATO and American policy	1. Prefer continuation of status quo (NATO) 2. Reject de Gaulle's foreign policy and expect it to be revised after de Gaulle
Europe	1. Favor loose confederation (if any at all) 2. Would exclude Great Britain	1. A little more European than Gaullist	1. Enthusiastically European and Confederationist	1. European	1. Nominally European 2. Would include Great Britain

links with the "Six" *and* with England. They hope that the status quo in NATO will continue. Believing that France can rely upon NATO and upon the American deterrent, they have no specific plans for the reform of NATO. In a sense they accept American hegemony as a "natural" fact. They reject the *force de frappe* and see in it only a Gaullist manipulation directed toward heightening the General's political position and his prestige. Since they do not believe it to be militarily credible, they look for its disappearance after de Gaulle. They see considerable stability in the "balance of terror."

Communists

The Communists are highly dissatisfied with the Fifth Republic regime and view its development as an entrenchment of technocratic, financial and business power at the expense of the French workers. They are highly critical of virtually all domestic aspects of de Gaulle's policy. They think the old parties are very much alive, and view their own electoral position optimistically.

With regard to world politics the Communists admit that the domination by the United States and Soviet Union is declining and that nationalisms are emerging. They are happy with the decline of American influence, apprehensive about the decline of Soviet influence and generally confused and worried about the strengthening of nationalisms. On balance, they disapprove of the regime's foreign policy. To them, de Gaulle is a neo-imperialist, "megalomaniac," and "anachronistic" figure imposing upon France goals well beyond her means. He is a "militarist." They are sure that de Gaulle's departure will bring about changes in foreign policy. Above all they fear a return to a pro-NATO stance or European integration.

The Communists say that France's deterrent is motivated primarily by prestige and political reasons. It is not credible; and it is "ruinous" for France economically. They hope that the *force de frappe* will be abandoned after de Gaulle, but are not at all sure it will be.

In the last analysis, the Communists join hands with the *Unreconstructed* in their preference for the present bipolarity and nuclear status quo to any alternative scheme.

Tables 2.1 and 2.2 show our summaries of the five types of French political elites in the Fifth Republic (ignoring, for the moment, the Communists). Using this typology as a basis, we categorized each of

Table 2.3

FRENCH RESPONDENTS ACCORDING
TO ELITE TYPE

Type	Number in Sample	Percentage of Sample
Gaullists	29	19.7%
Riders	20	13.6
Aspirants	34	23.1
Notables	48	32.6
Unreconstructed	14	9.5
Communists*	2	1.5
Total	147	100.0%

* Only two Communists agreed to be interviewed, claiming to speak "on behalf of the Party." We were thus forced to reconstruct Communist opinion on the basis of other evidence.

the 147 leaders whom we interviewed. The number of respondents fitting each category is shown in Table 2.3.

As indicated earlier, our respondents do not comprise a random sample of the French elite. For example, it is immediately apparent that we have too few Communists in our sample.[4] Nevertheless, our proportions are extremely suggestive. For example, in the first ballot of the election of 1962 the UNR (the bulk of the Gaullists and Riders) received 31.9 per cent of the total vote. Gaullists and Riders comprised about 33 per cent of our sample. In that same election the "old parties," represented in our sample mainly by the Notables and some of the Unreconstructed, received approximately 30 per cent of the vote. In our sample, the Notables and Unreconstructed accounted for about 40 per cent of

[4] The proportion of Communists in the French political elite at the present time is closer to six or seven per cent than to the 1.5 per cent that appeared in our sample. If we adjust the proportions of the various types in our sample to reflect the greater strength of the Communists, then we find that the proportion of Gaullists ranges approximately between 18 and 20 per cent; the proportion of Riders between 12 and 14 per cent; the proportion of Aspirants between 22 and 24 per cent; the proportion of Notables between 30 and 33 per cent; the Unreconstructed between 8 and 10 per cent; and the Communists between 2 and 7 per cent.

the respondents. What might be called the "Aspirant vote" in the 1962 balloting was spread among the *Parti Socialiste Unifié* (PSU), the Socialist party, the MRP and even the Gaullists. In our typology the Aspirants account for about 23 per cent of the respondents. The only significant discrepancy is that of the Communist popular vote in 1962 (21.8%) and our Communist elite percentage (1.5% or, if adjusted, 7%). But this can be explained on the generally accepted proposition that there are many fewer Communists among the elites than the electorate.[5]

Our categorization of respondents, therefore, could very well reflect something of the relative strengths of the various "types" among the French elite. It suggests fair representation among supporters of the Gaullist regime, but not necessarily any impressive strength because almost half of those who approve Gaullist policies are Riders who might well abandon both de Gaulle and the Fifth Republic in the event that "the game on the other table" proves more profitable for them to play. Then, too, the breakdown suggests a good deal of latent opposition to de Gaulle or to the Gaullist regime. If this deserves not to be called "opposition," then it should at least be called "dissatisfaction." Given this configuration of the elites in the Fifth Republic and our hunches as to their size and weight, one comes up with a picture of latent tension amid manifest, but perhaps temporary, stability. If this picture is accurate, we might have moved a step closer to answering the question "after de Gaulle what?", especially with regard to likely changes in the direction of foreign policy.

[5] In the presidential election of December 1965 de Gaulle received 44% of the vote, as opposed to about 33% of the vote of our panel comprising Gaullists and Riders. But again, as was the case with the election of 1962, a part of the Aspirant vote went to him. Furthermore the presidential election had inevitably plebiscitary overtones to which the masses are far more sensitive than the elites. What is extremely suggestive is that our figures indicated a widespread opposition to the President of the Republic. It may well be that only polarization between a Communist-supported candidate and de Gaulle saved the latter on the second ballot by a small margin (54.4% against 45.5%).

CHAPTER 3

Domestic Politics and Issues

The thesis advanced in various forms and with various qualifications by a number of writers is that the French political system has entered upon a period of rapid change that corresponds to major systemic changes of the French society. "New politics," it is claimed, are characterized by at least two major changes, both of which are largely reflected in the Constitution of the Fifth Republic as it was amended in 1962. First, as the society becomes increasingly modernized and industrialized, national issues are taking precedence over local ones, and, in addition, executive leadership and action increasingly replace parliamentary deliberation and initiative. A correlate of this is that the significance of local and other "intermediaries" between the people at large and their government is slowly declining and a closer nexus is being established between government and electorate. Second, the new politics are conducted by "new men" with a new approach and a new pragmatic policy orientation. The new politics and the new men both reflect and further enhance a new consensus that is slowly overcoming the old sectarian and ideological divisions of the French body politic and producing a political system that is highly legitimized.

Since we were particularly interested in gauging elite reactions to the above propositions, we probed their general satisfaction or dissatisfaction with the regime; the kind of positive or negative features they see in it; the extent to which they accept the present Constitution; and their general evaluation of the present states of the political parties and of their future.

SATISFACTION AND DISSATISFACTION

In attempting to gauge the degree of satisfaction or dissatisfaction with the regime, we realized that the best we could expect was to get a qualified composite picture that we could reproduce at the end. A "yes" or "no" answer is hard to come by and very few of our respondents gave it to us in those terms (and then only to qualify their responses later). With the vast majority of respondents who are satisfied with some aspects of the regime and some of its policies and dissatisfied with others, it is extremely hard to weigh accurately the degree or extent or intensity of satisfaction against dissatisfaction. A respondent may answer that he is satisfied with de Gaulle but that he considers the system a transient phenomenon. Another may declare himself satisfied with de Gaulle's Constitution, somewhat dissatisfied with his foreign and domestic policy and intensely dissatisfied with his military policy. In both cases it will require procrustean tactics on our part to weigh these answers and come out with an accurate picture of "satisfied" and "dissatisfied."

Answers then are highly qualified. Only nine per cent of respondents declared themselves highly satisfied, and only six per cent declared themselves highly dissatisfied with the regime. The rest fell into the two broad categories of satisfied (approximately 44 per cent) and dissatisfied (approximately 33 per cent). But the two categories, interestingly enough, overlap. Those moderately satisfied approve and disapprove of policy issues that are also approved or disapproved of by those moderately dissatisfied. (See Table 3.1.) Thus it is hard to establish "syndromes" of opinion among satisfied and dissatisfied respondents.

Table 3.1

SATISFACTION WITH PRESENT GOVERNMENTAL SYSTEM IN FRANCE

QUESTION: *Are you content with the present governmental system in France?*

	Number of Respondents	Percentage
Highly satisfied (enthusiastic about current regime)	13	9%
Satisfied (looks for no *major* changes)	27	18
Moderately satisfied (good in general, but some changes would help)	38	26
Indifferent (no better nor worse than previous regime)	11	7
Moderately dissatisfied (idea good, but many bad features)	25	17
Dissatisfied (looks for major changes)	24	16
Highly dissatisfied (negative toward idea and institution)	9	6
Don't know	0	0
Not ascertained	0	0
Total	147	99%

In general, it appears that there is considerable "satisfaction" with the present regime. Seventy-eight of 147 respondents (53%) consider themselves highly satisfied, moderately satisfied or simply satisfied. Only 58 (39%) are highly, moderately or simply dissatisfied. A small number (7%) declares itself to be indifferent. In the referendum of October 1962, by way of contrast, 61.8 per cent voted for General de Gaulle's constitutional reform measure, thus, according to many observers, registering their confidence in him, while 38.2 per cent voted against. On the second ballot of the presidential election, however, in December 1965, the figures were 54.4% against 45.5%.

POSITIVE AND NEGATIVE FEATURES

When we asked what the positive features of the present regime were, the answers given were extremely interesting. Sixty-five per cent of the respondents consider leadership to be the most important positive aspect of the regime—and by this the great majority means de Gaulle's personal leadership. Domestic policy is considered by 37 per cent to be the most important positive feature of the regime, and foreign policy is so considered by 35 per cent of the respondents. Only 10 per cent of the respondents see no positive features in the present regime. (See Table 3.2.)

In other words, an overwhelming majority of respondents associates the regime with General de Gaulle. There is no apparent association in

Table 3.2

POSITIVE FEATURES OF THE
FRENCH GOVERNMENTAL SYSTEM

QUESTION: *What are the positive features of the present form of government?*

	Number of Responses*	Percentage
Leadership	96	65%
Domestic policy	55	37
Foreign policy	52	35
Party system	8	5
Accessibility	0	0
Democratic nature	1	1
Elitist nature	14	10
No positive features	15	10
Don't know	0	0
Not ascertained	9	6
Total	250	169%

* Multiple responses permitted

Table 3.3

CHANGES IN THE
FRENCH GOVERNMENTAL SYSTEM

QUESTION: *To what extent is the governmental system changing due to the changing influence of groups?*

	Number of Respondents	Percentage
Fundamental systemic change	15	10%
Noticeable change (but won't change system)	26	17
Some change (minor)	76	52
No change at all	8	5
Don't know	2	1
Not ascertained	20	14
Total	147	99%

the minds of respondents between the regime and any systemic changes represented by structural modification of the society or the accession of certain groups to power—except for a general inclination to emphasize the influence of "technocracy." But this is not considered to account for any profound changes, as Table 3.3 indicates. The Gaullist system appears to be considered as a reflection of ephemeral or adventitious forces rather than an expression of systemic changes.

It is unfortunate that we included no specific question dealing with the negative aspects of the regime. A majority of respondents— even those who consider leadership to be its single most important positive feature—often implied that the "personal" character of the regime also constituted its single most important negative aspect. Leadership and the personal nature of the regime are reconciled in the growing acceptance of presidential government, in which, as we shall see, elites hope that leadership will become institutionalized and the personal, often arbitrary and discretionary, traits of the present regime will be carefully circumscribed. The obvious tension, therefore, between admiration of the regime because of its leadership and criticism of it because of its personal nature is only temporarily overcome.

THE CONSTITUTIONAL DEBATE

In the light of France's constitutional history, legitimization of the regime must be sought in the degree of agreement or disagreement with the present Constitution *and* on its viability. This Constitution, even if made by de Gaulle, is presumably the charter that will determine, if accepted, the future game of politics. If it is not accepted, however, de Gaulle's disappearance is bound to be followed by sharp conflict about the basic instrument of government that will undermine political action and decision-making.

The constitutional debate elicits remarkable areas of agreement but also ominous signs of disagreement. To begin with, virtually all respondents agree that there will be no return to the Constitution of the Fourth Republic. This negative type of agreement is not new. In 1944-45 only a very small fraction of the electorate favored a return to the institutions of the Third Republic. In the first post-World War II constitutional referendum on 21 October 1945, more than 95% of the voters opted for a Constituent Assembly to draft a "new" Republic. As became clear subsequently, however, this did not mean that the voters were in agreement as to what kind of new constitution they wished to have. It is likely that the same is the case today. Even so, disagreements are not as sharp and divisive as they were some two decades ago.

Second, a majority of respondents, including even many of the Notables, seems to be in agreement with constitutional provisions for a rationalized parliament. There is nonetheless a strong minority which interprets this simply to mean that parliament will not and should not again be able to make and unmake cabinets at will. The considerable, indeed in certain cases great, diminution of the legislative and control powers of parliament is not acceptable to more than half of the respondents. They believe that parliament ought to play "a more important role" both in legislation and control. How this control will be reconciled with cabinet stability is not clear. A number of schemes have been advanced by lawyers, political leaders and professors, and respondents repeat them. Some advocate in one fashion or another either the so-called "majority contract" or "automatic dissolution," and in many instances they advocate both. The device of a "majority contract" means that the "majority" in parliament will agree not to unseat the cabinet for the duration of the parliamentary mandate. If it did so, or, according to another version of the same scheme, whenever it did so, an "automatic dissolution" would be followed by elections.

Third, many respondents advocate a more "open" parliamentary system so that the executive cannot block all amendments and force a vote on its own measures. Many also advocate a more restricted use of the question of confidence by the prime minister so that he can no longer have his bills carried without majority support, as is the case now when he puts the question of confidence.[1]

Divergences about the functions and role of parliament are not so serious, however, when compared to two basic issues: the relationship between the president and the prime minister and the nature and scope of powers of the presidential office. As far as the presidential system is concerned, a majority of respondents accepts the basic mechanisms of the new Constitution as amended in 1962. For instance, an astonishing number—perhaps as many as 70%—accepts the "presidential system" itself as well as the direct popular election of the president. But they seem to disagree sharply on the nature of the presidency and the scope of its powers. Few respondents accept the "American system." Instead, two views of presidential government are advanced.

On the one hand, a majority of our respondents (Notables, some Riders, the Unreconstructed and many Aspirants) accepts the system as established by the Constitution of the Fifth Republic but rejects the Gaullist interpretation. They see no reason to change the letter of the Constitution but every reason to respect it. It is "our Constitution, not de Gaulle's," said a number of respondents (including numerous Notables). The president should not govern—he is an *arbitre*.[2] He should exercise the prerogatives of his office only when there is a parliamentary deadlock or grave emergency. The president is not now nor should he ever become a political leader and involve himself in elections, as de Gaulle has. The person that governs, according to Article 20 of the Constitution, is the prime minister as long as he has a majority in the National Assembly. He and his cabinet are the *responsible* government. All that is called for, then, is the resumption of cabinet government under

[1] The present Article 49 of the Constitution.
[2] This is the thesis expounded in Paul Reynaud, *Et Après?* (Paris: Plon, 1964).

the arbitration of the president. The latter should not use the referendum for political purposes or without the advice of his prime minister and should not attempt to modify the Constitution through referenda. Article 16—emergency powers—should be used in strict accordance with the Constitution.[3] When dissolution is decreed, a caretaker government should be appointed, and the president should remain neutral.

On the other hand, a strong minority of respondents (Gaullists, Riders, a few Notables and many Aspirants) favors a strong presidential executive. They feel, as we mentioned earlier, that the modernization of the society demands concentration on national issues, national participation and national leadership. But they differ on how a strong presidency should be institutionalized. Half of them, especially the political Aspirants, some Riders and the Notables, reject the Gaullist system. They advocate the establishment of an organic link between the president and the legislature through automatic dissolution. They further advocate the reduction of the presidential mandate to coincide with that of the mandate of the legislature. When the president dissolves parliament, he also must resign to confront the electorate and to assume his own political responsibility. Parliament could make the president do so by voting against his measures, thus forcing him either to accept the dictate of parliament or to dissolve parliament, and by so doing stake his own political future. But the other half of the Gaullists, the Riders and Aspirants (about 25% of all respondents) think that the system should continue *as it is*. The new electoral system provides for popular support and, once elected, the president continues to be the center of government. He has sufficient power to govern and adequate instruments to appeal to the public for support. Anything else, they argue, will force the system to slip back in one form or another to some kind of parliamentarism which once again will make for executive impotence.

Thus, the most salient feature of French political history—disagreement about the nature of the Constitution—continues to be present. *It may well be that the disagreement is narrowed in favor of a strong executive leadership—presidential or cabinet.* But this is an oversimplification. The very conflict about the type of presidential system and about the relations between the president and the prime minister may well be resolved by a compromise which, as many fear, may weaken the presidency and open the gates to parliamentary ascendancy. "Presidentialism"

---

[3] It should be invoked only when the enumerated conditions bring about "an interruption" in the "regular functioning of constitutional governmental authorities."

is a major source of contention overriding all other current constitutional issues. A sharp conflict over the institutionalization of the presidency, however, will not be an isolated affair. It will spill over into all other constitutional disagreements: the role of the prime minister, the electoral system, dissolution, constitutional reform, Article 16, use of referenda, and so forth, and will make compromise difficult.

POLITICAL PARTIES AND IDEOLOGIES

The whole issue of the type of executive leadership—whether presidential or cabinet—rests squarely on the existence of a majority that remains cohesive behind a political leader or around certain basic issues. The constitutional reform of 1962 and the means it provides for the popular election of the president is based upon the expectation that there will in fact be a majority to elect a president. But it is one thing to elect a president and another to produce a parliamentary majority that in one form or another will be cohesive enough to sponsor legislation and support the government. For this reason we raised in our interviews specific questions about the role and function of political parties —and the nature and intensity of ideological conflicts.

As Tables 3.4 and 3.5 indicate, the majority of our respondents believes that political ideologies, although they have not disappeared, are neither so intensive nor so divisive as they used to be. Most of the concrete responses (267 of 331, or 81%) refer to domestic issues—either policies, or overall ideological and class divisions. Fifty-one per cent of the responses specifically mention class and ideological divisions. But, of course, a number of other domestic issues are also indirectly class and ideological ones.

The persistence of ideological attitudes is clearly illustrated by the continuing significance attached by respondents to the Left-Right conflict. Almost half of our respondents considered it to be still important. What, then, are the specific ideological alignments and divisions of today?

The role of the state seems no longer to affect the ideological position of respondents in any way. Almost everyone believes that the state has an important role to play in social and economic affairs. There are, however, two issues that were constantly mentioned: *laicité*, and planning *vs.* liberalism. *Laicité* covers a number of attitudes. It is vague and

Table 3.4

MOST IMPORTANT CLEAVAGES IN CURRENT FRENCH POLITICS

QUESTION: *What are the most important cleavages and conflicts in French politics today?*

	Number of Responses*	Percentage
Class	20	14%
Ideological	54	37
Domestic political issues	81	55
Domestic current issues	53	36
Nationalism vs. supranationalism	42	29
Party political	15	10
Membership in Atlantic community	2	1
Armament issues	4	3
Other foreign policy issues	16	11
Other domestic cleavage (specify)	44	30
None	4	3
Don't know	2	1
Not ascertained	8	5
Total	345	235%

* Multiple responses permitted

diffuse opposition to the church, an equally diffuse rejection of "clericalism," and a more specific rejection of recent school reforms providing for subsidies to private (Catholic) schools. Communists and, among the Notables, the majority of the Socialists and some Radicals as well as some Gaullists and Riders consider this an important issue. It will not set people in a political family against each other as it used to, but it continues to shape conduct and attitudes and remains a stumbling block to unity.[4]

[4] It was the issue of *laicité* that was used by the leader of the Socialist Party, Guy Mollet, in order to block Defferre's efforts to form a broad federation of all parties other than the Gaullists and Communists in the summer of 1965—one year after our interviews.

Table 3.5

IMPORTANCE OF CONFLICT BETWEEN LEFT AND RIGHT IN FRANCE

QUESTION: *Is the conflict between Left and Right important today?*

	Number of Respondents	Percentage
Yes	71	48%
No	68	46
Don't know	1	1
Not ascertained	7	5
Total	147	100%

The issue of planning *vs.* economic liberalism cuts deeper and is extremely vital. In essence it is a slightly different form of the conflict between "socialism" and "capitalism" in its broadest political and philosophic connotations. It is a conflict that still—perhaps because of its diffusiveness—gives some meaning to the terms "Left" and "Right." Proponents of planning consider themselves heirs to Jaurés' humanistic socialism; they believe that through the state the collectivity should set economic and welfare goals and, indirectly at least, cultural goals. They feel that the competitive market system, like the American one, makes haphazard the allocation of resources and, by putting the profit motive above that of social and collective need, debases human nature and produces inequality. "Equality" is the great *idée force* of our century, many respondents say. A good number of them believes that it is this conflict that will determine the future of French politics. "Planners," it must be added, come from all categories of our respondents except the Unreconstructed.

There is yet a third ideological strand in contemporary French politics. French intellectuals and some political leaders are groping for some form of "guild socialism." Several term it *"démocratie participante."* It calls for increased participation on a decentralized basis of the various economic groups and professional groups in decision-making, particularly with regard to all problems that have economic and social character. This runs counter to the Gaullist conception of a strong central political state and of a strong political executive. It is the old conflict between executive power and legislative omnipotence couched in different forms. Many of the planners and guild socialists come from the ranks of those Aspirants who are reconciled to the presidential system. Thus, the contradictions between a strong executive leadership that many of them advocate and the decentralization implicit in their theory of professional representation is a portent of difficulties and frictions for the future.

POLITICAL PARTIES

Generally, respondents admit that there is an alienation from parties. They term the present state of things as one of *départisation* rather than *dé-ideologisation*. This has been caused, they agree, by a popular revulsion against the great number of political parties and their inability in the past to come to terms and support a government. They also point to the imperative need for party regrouping. In fact, many of them not only wish it but see it happening.

Yet, the parties remain very much alive in the eyes of our respondents (Table 3.6). And, asked what separates these parties from one an-

Table 3.6

CONTINUATION OF THE OLD PARTIES IN FRANCE

QUESTION: *Are the old parties dead?*

	Number of Respondents	Percentage
Yes	35	24%
No	103	70
Don't know	3	2
Not ascertained	6	4
Total	147	100%

other, 27 per cent see only superficial differences among them, 35 per cent see differences on domestic policy issues, 12 per cent see ideological differences, 5 per cent class differences and 10 per cent differences on foreign policy issues. Only a quarter of our respondents (mostly Gaullists and Riders) are prepared to bury the political parties.

A realignment and a merger of parties are deemed to be indispensable for the emergence of new democratic politics in the country. But our respondents see two major obstacles. The first is the Communist Party. It makes the combination of the "Left" into one or even two larger party groupings impossible. The second obstacle is de Gaulle himself. He may well continue to hold himself aloof from parties and to encourage a situation in which the parties will have no stake other than the presidency—a stake that they cannot hope to win while he himself is a candidate! A number of possibilities were suggested.

1. A radical reorganization of the Socialist Party under the leadership of the political Aspirants. It will unite the Left and attract a sizable number of Communists. It will not supersede the Communist Party but rather will establish a broad leftist, socialist, reformist party that will appeal to Communist voters, to many Notables and to a sizable part of the progressive Catholics among the Aspirants. This is the old dream of the Labor Party—a *Parti Travailliste*.

2. A Communist-led leftwing merger. Many leftwing intellectuals admit that, if the Communist Party were to change its ways and move in the direction of its sister party in Italy, this might not be impossible.[5]

3. France is likely to emerge with four large party groupings: the Communists, the Socialists, a Center Democratic Party and a Conservative Party. The Center will consist primarily of Radicals, MRP, some Socialists, some Independents (mainly from among the Notables) and perhaps a number of the UNR followers (mostly Riders). The Conservative Party will draw from the bulk of the UNR adherents and the great majority of Independents, that is, mostly from among the Notables, some Gaullists, the Riders and the bulk of the Unreconstructed.

4. France is likely to emerge with three large party groupings. The Communists, a broad coalition party of the Center and a Conservative Party, the latter represented by the Gaullists and the Riders. The establishment of a Center is based on the expectation that the Socialists will continue to lose strength and that the MRP and the Radicals will merge.

[5] Since the presidential election of 1965, the French Communist Party has been undergoing changes.

When we asked a leader of the Radical Party whether he was hopeful that this would come about, he answered, "Monsieur, you are asking me the question on which I have staked my political future." Many respondents hinted that his future was not very bright!

5. The establishment of a true Conservative Party will be modeled on the British Conservatives and will include, under the leadership of one of de Gaulle's heirs or heirs apparent, the majority of the Gaullists, Riders and even some of the Notables and Aspirants. The majority of respondents, however, is not very sanguine about this prospect and is more inclined to believe that the UNR will break up when de Gaulle disappears.

Thus, like the constitutional question, another central issue of the French political system—the future of political parties—is in the eyes of respondents filled with difficulties and uncertainties. There is no consensus. Since speculation about the future is very often based upon the political action respondents expect to take, the responses of our elites underline the existing fluidity. It may be that we are at the threshold of a major breakthrough and that parties will merge into three or four larger disciplined coalitions. But it is equally possible that the existing parties will hold on tenaciously to their organizations and their ideologies. As was the case with the Constitution and the presidential system, nobody wishes to return to the multi-party system of the Fourth Republic. But, though it is true that virtually all respondents know where they do not want to go, it is hard to tell where they are heading.

POLICY QUESTIONS

Divisions over policy issues that fed the traditional ideological conflicts of the French society appear to be less significant today. With the exception of a few, they are at least not so intensely felt as before. French elites almost unanimously consider Algerian independence and decolonization to be the most significant and positive aspect of Gaullism. De Gaulle's Algerian policy, whatever the equivocation and misunderstandings, "saved" the Republic from the extreme Right. Whatever the course of events and whatever the future developments in Algeria, the Republic is now safe. Connected with Algerian independence and the general approval of decolonization in Africa is the issue of the French Army. Again, despite the equivocations and delays, the manner in which de Gaulle managed to bring the Army under the control of civilian authority—even if it is his own authority—is generally approved.

While Algerian independence, decolonization and the taming of the Army are considered to be the most positive accomplishments of the Fifth Republic, virtually all other policy issues and decisions made by the regime are subject to differing evaluations and assessments. For many approval is fairly widespread, whereas for others there is on balance strong disapproval.

There is a general satisfaction with the development of the economy. The rate of growth is noted; the ability of France to hold her own in the Common Market is mentioned; full employment is viewed as an important accomplishment; the rise of productivity and of real wages is widely approved and is conceded even by the trade union leaders. There are, however, a number of qualifications and criticisms.

Despite the rate of growth, for instance, many claim that the economy is *not* moving as fast as it should and that, relative to Germany or even Italy, it is falling behind. *Economic planning*, especially with regard to the social sector of the economy, is slowly being undermined. Two reasons for this are advanced: (1) the commitment of the government to planning is giving way to a growing "flexibility" which gradually moves toward economic liberalism; and (2) even if some commitment to planning remains, the investments allocated and the efforts made are insufficient. There are at least three areas in which, despite governmental efforts, planning is seen as falling behind the needs of the people: housing, education and highway construction. Similarly, when it comes to an assessment of the fate of marginal groups—especially merchants, farmers and unskilled workers—it is generally felt that programs of rehabilitation, retraining and relocation are inadequate. Even Gaullists agree that the social sector of the economy is in need of serious attention. Recent reforms in agriculture are generally praised. Fears are expressed, however, that the reforms are not adequate and that there is still a fairly large number of uneconomical farms. More comprehensive measures in rationalizing agriculture are required, it is claimed, to direct in an orderly fashion the movement of people from the farm to the towns and to avoid or end discontent among certain groups of farmers in certain areas of the country.[6]

Criticisms are also voiced about *administrative reform*. "De Gaulle,"

[6] Many critical remarks were made against the then Minister of Finance who has since been replaced by Michel Debré.

said one respondent, "could have done anything in 1958 when he came to power or in 1962 when Algerian independence was granted." The government's interest in urban problems, especially in the Paris district, is mentioned with approval but, again, the progress of contemplated or initiated reforms is deemed unsatisfactory. It is primarily with regard to departmental reorganization that criticisms are more vocal. It is felt by many that the government should have eliminated many departments and consolidated them into larger administrative units. The old structures have been allowed to exist despite the fact that the need for direction and planning as well as the growth of communications make them anachronistic. "The regime has marked time," commented one respondent, and has in a sense obstructed the development of national politics by allowing departmental and regional interests to shelter the old political forces and the Notables.

Administrative reorganization, agricultural policy and economic growth do not appear, however, to be divisive issues. On balance, contentment and approbation—often qualified and unenthusiastic—is the general rule, for the regime has been effective. Criticism notwithstanding, few believe that another government or a different regime could have done better. In the eyes of the elite groups, when it comes to domestic politics, the positive aspects of the regime outweigh considerably the negative aspects. But it is also our impression that in the last few years there has been a reevaluation of the Fourth Republic. Numerous respondents, especially political Aspirants and Notables, said that de Gaulle continued many of the policies of the Fourth Republic and that indeed he very shrewdly had managed to exploit the successes and the structural reforms of the Fourth Republic while heaping insults and injuries upon its political leaders.

This general contentment appears to be reinforced by a belief that no major threat of upheaval confronts the society. When asked how French society would react to a major upheaval in the world, more than half (55%) of our respondents seem unable to envisage such an event. Most of the remainder (33% of the entire sample) refer to the death of a national leader, specifically de Gaulle. Only 10 per cent seem to envisage an economic crisis such as a depression.

THE FUTURE

Only a small minority of respondents believes that after de Gaulle things will continue as they are and that the succession problem will not be serious. They think that a man like Pompidou might unite the Right (Gaullists, Riders and some Notables) and that the UNR will also close ranks behind him. But even if the majority believes that the "regime" is likely to survive, they attach differing and contradictory interpretations. A good number of respondents is outrightly pessimistic. The word *"vide"* was used by almost a dozen of them; a number used the expression, *"il n'y aura rien."* Many used the suggestive shrug of the shoulders and "we do not know." "The problem of our future," said a member of the *Conseil d'État*, "is not political or constitutional, it is medical." The fact remains that a majority of respondents gives the regime a chance to survive (Table 3.7). Even if we were to eliminate from our calculations those who think the Fifth Republic "might" survive, there still would be almost 50 per cent who give the regime a strong chance of survival.

The preceding answers, however, call for two qualifications that

Table 3.7

EXPECTATION FOR SURVIVAL OF FIFTH REPUBLIC AFTER DE GAULLE

QUESTION: *What would be likely developments in French domestic politics over the next ten years? Will the Fifth Republic survive after de Gaulle?*

	Number of Respondents	Percentage
Definitely will survive	21	14%
Strong probability that it will survive	50	34
Might survive (some chance)	35	24
Undecided (doesn't know whether Fifth Republic will survive or not)	10	7
Slight possibility that it will not survive	1	1
Strong possibility that it will not survive	20	14
Fifth Republic definitely will not survive the death of de Gaulle	5	3
Not ascertained	5	3
Total	147	100%

become relevant when we ask our respondents directly, what will happen after de Gaulle? It appears that by survival of the Fifth Republic what most of them really mean is that they do not expect a return to the Fourth Republic. Second, many also think that one of the features of the Fifth Republic—the presidential regime with popular presidential elections—will continue after de Gaulle, but, as we have seen, with the considerable modifications. This is well illustrated, for instance, by responses about the role of political parties after de Gaulle. Forty-one per cent of the respondents believe that parties will play a "much more important role," and about eight per cent think that they "will dominate the political scene."

The likelihood that the Gaullist regime might outlive de Gaulle, however, did not give pleasure to our elites. A good part of the respondents believed that de Gaulle would run in December 1965—as he did—and stay in the presidency until 1972. If so, the regime might be legitimized especially among the younger voters. By 1972 more than 25 per cent of the voters will have known only the Gaullist system. Then, too, the UNR will be better entrenched in the various departments and localities than it is at present. This, of course, was no source of comfort to the Notables, the Aspirants, the Communists and the Unreconstructed. The strong vote against de Gaulle in 1965 may have been due, at least in part, to the apprehension of many that another seven-year term would in fact lead to the legitimization of the system and to the entrenchment of the UNR.

Thus de Gaulle, who dominates the present, casts a long shadow on the future. How and exactly when he will step out of the political scene, what will be the domestic and international situation and the party alignments at that time, are factors that cannot be weighed at this time. Few wish to see him go *now*, but many fear his prolonged stay in power. The ambivalence is rooted in the personal nature of the present regime. At the very moment when there is a large consensus, it is a fragile one deeply interwoven with the person of the man who embodies it.

CHAPTER 4

Foreign Policy and World Politics

De Gaulle, the architect of French foreign policy, means different things to different groups. His policy is perceived by our elite groups in many varying and often contradictory ways. This makes the task of the analyst very difficult: Tabulation of responses often distorts instead of clarifying opinion patterns since every answer is given in terms of a series of assumptions on the part of respondents. Only if the response is linked to these assumptions and conditions can we construct a dynamic picture of French elite opinion on foreign policy questions.

All we can do here is to show the complexity of the opinion patterns we detected and indicate the extent of ambiguity and contradiction. The latter, however, is extremely significant. The greater the ambiguity and the range of contradictions in the perception of foreign policy issues, the greater the possibilities of change when de Gaulle disappears.

THE IMAGE OF DE GAULLE

If we disregard the small minority that attributes to de Gaulle personal motives devoid of all other content, the great majority regards him as a "nationalist," a "pragmatist," a "Machiavellian" or a "realist," a "nineteenth-century man," but some see him as an "internationalist" and a "European."

French respondents realize that to call a man, and especially a French political leader, a "nationalist" is not saying much. Hence, the term is quickly qualified to mean a number of things. For a handful, his nationalism is "jingoism" with all that it entails—an assertion of narrow and petty national values, xenophobia, anti-Americanism and so forth. For many others, de Gaulle is primarily a Maurassian, a man who exalts the uniqueness of French national values and traditions to the exclusion of all others, a man for whom the destiny of France and French civiliza- tion is superior to all other nations and who would in the pursuit of the realization of France's superior destiny brook no compromise. Respond- ents who see in de Gaulle's nationalism the narrow aspects of "jingoism" or the loftier but perhaps equally confining aspects of Maurassian na- tionalism think that de Gaulle's lip service to "Europeanism" is an effort to reestablish French hegemony in Europe. But there is yet a third inter- pretation of de Gaulle's nationalism, borrowed from Hegel. According to this, de Gaulle's nationalism has two significant traits: first, an effort to realize, within the framework of a national entity, the best values of Western civilization—freedom, humanism and justice. In this sense de Gaulle's nationalism is a progressive force. The spirit, after flirting with Prussia, has now definitely settled on France. Second, the realiza- tion of Western values in France carries its own dialectic by paving the way toward a European community based on those values. Gaullism, which in its own way is doing just that, thus again plays a highly progressive role.

A fair number of respondents does not believe that de Gaulle has any philosophy of world politics. To be sure, he is a "nationalist" in the sense he has so often explained himself: The nation-state is the basic center of man's loyalty, and as yet nothing has emerged to replace it. De Gaulle's objective, therefore, is to enhance the strength of France. Implementation and tactics are subordinated to this objective. He will do different things at different times, will follow different alliance pat- terns, will eliminate considerations of "ideology" or "morality" if they block the accomplishment of his objectives, or will appeal to "ideology" or "morality" if that seems necessary.

De Gaulle is called a "nineteenth-century man" by a number of respondents. The term pinpoints what many consider to be the anachronistic aspects of Gaullism. After evoking the need of "great wholes," after taking a strong stand in favor of colonial emancipation, in short, after espousing the trends and developments that many respondents consider progressive, de Gaulle has re-entrenched himself behind French national barriers. Instead of urging cooperation that transcends the limits of national boundaries, Gaullism has glorified the nation and has re-introduced the system of classic alliances as the only acceptable means of international cooperation. Furthermore, by playing the game of balance of power himself, he has exacerbated internal antagonisms in Europe, and he has helped bring about what he prophesied to be inevitable and natural—nationalisms.

Few respondents see de Gaulle as an internationalist. Both his emphasis upon national states and his general contempt for the United Nations speak for themselves according to many. But a surprising number of respondents affirms de Gaulle's attachment to the Atlantic community and to the Atlantic Alliance (a point to which we shall return later). A good number also believes that de Gaulle is a genuine European in the sense of working for the eventual establishment of a European union. It is interesting in this respect to note that, 40% to 50% of the French public have, over the last five years, considered de Gaulle to be a "dedicated supporter of European unification."

SATISFACTION AND DISSATISFACTION

The regime's foreign policy is the subject of serious soul-searching and controversy among elite groups. They see nuances and make qualifications that are not present in public opinion polls. Half of them, however, approve "enthusiastically," "mildly" or "generally," while 46 per cent "disapprove" of the government's foreign policy. Only 3 per cent are "indifferent." (See Table 4.1.) If we were to ignore those who mildly approve or disapprove, then those who show positive approval and those who show positive disapproval split almost evenly at 33 and 35 per cent, respectively.

The stability of the institutions, the prestige of General de Gaulle

Table 4.1

FRENCH FEELINGS ABOUT THE GOVERNMENT'S FOREIGN POLICY

QUESTION: *Are you satisfied with the government's foreign policy measures?*

	Number of Respondents	Percentage
Enthusiastic approval of regime's foreign policy	21	14%
General approval of regime's policy without enthusiasm	28	19
Mild approval (more good features than bad)	25	17
Indifference (doesn't care)	4	3
Mild disapproval	16	11
General disapproval (without emotional involvement)	24	16
Vehement disapproval	28	19
Doesn't know about government's foreign policy	0	0
Not ascertained	1	1
Total	147	100%

and the economic recovery and relative military strength of contemporary France are all factors that account for the manner in which the majority of elites views France's role in the world. No matter what the reservations about the foreign policy issues may be, virtually all respondents, even those who are dissatisfied, view France's new role with pride. This can be understood against the background of the last 25 years—a background of defeat, occupation, progressive loss of status, and colonial retrenchment. It has a strong nationalistic flavor (one that has, however, a distinct compensatory character). It is linked with a restatement of France's "civilizing mission" and with the postulate that France's culture and humanism are superior to that of any other society.

Two basic ideas are associated with France's renewed national aspirations: first, the conviction among the great majority of elites (73%) that the bipolar division of the world was artificial and is breaking up—a trend they favor; second, the notion that Europe and particularly France (though, as we shall see, there is a tendency on the part of respondents to speak of Western Europe and France interchangeably) are too mature to be totally dependent upon the United States. These two ideas, developed by intellectuals, writers and political leaders (and not just Gaullist leaders), reflect de Gaulle's position as well. Most respondents, for instance, insist that some degree of equality between France (or Europe) and the United States in the development of strategy within NATO is logical, necessary and inevitable and believe that if the alliance is to continue there must be a broad functional division of labor, tantamount to independence, in which the "historic interests" of France in Europe and Africa are fully respected and supported and in which the United States and England revert to their traditional spheres of interest. Indeed, some respondents try to justify de Gaulle's more extreme pronouncements by saying that they are primarily tactical moves to force deliberation within NATO that would lead to more intimate consultations on strategy.

The great majority of respondents thus agrees that the old bipolar arrangements are breaking down. The world is moving toward multipolarity or multicentrism for the following reasons:

1. Bipolarity was impossible: (a) It ignored the pervasive and tenacious phenomenon of nationalism in Western and Eastern Europe and in other parts of the world. National states continue to evoke powerful symbolisms and attachments everywhere in the world. They remain the only viable centers of human solidarity. (b) In the conflict that developed between the "two centers," the Soviet Union and the United States were forced to appeal to national forces within their own respective blocs, thus undermining their own hold upon them.

2. The development of regional international blocs was equally inevitable. De Gaulle himself evoked the need of larger "ensembles" and felt that small nation-states had no hope of pursuing national objectives against or in cooperation with the superpowers. Thus, again, bipolarity was inevitably destined to give way to multipolarity.

3. The balance of terror between the Soviet Union and the United States made a confrontation in military terms between the two superpowers very unlikely. It, therefore, encouraged states that belonged to one bloc or another to pursue their own national aspirations, since intervention by either the Soviet Union or the United States was "deterred" by the fear that it might lead to war between the two. Under the

Table 4.2

FRENCH FEELINGS ABOUT TREND IN WORLD POLITICS

QUESTION: *Do you welcome the current trend in world politics?*

	Number of Respondents	Percentage
Strongly favors current trend (enthusiastic about current trend, whatever trend he thinks it is)	39	27%
Favors current trend but not enthusiastically	50	34
Favors current trend but with considerable reservation	30	20
Doesn't care one way or the other (or undecided)	7	5
Conditionally against current trend	10	7
Against current trend but not vehemently	7	5
Vehemently opposed to current trend in world politics	0	0
Doesn't know	0	0
Not ascertained	4	3
Total	147	101%

awesome nuclear umbrella of the two superpowers, national independence movements stirred and came into being.

What is more, a majority of respondents favors this trend, as may be seen in Table 4.2.

Yet the general belief that many centers of power are developing and the fact that our respondents favor this trend in no way means that they do so without reservations. Moreover, they do not favor the development of strong nationalisms and the proliferation of independent and sovereign nation-states. In fact 45 per cent of our respondents favor reduction of national sovereignty and an additional 38 per cent do so conditionally.

How do we reconcile this apparent contradiction? It simply requires a realization that, in favoring a trend away from bipolarity,

French elites do not necessarily envisage the proliferation of independent national states and independent foreign and military policies, but rather the development of a new "European" center of power. Discussion about the feasibility of an independent foreign policy for nation-states brought this out quite clearly. Despite the Gaullist propositions, when pressed hard, very few members of the French elite think that any country can have its own independent foreign policy with all that it entails. The logic of independence, they concede, does not apply even to the Soviet Union and the United States.

This again becomes clear when we asked respondents to choose between independent national action and cooperation in alliance. Only 25 per cent favor independent national action, whereas 62 per cent favor cooperation in alliance. A large number of respondents (32%) hedge their answers and couch their remarks in conditional terms: Under certain conditions they would favor either national action *or* cooperation in alliance. "Alliance," it must be clearly understood, does not necessarily mean integration.

The same is the case when respondents are asked to envisage the best way to defend the French national interest. Over three-quarters (77%) opted for alliances, 35 per cent for integrated international defense schemes (such as the European Defense Community), and one-third (33%) for other forms of international diplomacy—together accounting for 212 (67%) of the 318 responses given. Strictly national solutions account for only 95 (30%) of the 318 responses given. The preference for multilateral means of defense is clear.

FOREIGN POLICY ISSUES

As we have seen, French elites seem to be divided in the perception of de Gaulle's underlying philosophy and hold different images of the man. When it comes to specific policy issues, the divisions appear to be equally great.

Recognition of Communist China

The majority of respondents approves of the recognition of Communist China, but for different reasons. For some it is simply a logical imperative stemming from international law. The government controlling China should be recognized as the only legitimate government of territorial China. Some who agree that this is so deplore de Gaulle's manner and timing of the recognition. A minority finds the recognition to be a quixotic gesture that has only irritated the United States without providing any advantages to France. "What can we contribute to China?" is the question many ask; "What business do we have there?" And even if recognition were necessary, why not do it after consultation with the United States? Others see no purpose in the recognition except de Gaulle's intention to bring to the fore the issue of American global strategy. A person very close to de Gaulle told us that, when Dean Acheson was sent to Paris by President Kennedy during the Cuban crisis, de Gaulle asked him, "Have you come to consult me or to inform me?" Acheson reportedly answered that he was informing de Gaulle. De Gaulle is making every effort to force the United States to accept the principle of consultation. A small number of respondents sees in the recognition of China the implementation of the theory of the balance of power. A *rapprochement* between the United States and the Soviet Union may pose severe threats to the independence of France and Western Europe. The proper response is an alliance with China. De Gaulle is appealing to China as Canning appealed to the "new world" early in the nineteenth century, that is, to redress the world balance of power in favor of France and Europe. It is this attitude and the empiricism underlying it that is sharply criticized by a number of well-informed respondents. "First it was Russia in 1944; then England; then Germany and the Franco-German accord; then the Fouchet plan; now it is China." "The only outcome," many say, "will be to isolate us and to alienate all our friends."

Southeast Asia

According to a survey of May 1964, 52 per cent of the French people thought that France had no role to play in Vietnam; 21 per cent thought that she did; and 27 per cent could not or would not answer. De Gaulle's suggestion for a conference and for the neutralization of the area nonetheless appeals to a great percentage of the elites. First, there is the attraction of the very idea of neutralization to which many intellectuals remain nostalgically committed; second, there is the realization that an extension of the war might drag the United States into that area and commit its resources there; third, there is the fear that the war may escalate with all that that entails; finally, there is the prevalent feeling that France continues to have attachments in Vietnam and that French influence—political, intellectual, economic and even military—can be reaffirmed there if the United States, the Soviet Union and China were to withdraw. Even some who disagree with de Gaulle's basic aims are sympathetic to his suggestion for neutralizing Southeast Asia.

Latin America

More than anything else, de Gaulle's trip to Latin America was viewed with irony. "Millions will applaud de Gaulle and curse the Americans," a respondent said. "Then what? De Gaulle will give false hopes, arouse emotions, provoke anti-American incidents—and for what purpose? What can we give to Latin America even if we exalt the common Latin heritage?" But again de Gaulle's purpose, according to many, is to force the Americans to accept the principle of consultation in establishing global strategy within the Atlantic Alliance.

Eastern Europe

The official French position, shared by a great number of respondents, is that Yalta was a serious mistake. It indicated clearly the Americans' lack of diplomatic skill and showed how dangerous it is to let American policy-makers handle European problems. In a number of pronouncements de Gaulle himself sharply criticized the Yalta arrangements, attributing them in part to the fact that France was absent. The French position, then, is, if possible, to restore Europe to its pre-World War II boundaries (with some obvious qualification centering on the Oder-Neisse boundary, German reunification and rearmament).

The present balance of terror between the United States and the Soviet Union is so overwhelming, the argument continues, that neither country can afford to challenge the position of the other. If anybody had any doubts, this was shown conclusively during the Cuban crisis. The two blocs, therefore, are likely to be frozen. No matter what the United States would like to accomplish in Eastern Europe (liberation, "rollback" or something else), it is unable to do it for fear of causing friction with the Soviet Union that might escalate into a war. France, however, if given enough leeway, might be in a better position to provide for a "liberation" of the Eastern European countries. France is a natural source of attraction for Eastern European leaders; unlike the United States, it does not represent a threat to the Soviet Union, and, in addition, it holds the promise of an independent Europe from which both Soviet and American troops might withdraw. The French attitude provides for flexibility where there is rigidity, and for maneuvering where there is only the prospect of nuclear confrontation.

French elites generally believe that contacts with Eastern Europe are improving and that already there are signs that pent-up national emotions in Eastern Europe may find emancipation from Soviet rule. Contacts with France—as the July 1964 visit of the Rumanian Prime Minister and other subsequent visits show—provide opportunities for Eastern European nations that do not provoke Soviet antagonisms in the way that American aid and support do. Such a development is further facilitated by the Sino-Soviet dispute which may well force the Soviet Union to align itself with the "West." The obvious price the Soviets will have to pay is a relaxation of their control over Eastern Europe. Then the Gaullist idea about a Europe from the Atlantic to the Urals may become a reality.

There is widespread sympathy among the elites for this position and considerable hope that it might come about. In other words, the French elites would like to see the ante-bellum Europe restored in a way (that is, without a strong unified Germany) that will strengthen the position of France. This hope, incidentally, is one of the reasons why the thesis of an independent Western Europe is supported and why even reservations about a long-term presence of American troops in Europe are expressed by some respondents.

Germany

The status of Germany[1] was once declared by General de Gaulle to be the central problem of our universe. The anti-German attitude of the French public and elites immediately after World War II seems to have disappeared almost entirely. Public opinion polls reported in *Sondages* or gleaned from the files of the *Institut Français d'Opinion Publique* (IFOP) also show a reversal of public attitudes on the suitability of Germany as an alliance partner. In April 1964, for instance, to the question, "If you had a choice between West Germany and England as a principal ally, which country would you choose?" 41 per cent chose West Germany, 37 per cent England, and 22 per cent did not know. (In a similar question asking for a choice between the United States or England, 56 per cent were for the United States and 19 per cent for England; between the United States or Germany, 50 per cent were for

[1] Virtually all interviews were concluded before the visit of General de Gaulle to Bonn in July 1964.

the United States, 29 per cent for West Germany and 21 per cent did not know.) This, however, does not mean that there is a widespread affirmation of confidence and trust in West Germany among French elites. They tend to be more reserved, to qualify in a number of ways the Franco-German *rapprochement*, to express serious doubts about de Gaulle's efforts to make the cornerstone of his European policy out of a Franco-German alliance and to fear a revival of German strength.

Strong traces of diffidence toward Germany are noticeable. There were repeated assertions that Germany "cannot be trusted" and expressions of a lingering fear that she might return to her old ways. The majority of respondents also feels that West Germany is actually and potentially far more powerful than France and that, if Europe were to be left to France and Germany, Germany would assume and play the dominant role. A recurring criticism against de Gaulle is that his effort to make the Franco-German alliance the cornerstone of his European policy, to the exclusion of Great Britain and the United States, is paving the way to a situation that may underwrite German power and French inferiority.

Elite feelings about Germany come out openly when we discuss the question of reunification. Twenty-nine per cent favor it, but 24 per cent only conditionally. Thus, those who favor it unconditionally amount to only five per cent of our sample—eight respondents in all! Those who are against it comprise 40 per cent, of whom half are solidly against and another half conditionally against German reunification. Only 17 per cent think that German reunification would enhance French security, whereas 31 per cent consider it to be a threat. Forty-eight per cent of our panel fell into the category of "not ascertained" because they had made it quite clear that they would not entertain the thought of a unified Germany and that, therefore, it was superfluous to ask the question. With this in mind, we venture the guess that more than two-thirds of our panel of 147 consider German reunification to be a threat to French security. This latent fear may in part account for the fact that a majority (51%) of our panel does not foresee German reunification for at least the next 25 years.

Virtually no one advocates either granting nuclear capabilities to West Germany outright or effective West German participation in deciding overall nuclear strategy for a European atomic force (if and when such a force is established). The same respondents who argue so well on the basis of logical inferences drawn from basic postulates refuse to see that the same arguments apply also to a West German nuclear force. "Politics is not logic," one master of dialectics said when we came to this point: "The Germans just cannot be allowed to play with atomic toys." A respondent who demolished NATO so brilliantly, by showing us that it no longer corresponds to the needs and situations that existed when it was established in 1949, invoked the Paris accords and the ABC clause as a definitive argument against German possession of nuclear weapons.[2]

Returning to the Franco-German alliance, to de Gaulle's "Grand Design" for Europe, a majority of respondents feels that it has been a failure. Germany and France have not followed the procedures laid down in the Treaty of 1963, and each nation is more prone than ever to follow its own policy without consulting the other. Several blame Erhard; others see in the treaty itself the signs of German independence and reaffirmation of national strength; some blame the United States; but a majority comes back to criticize de Gaulle's nationalism, his "No" to English membership in the Common Market, his attitude toward the United States and his general reluctance to work effectively for a unified Europe.

At a time when the French people look upon Germany with growing confidence and warmth and consider the Gaullist policy to be consistent with European union, the French elites see in it not only a threat to France's position in Europe but also a gamble that is potentially disruptive of the European movement. More than in the past, they consider Britain's participation in the Common Market to be necessary in order to offset France's relative isolation and to balance France's relative weakness vis-à-vis West Germany.

FRANCE AND THE UNITED STATES

Relations between France and the United States are viewed in so many different contexts, in terms of so many conditions and with such a degree of emotion that simple answers on this topic cannot be given.

[2] Article 1 of Protocol No. III of the Paris Agreements reads in part: "The High Contracting Parties, members of Western Europe Union, take note of and record their agreement with the Declaration of the Chancellor of the Federal Republic of Germany (made in London on 3rd October, 1954, and annexed hereto as Annex I) in which the Federal Republic of Germany undertook not to manufacture in its territory atomic, biological and chemical weapons."

The most prevalent attitude is that of the ambivalence that children and parents often display in their feelings toward each other.

Resentment stems from many sources. The liberation of France is a debt that cannot easily be paid off. It is often ignored, and history is beginning to be rewritten. The lack of confidence in the French so often voiced by American leaders in the past is now fully reciprocated. A society, such as the United States, which devotes at least one out of every four years to electioneering for the highest office in the land is not a stable society. The perennial questions, "Which French government?" or "How can we trust the French when we do not know their government?" are now directed toward the United States by the French. The majority of the French elites is convinced, for instance, that between the time of President Kennedy's assassination and the election of November 1964—a full year—the government of the most powerful nation of the West remained stalemated and immobilized. The Gaullist plea for "independence" is, therefore, strengthened.

Still another and quite significant source of distrust lies in the operation of the economic system of the United States. Quite a few of the Gaullists and the Aspirants see in the American system an unadulterated exploitive capitalism that accounts for the subjection of the American Negro, the perpetuation of crude materialistic values and the satisfaction of frivolous wants ("gadget production") through an uncontrolled market system. A prevalent image of the United States is that of imperialism—an attitude that generally accounts for French pessimism about American foreign policy in Latin America, Southeast Asia or Africa. American power cannot be used intelligently, they say. This image of American imperialism is also the source of another fairly prevalent attitude; fear of American domination of the European markets through increased American investments.

Generally speaking, French elites feel that Franco-American relations are deteriorating. Reasons given for this deterioration are many (Table 4.3), but most respondents think that the only serious conflict between France and the United States lies in the realm of defense, that is, the *force de frappe* and NATO policy. A number of respondents (14%) mentions trade policies, "economic penetration" or "American investments."

Despite the controversies between de Gaulle and the United States, the general and widespread criticisms of American actions, both economic and political, and despite the general attachment of those, who

Table 4.3

MAJOR SOURCES OF FRICTION BETWEEN FRANCE AND THE UNITED STATES

QUESTION: *What are the major sources of possible friction between the United States and France?*

	Number of Responses*	Percentage
NATO policy	101	69%
Force de frappe	96	65
Southeast Asia policy	34	23
Trade policies	20	14
Personal characteristics of de Gaulle	19	13
French desire for greater independence	15	10
Policy toward China	13	9
Policy toward non-Western countries (excluding China)	13	9
Insufficient consultation by United States	8	5
Policies toward European unity	7	5
Policy toward Russia	2	1
Other	4	3
No recognizable friction	4	3
Not ascertained	3	2
Total	339	231%

* Multiple responses permitted

criticize de Gaulle, to the European idea as the most desirable alternative to Gaullist policies, 87 per cent of our respondents mention the United States as a country with which France has had and will have common interests over a long period of time (Table 4.4). Only the countries of the Common Market take precedence with 88 per cent. It is also worthy of note that over half (52%) of our elite respondents consider England to have long-term interests shared with France.

Whatever the nature of the American system, it is argued by many

Table 4.4

COUNTRIES OF PERCEIVED COMMON
INTEREST WITH FRANCE

QUESTION: *With which countries will France continue to share common interests for a long period?*

	Number of Responses*	Percentage
EEC countries	130	88%
United States	128	87
Great Britain	76	52
Germany	55	37
Russia	8	5
Other responses	9	6
No other country	0	0
Don't know	0	0
Not ascertained	2	1
Total	408	276%

* Multiple responses permitted

that France needs the United States until a united Europe is established. The basic international realities are such that France "cannot do without the United States" for the time being. Both in diplomacy and in defense, and perhaps even in order to build Europe, France needs American support: French independence must be qualified by the realities of American power and the need for American support. The public also shares this view: More than 50 per cent chose the United States as an ally in preference to any other nation.

TRENDS

French elites overwhelmingly identify de Gaulle's death as virtually the most important domestic event likely to bring about a change in the nation's foreign policy. About 90 per cent, or 132 out of our 147

Table 4.5

FRENCH FOREIGN POLICY AFTER DE GAULLE

QUESTION: *Which features of French foreign policy, if any, are likely to remain after de Gaulle?*

	Number of Responses*	Percentage
Franco-German rapprochement	72	49%
Policy toward United States	70	48
Policy toward East	46	31
Policy toward relations with non-Western nations	37	25
Policy toward NATO	34	23
Policy toward European integration	10	7
All of the above (i.e., whole foreign policy)	6	4
Other responses	19	13
No features will remain	15	10
Don't know	0	0
Not ascertained	13	9
Total	322	219%

* Multiple responses permitted

respondents, said so. But what changes will his disappearance produce? Table 4.5 clearly shows that the most controversial issue is Europe. Only 7 per cent of the respondents affirm that the present policies toward European integration are likely to continue. Thus, by inference, we may expect significant changes in the direction of European integration. By way of contrast, 52 per cent believe that de Gaulle's policy toward the United States (primarily his demands for equality in the development and implementation of global strategy) is likely to continue.

CHAPTER 5

Europe and NATO

It is the Gaullist policies with regard to Western Europe and particularly the Common Market that appear to be the most controversial ones today. As we saw earlier, most of our panel members view the world as moving in the direction of multipolarity. It is therefore not startling for them to perceive the policies of states as "increasingly nationalistic in flavor." However, they seem to be quite unhappy with this trend. About five-sixths (83%) of our panel favor further limitations of sovereignty, either "enthusiastically," "generally" or "conditionally." Only 16 per cent are indifferent or opposed. Of those in favor, 45 per cent are unequivocally so, while 38 per cent favor it conditionally.

Who are those who favor limitations upon national sovereignty? What are the conditions for those who conditionally favor it? What limitations are envisaged?

It is hard to answer these questions. Table 5.1 may provide some answers. Less than half of the respondents (47%) favor international pat-

Table 5.1

FRENCH PERCEPTIONS OF EUROPEAN INTEGRATION

QUESTION: *What form of union most nearly describes an integrated Europe as you generally think of it?*

	Number of Responses*	Percentage
International system (no more supranationality than at present; cooperation and coordination only)	20	14%
Mixed system with certain functions supranationally controlled and others nationally controlled; national dominance	49	33
Confederation	26	18
Mixed system as above; supranational dominance	39	27
Federal system (one European state)	30	20
Unitary European state	3	2
Don't know	2	1
Not ascertained	8	5
Total	177	120%

* Multiple responses permitted

terns and alliances that emphasize "national dominance," whereas 67 per cent of the responses favor some kind of "supranational dominance": 18 per cent are for confederation, 27 per cent for a "mixed" system with supranational dominance, 20 per cent for a federal system and two per cent for a "united" Europe. The "European vocation" in evidence here and the emphasis upon supranational arrangements are an indication that French elites are restive with the Gaullist themes.

There is nonetheless an apparent contradiction between nationalist views, quite prominent in France today, and the rather impressive figures favoring limitations on national sovereignty and supranational arrangements. *This contradiction can be resolved, as we have mentioned earlier, only by realizing that a "European vocation" is at one and the same time a manifestation of nationalism and a commitment to supra-*

nationalism. It is not only an acceptance of multicentrism but also an affirmation of a supranational arrangement that transcends nationalisms. In other words, one can be a French nationalist *and* a European; it is no longer inconsistent to argue for both forms of "independence." De Gaulle's ninth press conference of 23 July 1964, in which he stated in effect that France's policy was the policy of Europe, should not have caused surprise. French elites also use "France" and "Europe" interchangeably. The interests of the one are inextricably associated with the interests of the other; they have no longer separate and distinct entities. Indeed, many, even Gaullists, believe that national entities can sustain themselves only in the European context. It is not astonishing, therefore, to have the very same respondents who see a growing multipolarity in our world, and who favor this trend, also favor a European "entity" or "unity," and therefore, a reduction in national sovereignty.

When we move from these generalities to specific questions, the answers call for careful qualifications. What is Europe after all? What is the role of the Common Market? What form is unification to take? What will be the role of "Europe" if it is ever established as a political entity? How will it relate to the United States? What are the positive and negative aspects of Gaullist policy, and how likely is it that this policy will be modified?

THE FRENCH VIEW OF EUROPE

By "Europe" most respondents mean either the Six of the Common Market or the Six and England. In fact, the Six and England, despite de Gaulle's "no," come first with 35 per cent of the responses (Table 5.2). The Six alone was the choice for 22 per cent of our respondents. In realistic terms, the choice seems to be limited to these two combinations. Only 14 per cent mention the "Six and the Seven," and a mention of the famous "Atlantic to the Urals" theme (with or without the Soviet Union) is injected by only seven per cent of our respondents.

There is, however, no agreement on the objectives of European unity. Our respondents may be divided into three clearly defined groups (Table 5.3). The greatest number of answers supports the political and economic vision of European unity particularly as a solution of problems that can no longer be solved within the nation-state. The idea

Table 5.2

FRENCH VIEW OF FUTURE COMPOSITION OF A EUROPEAN UNION

QUESTION: *In your opinion, which countries should be included in such a European union?*

	Number of Respondents	Percentage
The Six	33	22%
The Six and England	51	35
The Six and the Seven	20	14
The Six and the Seven; Eastern Europe	12	8
Europe from the Atlantic to the Urals	10	7
Other configurations	13	9
Don't know	2	1
Not ascertained	6	4
Total	147	100%

of a "Third Force"—vis-à-vis Communism, the United States or both, or merely as reinforcement of the European bargaining position in world politics—also finds a prominent place in the thinking of French elites. Defense and military considerations are mentioned only by few.

Although a majority of our elite panel favors some kind of supra-national European arrangement, it is less sanguine about the possibility that such an arrangement will be realized. Only 19 per cent of our panel give it any chance of achievement in the coming ten years. Almost half (47%) feel that it probably or definitely will not be achieved in the coming ten years. An additional 30 per cent may be considered as somewhat hopeful, but their mild optimism is tempered by so many contingencies that it may well turn out to be no more than wishful thinking. Thus, while "Europeanism" in the sense of stronger political and economic ties in Western Europe (with or without England) appears to be the strongest single policy supported by our elite panel, hopes for its fulfillment appear to be at a low level.

Table 5.3

FRENCH VIEW OF THE PURPOSE OF EUROPEAN UNIFICATION

QUESTION: *What, in your thinking, would be the primary value of a united Europe? That is, what do you think is the purpose of European integration?*

	Number of Respondents*	Percentage
Generally, to give Europeans the means and resources to solve economic, social and political problems currently insoluble by nation-states acting alone	83	56%
Economic betterment of the European peoples	78	53
To reinforce the European bargaining position in world politics	63	43
To strengthen the European position vis-à-vis the United States	41	28
To strengthen the West against Communism	39	27
Better protection from military threat	28	19
To serve as a "Third Force" counterpoise to both East and West	19	13
To enhance French national power	1	1
To aid underdeveloped countries	1	1
No purpose in European integration	3	2
Don't know purpose	1	1
Not ascertained	3	2
Total	360	246%

* Multiple responses permitted

THE FRENCH VIEW OF NATO—AS OF 1964

The development of European institutions deeply concerns but also divides the French elites. It is also one of the strongest areas of criticism against de Gaulle and an area in which changes may be expected after the General's departure. This is not the case with NATO. Although many differ with de Gaulle, only a very small minority is satisfied with present NATO arrangements.[1]

French elites are dissatisfied with NATO on three related counts. First, it should not be the primary defense structure on which France must rely for its own security, to say nothing of the protection or advancement of its legitimate national interests. Second, cooperation within NATO is inadequate to allow for full French participation in the development of overall strategy. The monopoly of the United States in this regard is considered both unjustified and dangerous. Third, NATO was signed when the conditions were such as to make American protection a compelling need for the French and the Europeans. This is no longer the case. The Soviet threat against which only the United States could protect Western Europe has subsided; and, moreover, the Western European countries, and France in particular, are much stronger than they were in 1949. Hence, the need for American protection and with it French acquiescence to American leadership are no longer justifiable.

This is in summary form the overwhelming consensus of the elites we interviewed. It does not exclude the realization on the part of our respondents that the American umbrella and the presence of American troops are necessary. It simply means that, in the equation of forces, the weakening of the Soviet danger together with the strengthening of Western power makes the American presence and the American strength only *one* but not *the* principal factor of defense.

In the eyes of Gaullists and Riders, three additional reasons account for the further weakening of NATO: the United States cannot be relied upon to come to the defense of its Western allies with nuclear

---

[1] The reader should be reminded that all the data on which this analysis is based had been collected in the summer of 1964. Withdrawal from NATO was formally announced in March 1966. In the presidential election of December 1965 only Lecanuet could be considered as an Atlantic candidate. He received 16% of the vote on the first ballot. According to our interviews, elite opinion did not favor withdrawal from NATO but strongly favored a NATO reform. It appears that emphasis upon the MLF arrangements—efforts to develop special ties with West Germany at the expense of France—alienated many of the elites from NATO. The escalation of the war in South Vietnam and the increased commitment of American forces there provided support for de Gaulle's arguments. Thus, the break from NATO did not provoke serious political conflicts. A motion of censure in the French National Assembly against the government's withdrawal received only 137 (out of 482) votes, mostly from among the "old parties." Indeed, our elite interviews clearly indicate that the pro-NATO stance of the elites was weak and that their advocacy of reforms could ultimately lead, as it did, to a break, though the latter was not anticipated at the time we held our interviews.

Table 5.4

FRENCH PERCEPTION OF THE RELIABILITY OF NATO

QUESTION: *At the present time, to what extent can France rely upon NATO to protect her?*

	Number of Respondents	Percentage
It can rely upon NATO completely (NATO offers the greatest security possible under present conditions)	15	10%
NATO can be relied upon to a considerable extent	77	52
NATO can be relied upon to a limited extent	37	25
NATO cannot be relied upon at all	7	5
Don't know	1	1
Not ascertained	10	7
Total	147	100%

weapons; confronted with non-Western problems and conflicts, the United States may withdraw its forces from Europe and virtually abandon its commitment to defend Europe; and, finally, it is not unlikely that an agreement between the United States and the Soviet Union may be made at the expense of the vital interests of the European countries. Only a small minority of respondents, however, believes that American withdrawal is likely or possible, and a still smaller group believes that an agreement between the Soviet Union and the United States will be made in the near future at the expense of Western European interests. Such a sentiment comes from the most articulate of the Gaullists. The reform of NATO, in the eyes of our elite panel members, is nonetheless an overwhelming and urgent question for France's defense and security.

Despite governmental orchestrations against NATO, only five per cent of respondents feel that NATO cannot be relied upon (Table 5.4). Over half (52%) feel it can be relied upon to a considerable extent and 25 per cent to a limited extent. One in ten respondents feels that NATO can be relied upon completely. Few members of the French elites wish to move out of NATO. Even de Gaulle and his associates, so quick at times

79

with threats directed against existing arrangements in Europe or the Atlantic Alliance, did not openly proclaim their desire to dissociate themselves from NATO, at least not until the press conference of 9 September 1965. The reasons for this are made abundantly clear in our responses. No matter what, the American nuclear guarantee in one form or another will be indispensable to France for many years to come. Ironically enough, it is this guarantee that gives to de Gaulle all the elbow room he needs to maneuver from a position of strength, albeit a borrowed one. But there is an additional reason: To scrap NATO or to withdraw from it would also mean to abandon any hope of reforming it from within. In doing this France would abandon all hope of participating in the formulation of global strategy. Since policy is the art of the contingent, it is better to keep all alternatives open. NATO remains one, provided it can be reformed.

Almost half of our respondents favor a reformed NATO. Only a small group (mostly Gaullists and Riders) is in favor of scrapping NATO entirely or rather substituting for it an alliance constructed along classic lines. This group, however, would swell into a majority consisting of many Riders, most of the Notables and Aspirants and the Unreconstructed if Europe were unified. A very small minority remains indifferent to NATO. Let us discuss the attitudes of each one of these groups.

NATO Reformers

Those whom we may call NATO Reformers are in agreement that the organization now simply consecrates the supremacy of the United States. The United States has a monopoly of power within NATO and freedom to act as it wishes outside NATO. Even more important, American freedom to act within or outside of NATO is discretionary. It is not bound by any prior consultation on strategic objectives. Two former members of the NATO Standing Group claimed that they had made all efforts possible to devise a deliberative process for the body so that overall strategy could at least be discussed if not elaborated and so that American might could be harnessed to the implementation of agreed objectives. They claimed that their efforts failed. Policy was made in Washington; and NATO and its various agencies were nothing more than ingenious cloaks to hide the American monopoly.

The great majority of respondents agrees that NATO should be reformed to provide for genuine deliberative channels on strategic questions among the participants on a footing of equality. One influential member of our panel went so far as to argue that this arrangement should not necessarily involve a dispersal of atomic weapons among participants. He was willing to allow the American president to be the sole man with the finger on the trigger, but he added that his role should be that of a simple executor of decisions made and policies agreed upon.

Participation in the deliberations on strategy should not, of course, be open equally to *all* members of NATO. Most respondents consider this an exaggeration verging upon the absurd. The ideal solution would be the formation of a small group within NATO—a *directorate*—consisting of the United States, France and Great Britain. De Gaulle's original suggestion for the formation of such a directorate is, then, very much alive in the minds of many. What is more, some well-informed respondents claim that de Gaulle would still favor it. Other respondents, however, are no longer satisfied with it. In addition to the development of a deliberative agency in which decision-making would be entrusted to the three strongest members of NATO, they would propose the following: free exchange of information of atomic secrets among the three members of the directorate; the availability of atomic weapons to all three members, to be used by them to protect their vital national interests; and a more rational reorganization of regional commands and responsibilities.

For the "Europeans" there is a variant to the above theme. It involves a NATO in which integration of forces and deliberation on common strategy would involve primarily, if not exclusively, the government of the United States and that of Europe, on a footing of equality, with a clear division of responsibilities and a clear-cut global division of strategic commands. There are, however, two important stumbling blocks. First, there is no "Europe"—yet. This fact merely intensifies the opposition of the "Europeans" to de Gaulle. Second, it is doubtful that the United States will go along with this scheme. This fact makes them fall back upon the idea of an independent European nuclear force, if and when there is a political Europe. It is interesting to note that at no time do French elites consider the full participation of Germany in the directorate as they envisage it. They would accept German participation in some stages of NATO deliberation, of course, and would reconcile themselves to perhaps a quadripartite formula, but they reject outright West German possession of weapons and atomic secrets.

NATO Reformers comprise about 46% of our panel. But as Table

Table 5.5

FRENCH SUGGESTIONS FOR NATO REFORM

QUESTION: *Could NATO be reformed in such a way that France can rely on it for protection? How?*

	Number of Respondents	Percentage
No reform can make NATO a better protector of the nation's security	17	12%
European NATO members should have more influence	15	10
United States, England and France should have more influence	13	9
Fewer states should have influence in NATO policy-making	12	8
A special NATO body should control NATO policy-making	11	7
France should have more influence in NATO policy-making	10	7
England and France should have more influence	8	5
There should be a greater measure of equality among NATO members	7	5
NATO forces should be strengthened	4	3
United States, England, France and Germany should have more influence	3	2
NATO is outmoded	3	2
NATO conventional forces should be integrated to a greater extent than at present	2	1
Germany should have more influence in NATO policy-making	0	0
All members should have more influence in planning	0	0
England, France and Germany should have more influence	0	0
NATO should have an integrated nuclear force	0	0
Other reform	9	6
Needs no reform	3	2
Not ascertained	30	20
Total	147	99%

5.5 indicates, they split into many groups when it comes to suggesting specific reforms. Few argue for "integrating," and *nobody* suggests a "nuclear integration" of any kind.

"We Don't Care About NATO"

The second group believes that any effort to reform NATO is futile. They argue that the overwhelming preponderance of American strength effectively gives to the United States the first and last word in the development and implementation of global strategy. Hence, a reformed NATO, *no matter* what the reforms, will continue to underwrite European dependence upon the United States while allowing the United States freedom to act. "There can be no interdependence between two unequal powers," we were told many times; "You are so strong that we cannot cooperate." "You dwarf us," was the comment of one respondent. Further, irrespective of the degree to which technical information about nuclear weapons is disseminated, America is so advanced that other states will, quite naturally, tend to rely upon the United States for nuclear developments and for weapons. Finally, a reformed NATO means a continuing entanglement between the United States and Europe. This is not necessarily desirable. "Flirtation, yes; liaison, perhaps; marriage, no," said a respondent. In this exciting and changing world, many French feel like twelve-year-old boys who are beginning to flex their muscles. They begin to look forward to the "poisons and the delights" of the atomic age. Military integration with the United States will jeopardize whatever freedom they are regaining after almost a generation of dependence.

For the "We don't care about NATO" group, the best solution lies in the scrapping of NATO as an integrative type of alliance and its replacement with an alliance between the United States and France (or Europe when such a united Europe becomes a reality). Such an alliance will be primarily a military alliance in the classic tradition. In it information can be exchanged; weapons can be standardized or not; common security and defense arrangements can be made or not as it suits the two allies. Preferably, of course, the French would like to see an exchange of atomic information and know-how.

The "We don't care about NATO" group was represented by not more than 15 per cent of our panel—a suspiciously small percentage. What accounts for this? Simply the fact, again, that those in favor of reforming NATO are also those favoring European unity. In other words, many pro-Europeans appear in our tables as favoring (a reformed)

NATO rather than being indifferent or opposed to it. Many of them would favor a European arrangement rather than the status quo if they had a choice, thus joining the "We don't care about NATO" group. It is likely that United States unwillingness to consider drastic reforms forced them into this position by 1966.

It is, thus, in the light of their attitudes toward European unity (and a European nuclear force) that the views of our respondents on NATO become more sharply focused. Many Europeans prefer to see a politically unified and nuclear armed Europe, allied or not with the United States. NATO, *as it now stands*, appears to be an obstacle to the realization of this objective. American preponderance in Europe constitutes a disruptive element forcing the European nations individually to vie for American favors and putting the United States in a position to dispense or to withhold these favors as it sees fit. It subordinates European policies and institutions to American counsels. It deprives the Europeans of know-how and responsibility. Even if the possession of nuclear weapons and the freedom to contemplate their use serves only a maturing and educational function, the Europeans must get them. You must be exposed to sin before you can discourse on virtue.

There is also, many of our respondents feel, a relationship between nuclear power and influence in global strategy and decisions. Any form of integration and interdependence will underwrite French dependence. In such a situation France will be unable to bring pressure to bear upon the United States. If France has nuclear weapons, however, then the United States will have to think twice before making decisions that affect the peace of the world. Fear of displeasing an independent and armed nuclear force such as Europe will serve as a deterrent to American strategy and policies—a restraint far more potent, many claim, than any that the Europeans or the French would be able to exercise within the councils of an integrated NATO. Public opinion polls also support this point of view. In February 1963, 20 per cent of French respondents felt that there ought to be a European joint nuclear force independent of American control, while 18 per cent opted for NATO including the United States. In May 1964, 45 per cent of the French public favored moving toward a unified Europe independent of the United States rather than one closely linked with America (31%). But the same poll also revealed that 37 per cent favored closer ties with NATO, 23 per cent were in favor of greater independence, and 40 per cent did not know.

In our elite sample, only 12 per cent favor enthusiastically or

Table 5.6

FRENCH VIEWS OF A EUROPEAN NUCLEAR FORCE

QUESTION: *Would you favor a European nuclear force independent of NATO?*

	Number of Respondents	Percentage
Strongly favor (enthusiastic)	24	16%
Favor generally (not excited about it)	29	20
Favor conditionally (if certain conditions prevail or develop)	43	29
Indifferent, undecided	13	9
Oppose conditionally (if certain conditions prevail or develop)	7	5
Oppose generally	13	9
Oppose vehemently	3	2
Don't know	2	1
Not ascertained	13	9
Total	147	100%

generally a NATO-controlled nuclear force and 19 per cent are "generally" or "vehemently" opposed. The largest single group (about 44% of our panel) is in favor or opposed *conditionally*. If such a force is to be created, however, there seems to be an inclination to lodge its control in the hands of the United States, France and Great Britain. Only five respondents favor the inclusion of Germany in any such control council.

The crucial question of the creation of a European nuclear force independent of NATO elicits a strong sentiment (in the terms in which the question was put) in favor of a European integrative military arrangement (Table 5.6). Over a third (36%) of our panel favor the idea strongly or in general; only 11 per cent are vehemently or generally opposed; 29 per cent favor the idea conditionally; and 5 per cent oppose it conditionally. Therefore, those in favor (including the "conditionals") amount to a solid 65 per cent of our panel and those opposing it (again including the "conditionals") to a mere 16 per cent. Slightly over a

Table 5.7

PREFERENCE FOR DIRECTION OF EFFORTS— EEC OR NATO

QUESTION: *Do you feel that France should rather endeavor to strengthen NATO, or European unity [EEC], or both?*

	Number of Respondents	Percentage
Work primarily to strengthen NATO	5	3%
Work to strengthen both	61	41
Work primarily to strengthen EEC	50	34
Work to strengthen neither	6	4
Work to weaken NATO	0	0
Don't know	2	1
Not ascertained	23	16
Total	147	99%

quarter (28%) claim to be indifferent, do not know, or did not make their views known. At this point in the interview, we ventured a question about the feasibility of a revitalized European Defense Community (EDC). Results were inconclusive since 96 out of our panel of 147 did not wish to answer or were so taken aback by the question as to avoid it. Of the remaining 51 panelists, 19 (37%) favored the idea in general or conditionally and 15 (29%) were opposed to it generally or conditionally. The moment NATO and the Six are compared as integrative patterns and the choice between working to strengthen one or the other is posed, then only 3 per cent of the respondents favor NATO (Table 5.7). About a third (34%) prefer to work to strengthen EEC. The largest number, however, would work in order to strengthen *both* (41%)—another reason for the apparently large percentage of NATO Reformers.

Status Quo

A small number of respondents not only seems to be satisfied with the status quo but would work actively to maintain it. They include primarily the Unreconstructed and some of the Notables. Their position is that the present balance of terror is adequate; that NATO under the present arrangements gives, as it should, a preponderant position to the strongest partner (the United States); and that it is American strength that sustains the alliance and deters the Russians.

The Communists are also favorably disposed to the status quo at this stage. They surely would wish to dismantle NATO but cannot support de Gaulle's efforts to do so since this would virtually force them to jump from the frying pan into the fire. De Gaulle's image of a nuclear France—with or without England, with or without Europe—is a most unpleasant prospect to them. They would rather follow the Soviet policy because they have always done so and because it happens at this stage to be against proliferation, to emphasize coexistence and the support of the Moscow Test-Ban Treaty of 1963 and to encourage limited agreements with the United States—in short, the status quo!

Support for the status quo comes, therefore, in great part from sources that are far from being friendly to the United States or to NATO and which will shift radically over time.[2] It comes from the Communists, some Notables, most of the Unreconstructed. It reflects tactical positions advocated mostly by disgruntled individuals and groups.

A TYPOLOGY ON NATO AND EUROPEAN ISSUES

On the basis of our interviews, we attempted to devise a tentative typology of our respondents with regard exclusively to their attitudes toward NATO and Europe. We identified these types as "National," "European" and "Atlantic."

Nationals

The Nationals are primarily loyal Gaullists, although they include some Riders and Notables as well. They favor the resurgence of the unqualified nation-state. These are the people for whom Europe is only a camouflage to hide French aspirations to become Europe's master at the very time when it pretends to be its servant; who believe that the French bomb will remain French; who openly express fears about German military strength; who believe that bilateral alliances will revive France's position in the world and perhaps restore it to its pre-World

[2] Such a shift seems to have already occurred in the Communist Party.

War II position; and who are hostile to NATO. They comprise at most one-third of our sample.

Europeans

Europeans include most of the Notables and the Aspirants, a number of the Riders and all of the Unreconstructed. Europe is a mystique for some; for others a necessity; for still others a convenience. It should be strengthened to protect France and the other European nations against a world full of hazards. For these Europeans economic integration is not enough, nor can it be counted upon to bring about political union at some future date. For most of them, England's entry is necessary; for a good number it can be postponed until England is ready.

It would be extremely naïve to assume that the "Europeans" are united. Some are *gradualists* and, like some of the "Nationals," advocate a European unity only for the remote future. Political union, yes, but not until the people are ready. And, quite clearly, the "people" are not yet ready. It may take decades. Also, when it comes to the envisaged institutions, they simply suggest minor institutional changes in the Common Market, such as the unification of certain agencies. They invariably shy away from giving to "supranational" organs genuine political and legislative functions that are directly enforceable upon the member states.

Another group, and perhaps the largest one among the "Europeans," comprises *confederationists*. They urge some form of confederation in which a few functions will be delegated to a central body while the bulk of decisions will remain in the hands of the sovereign states. Many who have thought about the matter carefully favor strongly reinforced majorities coupled with a national veto or nullification. They are manifestly not prepared to accept the idea that a European parliament or executive will make decisions for France. Since they are projecting loose confederal relations, they feel not only that England should join, but also that its participation will avert a show of strength between Germany and France. But the same respondents also tend to be sympathetic to the idea of Atlantic ties, especially with the United States. Though they are more optimistic about European unification than the gradualists, they do not anticipate its emergence in the near future. They are nonetheless critical of de Gaulle for not initiating a policy that will pave the way to European political institutions. They feel that Europe has been slowed down and that Gaullist nationalisms may proliferate and impede developments to the point of undermining

"Europe" seriously. Confederationists assert with conviction that eventually the French atomic force will have to become European but they, too, are uncertain of when and how, especially since common defense is not to be one of the prerogatives of the confederation. They state that if military policies are adequately coordinated in the context of evolving European institutions, the Europeanization of the French atomic force is not a critical question: First, because they assume that, if England were a part of a loose European confederation, an Anglo-French atomic force in cooperation with the United States would be effective from the very start; second, because many of them *also* favor the strengthening of a reformed NATO.

A third category of "Europeans"—*federalists*—is outright European with or without England. For them the Common Market has gone about as far as it can go. The need for strong supranational institutions is imperative. Moreover, these respondents are federalist in the proper sense of the term. They want a common executive, a common legislature, a European court, popular elections, a common foreign policy and common defense institutions, possibly even the revival of the EDC, with atomic weapons. Only a minority of respondents, as we have seen, takes this view but by no means is it a negligible minority. Notables who advocate the EDC and integrative European institutions as well as many Aspirants and even some Riders favor it. Furthermore, it is not simply an affirmation of a mystique. It is, too, based upon solid and cogent arguments. First, such a Europe will bring West Germany irreversibly into Western Europe and will postpone the problem of German unification. Second, it will turn Europe into a power complex equal to that of the United States and the Soviet Union—a view, by the way, which according to opinion polls is also shared by the public, and gives real substance to the Gaullist call for "independence," but in European terms. Third, it will provide common resources for an independent military and atomic policy that France alone cannot sustain for any great length of time. It may well be that a directorate composed of England and France will control the bomb, a development that might satisfy both the Americans and the Germans. Fourth, a united Europe will provide opportunities to pursue a constructive policy of aid to underdeveloped peoples in the world. Fifth, the attraction of such a Europe may prove irresistible to Soviet satellites in Eastern Europe. The Soviet Union, hard pressed by China, may be more willing to make concessions to a European government than to the United States. Last, but not least, such a European political entity will, in the minds of many, preserve and promote the cause of European culture. United Europe will also be best suited to resist the capitalist infiltration of the United States or the political totalitarianism of the Soviet Union.

Atlantics and Globalists

By Atlantics, we mean those who, whether "European" or not, view as necessary close ties with the United States and other members of the Atlantic community, preferably within NATO. Without supporting the idea of an Atlantic federation (not more than three or four respondents evoked it even as a possibility), they nonetheless believe that at various levels—cultural, political, economic and military—the maintenance of ties among Atlantic nations is necessary and that efforts should be made to strengthen them.

The Globalists, by way of contrast, are those few French leaders who tend to think in terms of larger international organizations, such as the United Nations, and who insist that ultimately the establishment of supranational authority is desirable. Generally speaking, we did not find that attachment to a world supranational organization was significant

---

Table 5.8

GENERAL AND FOREIGN POLICY TYPOLOGIES IN FRANCE

General Political Profiles	FOREIGN POLICY PROFILES				
	National	European	Atlantic	Other	Total
Gaullist	24	1	3	1	29 (20%)
Rider	13	5	2	0	20 (14)
Aspirant	5	14	14	1	34 (23)
Notable	11	28	6	3	48 (33)
Unreconstructed	1	4	8	1	14 (9)
Communist	0	0	0	2	2 (1)
Total	54 (37%)	52 (35%)	33 (23%)	8 (5%)	147 (100%)

---

among French elites. Indeed, the United Nations was mentioned by no more than five of our respondents.

A cross-tabulation between the political groups we outlined in Chapter 2 and the foreign-policy attitudinal profiles discussed previously are shown in Table 5.8. Sixty-three per cent of our panel are shown to be Europeans *or* Atlantics—but only 37 per cent are "nationals."

We shall return to these profiles in discussing future trends *after* we discuss in the following chapter the issue of the French *force de frappe* and matters of arms control and disarmament.

CHAPTER 6

Force de Frappe and Arms Control

FORCE DE FRAPPE

In discussing NATO and Europe with our respondents, the *force de frappe* came up constantly, long before we ever mentioned it. However salient the issue of a French nuclear force is, our elites seem confused and divided. Only at the risk of doing violence to the complexity of the issues involved is it possible to delineate some attitudinal profiles based on the responses.

Support for the Force de Frappe

Looking at the attitudes apparently underlying their expressions of opinion, we divided the proponents of the *force de frappe* into three groups. The first of these, mostly Gaullists and Riders, may be termed "Nationals." They accept most of the arguments in favor of the bomb as a national force. The second group, "Europeans," argue for the bomb, but only because it must sooner or later (depending upon the strength of European sentiment of these respondents) become a European force. The third group of proponents may be termed "Franco-British." They accept the bomb but, for a number of reasons, see that its destiny is bound to be toward a Franco-British nuclear force and directorate. Many of the respondents in this category are "Europeans"; only a minority can be classified as "Nationals."

Several arguments are advanced in favor of maintaining and enhancing the *force de frappe* as a part of French national defense.

1. The bomb is an indispensable instrument for national defense, prestige and the implementation of national interest. Without it, no country can be truly independent.

2. The bomb is in the long run cheaper than conventional weapons.

3. The bomb is indispensable in terms of the impact it has upon technological and industrial developments in any modern nation.

4. The bomb helps scientific research.

5. The purpose of the bomb is genuinely military and strategic. It provides a deterrent. The bomb in the possession of a relatively smaller nation like France—and the argument even applies to smaller units, such as Monaco—deters attack and invasion since the prize to be gained by the aggressor is very small compared to the destruction that he might invite upon his own territory.

6. The purpose of the bomb is uniquely political. Its possession by France will force the United States to reconsider NATO seriously, and to accept the principle of consultation on the development and implementation of global strategy.

7. The bomb, even if it has little or no credibility, may nonetheless play the role of triggering the American bomb. In this sense it serves as a nuclear trip-wire that might deter prospective aggressors.

Opposition to the Force de Frappe

Those of our respondents who oppose a French nuclear force do so on various grounds. Some fear the cost of the bomb. Some favor conventional weapons for reasons of strategy. Others feel that the bomb should be Europeanized. Finally, some respondents are in principle opposed to nuclear weapons, fear their proliferation, favor disarmament or arms control, are pacifists, do not believe that an independent French nuclear force will ever be credible to potential enemies or simply are satisfied with the existing balance among the powers. These opponents of the *force de frappe,* who for the most part are the Unreconstructed, Notables, Aspirants and, of course, the Communists, suggest several arguments to support their attitude:

First, a solid majority agrees that France alone cannot sustain the economic effort of nuclear production. Though many agree that the cost of nuclear weapons is not higher than that of maintaining an adequate conventional force, most fear that the projected outlays will prove inadequate and that, as the American experience shows, these costs will increase and put an intolerable strain upon the French economy. Their concern is not only that France will face severe difficulties in the future stemming from the compression of expenditures for investment in productive sectors of the economy, but also that the French economy will become progressively weaker compared to that of the other Common Market countries.

Second, many of the respondents—especially the scientists we interviewed, some of whom are in very responsible positions—believe that the effort to create a nuclear defense does not promote research. Further, they say, its impact upon industrial and technological development is unfavorable.

It is for these two reasons, among others, that Europeanization or an Anglo-French arrangement is often advocated. "Europe can do it," they say; "we can't." Expenditure estimates are not reliable. "It is like going on a vacation," somebody told us; "anticipated expenses must be multiplied by a factor of two or three." It is among these persons that President Kennedy's proposals to England—a greater exchange of information and of nuclear know-how—look attractive if applied to France. Participation in MLF arrangements might give France the prospect of both a national force to be used in case her vital interests were at stake and greater participation in common nuclear strategy and defense.

Third, this consideration is reinforced by our respondents' appraisal of the deterrence and deterrent credibility of the French force now and for the coming five or six years. Only 31 per cent believe that the French deterrent is credible to France's potential enemies as opposed to 51 per cent who do not consider it credible (Table 6.1). Some concede a limited degree of deterrence and credibility of the bomb given the present government. "De Gaulle will use the bomb if Germany were attacked," stated, in identical terms, a strong anti-Gaullist and a strong Gaullist. But neither one was sure that future governments in different situations will seriously entertain making use of the bomb.

Fourth, opponents claim that de Gaulle's efforts are primarily political: An independent French nuclear force will make necessary a reconsideration of NATO and of Franco-American relations. These respondents feel that such an attitude on the part of France is a gross error. It will undermine relations with European nations and ultimately with the United States. America may find it imperative to stress its relationship with West Germany; the other European nations would rather be protected by the United States than by France anyway; and France may simply end up brandishing a small and noncredible weapon alone. If the bomb is to force a reconsideration of NATO, then, these opponents say, France would have a better chance to do so from within NATO rather than by withdrawing further. They also feel that the logic of the French position invites proliferation of atomic weapons and introduces an element of great instability into the existing balance of terror.

Thus, according to Table 6.1, 41 per cent of respondents feel that a *force de frappe* is a condition for national independence, that is, for a national defense system and a national foreign policy. Over half (52%) reject this, and only seven per cent do not answer. Similarly, only 29 per cent feel that a *force de frappe* is necessary for the nation's prestige and almost twice that many (54%) do not think so. When we raise the thorny question of whether the national deterrent is worth the cost, the positive (43%) and negative (44%) responses divide almost evenly. Many who claim that the *force de frappe* is worth the cost do so, however, for such non-military reasons as technological, economic and industrial expansion. What will happen to the *force de frappe* when de Gaulle disappears? As against the 22 per cent who believe that it will be kept and strengthened, over twice as many (48%) think that it will be supranationalized (in most cases "Europeanized" would be a better term), and only a small percentage (6%) believes that it will be abandoned. Almost a quarter (24%) of the respondents refused to answer or did not know.[1]

[1] On 20 March and 10 April 1964, public opinion surveys indicated an even split between those favoring a national deterrent (40%) and those opposed (40%), with 20 per cent without opinion. A majority, however, felt that the country could not afford the cost.

Table 6.1

FRENCH VIEWS OF A NATIONAL NUCLEAR DETERRENT

	Number of Respondents	Percentage
QUESTION: *It is often said that a national deterrent is a prerequisite of a country's independence. Do you share this view?*		
Yes	61	41%
No	76	52
Don't know	4	3
Not ascertained	6	4
Total	147	100%
QUESTION: *Is an independent deterrent necessary for a nation's prestige in the world?*		
Yes, increases prestige	43	29%
No effect upon prestige	79	54
Don't know	4	3
Not ascertained	21	14
Total	147	100%
QUESTION: *Is an independent deterrent worth the cost?*		
Yes	63	43%
No	64	44
Don't know	11	7
Not ascertained	9	6
Total	147	100%
QUESTION: *Is a national deterrent credible to France's enemies?*		
Yes	46	31%
No	75	51
Don't know	14	10
Not ascertained	12	8
Total	147	100%

	Number of Respondents	Percentage
QUESTION: *What would happen to the* force de frappe *if de Gaulle left the political scene?*		
Force would be kept and strengthened	33	22%
Force would be supranationalized	70	48
Force would be abandoned	9	6
Don't know	23	16
Not ascertained	12	8
Total	147	100%

THE DEFENSE OF FRANCE

Moving to the broader question of French national defense, we find that 72 per cent of respondents consider that French security ultimately depends completely or in large measure upon the American deterrent. Another 15 per cent believe that it depends ultimately but to a limited extent upon the American deterrent. Thus, 127 out of 147 respondents, including many who favor a *force de frappe*, are willing to concede that the security of France is in some measure (and generally a substantial measure) dependent upon the American nuclear deterrent. There is a marked reluctance to consider integrative schemes (Table 6.2). Alliances with conventional or nuclear weapons are mentioned by 69 per cent of the respondents. A national defense posture, nuclear or conventional, ranks second highest among the responses at about the same level as those advocating an integrated European nuclear force. An *integrated* Atlantic defense system is *lowest* among our respondents' preferences. Thus, the national stance remains strong, especially since those preferring alliances do so as simple and temporary techniques of national accommodation.

The controversy about either the trigger-happiness of the United States or its unwillingness to use the bomb except to protect its own country does not seem to have seriously affected the good judgment of French elites. An astonishingly high number accepts the official United States position that we shall use the bomb to retaliate against any attack upon all or some of our European allies. The notion of a preemptive strike is rejected; but so is the notion that we shall use the bomb only

Table 6.2

FRENCH VIEW OF BEST DEFENSE AGAINST
A MILITARY THREAT

QUESTION: *In your opinion, what would be the best defense against a military threat?*

	Number of Responses*	Percentage
National conventional arms	12	8%
National nuclear arms	50	34
Alliance in conventional arms	3	2
Alliance in nuclear arms	9	6
Alliance in conventional and nuclear arms	102	69
Integrated European conventional forces (i.e., supranational command)	7	5
Integrated European nuclear forces	33	22
Complete integration of all European defense forces	25	17
Integration of nuclear forces of Atlantic Community	6	4
Integration of all defense forces of Atlantic Community	13	9
Other	3	2
Don't know	1	1
Not ascertained	7	5
Total	271	184%

* Multiple responses permitted

in case the territory of the United States is attacked, given by only six respondents (or about 4 per cent of the sample).

ARMS, ARMS CONTROL AND DISARMAMENT

Arms limitations is a subject that heavily taxed the patience of the respondents and the endurance of the interviewers. It is one for which the interest, if not the level of information, of respondents is very low. Indifference seems to be the rule. The great majority of respondents had heard of most of the plans for disarmament that have been advanced in the last ten years, and though they consider disarmament talks a "good thing," they are not sanguine. Only 41 per cent of our sample feel that progress on disarmament can be made at the present time; over half (51%) nonetheless approve (strongly, generally or conditionally) of the 1963 Limited Test-Ban Treaty, and two-thirds (66%) favor further arms control agreements between the United States and the Soviet Union.

Hope and a positive affirmation of belief in principle are matched at least at times by what was to us a most exasperating disregard for detail. Lurking behind the answers of quite a few respondents is the sentiment that "arms control" has been devised by the "Anglo-Saxons," in this case the Americans, as a means to continue their arms race with the Soviet Union. To the extent to which the Soviet Union is also a participant, some respondents fear that "arms control" may be designed to perpetuate the preponderance of the two superpowers and to consolidate this predominance by obstructing the development of other national nuclear powers.

French elite opinion on arms control and disarmament can be broken down into three major groups: the "Politicals" who view the problem exclusively in terms of its political connotations (about 35%); the "Knowledgeables," those who are aware of some of the technical problems of arms control and disarmament (about 30%); and the ignorant or indifferent or both (about 35%). Even among the Knowledgeables, it must be added, only a small minority (not more than 10% of the total sample) is able to answer questions on arms control and disarmament in a sophisticated manner.

Politicals

For these respondents arms control and disarmament are political matters. When political conditions make it possible to come to agreement an agreement will be found; so long as such political conditions do not exist, technical discussions cannot and will not amount to much. Arms control is only another indication of the American belief in "gadgets," in technical arrangements. Although most respondents who voice their opinion on the subject favor (strongly, generally or conditionally) coupling any arms control plan with inspection (Table 6.3), they seem to agree that no system of inspection can ever be foolproof; no "arms

Table 6.3

FRENCH FEELINGS ABOUT INSPECTION

QUESTION: *Should an East-West agreement on arms control be coupled with inspection?*

	Number of Respondents	Percentage
Strongly favor (no other way to enforce an agreement)	24	16%
Favor generally (not excited about it)	14	10
Favor conditionally (but can have agreement without it)	13	9
Indifferent; undecided	31	21
Oppose conditionally (if certain conditions prevail or develop)	0	0
Oppose generally (just an excuse for not reaching agreement)	0	0
Oppose vehemently	1	1
Don't know	16	11
Not ascertained	48	33
Total	147	101%

control" mechanism can be trusted by either party unless both parties agree not to violate it. Why discuss the state of the patient's teeth— even if atomic—before taking a hard look at his overall state of health?

Knowledgeables

Generally, the position of the Politicals is also that of part of the Knowledgeables. The only difference is that many of the latter were drawn further into the discussion and speculated on the specific arrangements that might pave the way to disarmament. Most of them agree that general nuclear disarmament involving destruction of stockpiles and delivery capabilities should be the ultimate goals. They also agree, though without much enthusiasm, that the Geneva discussions might be a fruitful way to attain these goals. They deplore—and this applies to the majority of respondents—the fact that France does not participate in the Geneva talks. "Obviously no good will come out of them, but one does not know," said one respondent. And, in any event, "it is wrong for France not to be present." Inspection sites could be created or other means of detection installed and, if they were agreed upon by the United States and the Soviet Union, there would be no objection to having them in other countries, including France, as the occasion demands.

"Disengagement" might be another plausible way of reducing conflict, according to a few respondents. They would object to neither a nuclear neutralization of Central Europe, particularly if this meant East and West Germany, nor even to a disengagement of conventional forces on the basis of reciprocity, particularly if this were to mean the withdrawal of American and Soviet forces from Western Europe and Eastern Europe respectively. Only a minority, however, would seriously entertain and approve of this thought. In general, those opposed to the neutralization of Central Europe outnumber those favoring it. Twenty respondents were in favor and thirty-eight against, but the majority (52%) refused to answer a question that appeared to them highly speculative. Nor are French elites convinced that the denuclearization of Central Europe would even ease tension there. Moreover, a majority, including even Gaullists and proponents of the French nuclear force, feel that the time for American withdrawal has not yet come. "The first soldier to die in case of a Soviet attack must be an American," two very influential political leaders said. One offered his apologies and the other his condolences! A great number refuses to consider seriously a demilitarization of Germany, since they consider the German conventional army to be their first line of defense.

Only a minority of the Knowledgeables is willing to discuss the techniques of arms control in detail. They represent not more than ten per cent of the total sample: five of the military; three young political leaders; and four or five of the intellectuals and political Aspirants. The "business community" and respondents from "other professional groups" generally were uninterested, uninformed or downright ignorant.

A strong case is made by some of the Knowledgeables that the French nuclear force is in the nature of things an important deterrent to war. Two respondents—a general and a Gaullist political leader—argued that the proliferation of atomic weapons would create a balance that would be an effective deterrent. When small powers have the bomb, they said, neither of the superpowers would dare attack them since the possible benefits of military victory would be heavily outweighed by the amount of retaliatory power upon the aggressor that a small but nuclear armed state could deliver.

Some feel that, when France has become a nuclear power, then the question of arms control will become crucial to the country. This is particularly true with respect to nuclear proliferation and to the atomic status of West Germany. They, therefore, feel that the problem is urgent and that France ought to begin considering it now. Arms control, however, should be a genuine device for peace rather than an instrumentality to preserve the nuclear status quo. Otherwise, neither France nor other potential nuclear states could accept it. An agreement to destroy stockpiles and delivery missiles on the part of the superpowers should be the first step.

Elite opinion in June 1964 did not differ very much from a nationwide survey undertaken at that time by the *Institut Français d'Opinion Publique* (IFOP). To the question "When you hear people talk about disarmament or arms control, what do you think?" a third (33%) of the French public said it was a utopia; 27 per cent that it was "a good thing"; 14 per cent that it would put an end to war and usher in peace; six per cent that it would be good under certain conditions; and four per cent that it would lead to lighter taxes. Five per cent were opposed to any form of disarmament. The interesting thing is that almost three-quarters of the sample couched their answers in general and abstract terms. This vagueness and, in effect, inconclusiveness is reinforced by the answers to a second question: "Do you think that in the coming years there will be very substantial progress in the direction of disarmament?" A third (33%) felt that very important progress will be made; 32 per cent did not think so; and 35 per cent refused to answer. The 35 per cent expressing no opinion corresponds well to the percentage of elite respondents who simply shrugged their shoulders, suggesting they could not or did not want to discuss the matter of arms control.

Barring general nuclear disarmament, gradual and selective disarmament offers some hope. It is a possibility, however, that does not appear to concern French elites directly. The disparity between French strength and that of the two superpowers is such that it will take many years before progressive and gradual disarmament on the part of the United States and the Soviet Union can reduce their nuclear firepower and delivery capabilities so as to bring France up (or rather the United States and the Soviet Union down) to even a semblance of parity.

Arms control arrangements between the two superpowers, according to the majority of Knowledgeable respondents, should be encouraged. If nothing else, recent agreements reached have promoted goodwill. This is a positive sign. Gradual disarmament should begin with the gradual elimination of the most powerful nuclear warheads, so that the two superpowers may gradually be limited solely to the possession of tactical atomic weapons. Simultaneously, a gradual elimination of delivery missiles ought to be undertaken. The majority of knowledgeable respondents would start by insisting upon the elimination of what France does not yet have—ICBMs.

The question of policing or enforcing such agreements between the two superpowers is viewed as a real problem. Knowledgeable respondents believe that inspection and detection are necessary but are not quite sure of how this is to be arranged. On-site inspection by United Nations teams is favored by some; aerial reconnaissance by both superpowers is stressed by others; the presence of American teams on the Soviet territory and of Soviet teams on the American territory was mentioned by two respondents. But almost everybody is sensitive to the possibilities of deception and evasion. A majority accepts the need to ban further tests of nuclear devices and feels that, in this area at least, detection is facilitated through technical devices that do not call for on-site inspection of any kind. Some think that France will also accede to the Test-Ban Treaty *after* it has satisfactorily exploded her nuclear devices. A strong minority, however, favors immediate adherence to the Moscow pact.

When missiles and nuclear weapons are effectively reduced by the two superpowers a reconsideration of French strategy will be necessary. France need not undertake any strategic soul-searchings. Strategy will be modified and qualified as France's first generation weapons give birth to second generation weapons and as the future of Europe takes shape. Two generals, for instance, told us that there is no alternative to the counter-city nuclear strategy of France. Their rejection of the McNamara graduated deterrence strategy is based upon the limited number of weapons available to France. "We do not have the types and range of weapons you have," they said; "if we did we would also vary our strategy accordingly."

But weapons are not the only reason for the current French strategy of massive retaliation, reminiscent as it is of the Dulles strategy that French elites decried a few years ago. It is also based upon the realiza-

Table 6.4

FRENCH PREFERENCES FOR SPECIFIC
ARMS CONTROL PLANS

QUESTION: *Which of the various arms control and disarmament plans would you favor?*

	Number of Responses*	Percentage
General and complete disarmament	13	9%
Complete destruction of nuclear weapons	8	5
Freeze in production of nuclear weapons	8	5
Reduction of nuclear weapons stockpiles	19	13
Complete elimination of conventional weapons	0	0
Freeze in production of conventional weapons	3	2
Reduction of conventional weapons	1	1
Denuclearization of Central Europe	4	3
Troop withdrawal in Central Europe	2	1
Neutralization in Central Europe	4	3
Neutralization in other areas	1	1
Banning atomic weapons testing	13	9
Inspection of weapons	20	14
Any and all plans	17	12
Favors no plans	52	35
Don't know	8	5
Not ascertained	23	16
Total	196	134%

* Multiple responses permitted

tion that any form of graduated deterrence, and any implicit acceptance of this strategy by the United States and the Soviet Union, will have a double effect on French security. First, it will reduce the credibility of American nuclear riposte against the Soviet Union; and, second, it will delay such a response in case there is a Soviet attack. It is the second prospect that frightens the French, since a graduated strategy may in case of conflict induce both sides to select targets that are outside their own national territories, presumably in Europe! (See Table 6.4 for data on preferred arms control plans.)

Despite the general criticism of the Moscow Limited Test-Ban Treaty and the unwillingness of the French government to accede to it, 51 per cent of our panel approve more or less strongly of this agreement. Only 17 per cent disapprove somewhat, generally or vehemently. Yet 24 per cent are "indifferent," and in this context indifference should be construed as tantamount to disapproval. It is an attitude shared primarily by those who in principle are in favor of a treaty banning nuclear tests, but who consider the timing of this particular treaty to have been directed against French efforts to build their own bomb. For similar reasons, almost half of our panel (49%) believes that it makes no difference whether their country was consulted or not. Furthermore, 66 per cent of the panel favor further arms controls agreements between the United States and the Soviet Union, irrespective of what France does. Only a handful (5%) are opposed to further agreements. In the event of such agreements, 60 per cent of our respondents feel that France should be consulted, while 26 per cent remain indifferent. Even if France is not consulted, and the skepticism prevailing among French elites about arms control notwithstanding, over half our panel (57%) favors arms control agreements; 27 per cent remain indifferent, and only a very small fraction (3%) are opposed.

Discussion in our interviews of deterrence and nuclear weapons inevitably brought up problems of proliferation and questions about which countries should possess atomic weapons. An overwhelming 70 per cent of respondents are in favor of arresting further proliferation; only seven per cent of our panel are against such efforts and about a quarter (23%) did not respond to our question. But a majority (58%) of our panel says that countries already possessing nuclear weapons should be permitted to retain them. Only 15 per cent of respondents explicitly wish to see France give up its weapons.

FRENCH ELITES AND ARMS CONTROL ATTITUDES

What accounts for the relative silence of our French elite respondents—men who are so articulate on other subjects—on questions of arms control and disarmament? A number of possible reasons comes to mind. First of all, there is a widespread belief that nobody actually threatens France; the majority of respondents agrees, however, that if there is a threat it is likely to come from the Soviet Union. Second, the proposition is generally accepted, despite the uneasiness it provokes, that nuclear parity between the United States and the Soviet Union is an adequate and effective deterrent. Third, most respondents (as well as the public) do not believe that there can be a nuclear war. This is the phenomenon of "atomic incredulity" to which Raymond Aron has alluded. To the extent to which there were lingering fears and doubts, Cuba dissipated them. This is one reason, we think, why the Gulf of Tonkin crisis in the summer of 1964 and the subsequent aggravation of the South Vietnam situation has failed to stir French mass or elite opinion appreciably—at least until the end of 1965. Fourth, there has been a basic and rather drastic change in the French elite perception of the Soviet Union. Since Stalin died, things have changed, and Communism, no matter what its ultimate aspirations, appears to our respondents to have lost its aggressive character. Fifth, Soviet Communism, threatened by the Chinese, is likely to align itself increasingly with the West. Since elite opinion is more confident today than ever before that the United States will not provoke war, the expectation of any involvement in war has greatly weakened.[2] Finally, the fact that, until recently, the French possessed no national nuclear force has not made it imperative that French leaders consider and speculate about arms control. Only in the last few years, and more particularly in 1964 and 1965, have publications by intellectuals, political leaders and military experts brought the problem to the attention of the educated public.[3] There is no doubt in our minds that, as the nuclear effort of France continues, elite opinion will become increasingly more alert to and sophisticated about issues of arms control and disarmament.

[2] This at least seemed to be the opinion of the elites in the summer of 1964.
[3] Recent publications on French nuclear strategy are rapidly increasing in numbers. In addition to Raymond Aron's *Le Grand Débat: Initiation à la Stratègie Atomique* (Paris: Calmann-Lévy, 1963); the following should be mentioned Général Pierre Gallois, *Stratégie de l'Âge Nucléaire* (Paris: Calmann-Lévy, 1960); Alexandre Sanguinetti, *La France et l'Arme Atomique* (Paris: Julliard, 1964); Jules Moch, *Non à la Force de Frappe* (Paris: Laffont, 1963); Général André Beaufre, *Introduction à la Stratégie Nucléaire* (Paris: Colin, 1963) and *Dissuasion et Stratégie* (Paris: Colin, 1964); Club Jean Moulin, *La Force de Frappe et le Citoyen* (Paris: Editions du Seuil, 1963); and Club de Grenelle, *Siècle de Damoclès: La Force Nucléaire Stratégique* (Paris: Couderc, 1964).

CHAPTER 7

Trends and Perspectives

The results of our interviewing indicate clusters of "attitudes" and "opinions." There is, of course, a gap between these opinions and actual behavior. Opinions generally reflect *desirable* courses of action; behavior is more often determined by *feasible* courses of action. In the case of the French elite and the "new politics" of the Fifth Republic, however, we think it quite valid to argue that feasible political developments, for both the present and the near future, can to some extent be gauged by the degree of elite consensus upon desirable developments. In other words, current opinions about domestic and world politics, even if they deal with what is desirable, will necessarily have a bearing upon future developments. How much is hard to say. Between those who claim that the knowledge of such opinions cannot help us see ahead into the future and those who rely almost exclusively upon them in predicting trends, there is a middle ground. Elite opinions, we feel, give us a basis for careful and qualified "guessing."

According to one theory, it is the internal situation, both political and economic, that constitutes the single most important independent variable for the study and understanding of the evolution of opinion. If we were to accept this theory, then future development can be "predicted" with a reasonable degree of reliability while de Gaulle is in power and the Gaullist institutions in operation. But de Gaulle is not likely to stay in power for too long and the Gaullist institutions are so intimately linked with him that their stable functioning is, as we have seen, by no means certain. We have to assume that in the relatively near future these institutions of the Gaullist Fifth Republic will be challenged and that the changing and shifting internal political situation will then modify the world outlook of the elites. International changes will also have a much more direct impact upon internal politics, and this, in turn, will snowball into a rapid change of French opinions and attitudes on world matters. The task of predicting elite opinion in France is thus far more difficult than that of predicting it for England, the United States, the Soviet Union or any other country where internal stability can be taken for granted.

THE INTERNAL DIMENSION

A crucial question to which we addressed ourselves in the interviews was whether or not there is developing in France a new and stable polity: a constitutional structure with the executive rather than the parliament dominant; rationalized rather than fragmented in party structure; and pragmatic rather than ideological in policy orientation. We found a modicum of consensus: (1) There is general agreement that de Gaulle today dominates completely not only the government but public opinion as well. (2) Only a small minority of respondents believes that after de Gaulle things will continue as they are (indeed, few would choose to keep things exactly as they are) and that the succession problem will not be a serious one. (3) Virtually all respondents reject a return to a system resembling that of the Fourth Republic. (4) Most respondents, even among the Notables, seem reconciled to a presidential system. (5) Most respondents agree upon the need for revamping the French party system through some kind of meaningful and stable reduction in the number of parties. (6) A majority of respondents recognizes the old instability to be rooted in ideological incompatibilities and further recognizes the obsolescence of ideological bickering in a modern political system where complex problems must be solved. (7) In sum, most of the French elite respondents whom we interviewed *desire* a "new politics" for France.

Despite this widespread desire for stability, it does not seem that the development of a more stable and more consensual polity in France is likely. The results of our interviewing also showed that de Gaulle and the Fifth Republic, while giving the French a new experience in stability, have stimulated at the same time new orientations to politics in France. New political outlooks have been born. Men sharing these new outlooks represent new groups or forces in French politics. But many of these new attitudes seem just as contradictory as those harbored by the ideologically committed who belonged to the old parties of the Fourth Republic. In other words, though virtually all the respondents reject the Fourth Republic and though almost all would also like to see some changes in the system or processes of the Fifth Republic, there is actually little consensus as to what these changes should be. Many of the respondents who predict that the Fifth Republic will survive de Gaulle differ widely in their images of a successor system. To take one example of this situation, in which the *desirable* becomes *unfeasible* by virtue of contradictory thinking, we found in French elite opinion, as reported, that there appears to be an attachment to the institutions of the Fifth Republic that transcends de Gaulle's person. Despite this consensus in the value of the presidential system, however, 49 per cent of our respondents expect that political parties will play a much more important role after de Gaulle, and a great majority also believes that the only party which has a chance of becoming a majority or at least the center of gravity for a majority—the UNR—will disintegrate after de Gaulle. How can one expect that the presidential system will survive when many expect, and some prefer, that the foundations of presidential power will be undermined? It was also made abundantly clear in the interviews that "presidential government" means different things to different elites and that the constitutional debate that will follow de Gaulle's departure is very likely to undermine the legal and structural basis of the power of his successor.

The many alternative, and very often contradictory, plans for political stability in France expounded during our interviews lead us to the conclusion that the best-fitting model of the "new politics" of the Fifth Republic and the "new politics" of succession after de Gaulle is a model of *relative instability*. Our respondents by and large desire stability, but differ so markedly in their proposals for achieving this stability that the confrontation of alternative designs can only mean instability.

Our model of relative instability is based upon the historical experience of the Fourth Republic. As it applies to the future it is based upon two assumptions, neither of which is beyond reason. First, we assume the continued existence of a strong Communist electoral vote. Second, we assume the weakening of the UNR after de Gaulle and a scattering of its adherents and votes among some of the old political formations. In this situation the Riders will reestablish some of their earlier political ties (as did the Gaullist deputies in 1952 and the Gaullist electorate in 1956). The Aspirants, in this context of a splintering UNR and the reemergence of the old parties and alignments, will in all likelihood fail in their effort to create a new comprehensive political formation. In such a chain of events, as the old parties take a new lease on life, the Notables may retain their strength and regain their positions. If historical experience is any guide, the result of these interrelated developments could very well be the disappearance of a coherent "governing" majority and a renewed need for coalition cabinets.

FOREIGN POLICY

To what degree have Gaullist foreign policy trends been accepted by French elites? Despite considerable empathy and often identification with de Gaulle, both as a symbol and a vehicle of France's renewed power, the elites seem quite divided. The issues of European unity, of the future of the Atlantic world and of the nuclear deterrent appear to us to be the ones most fraught with conflict and most likely to undergo serious changes after de Gaulle.

Europe

Although the public perceives de Gaulle to be a "European," elites, as we have seen, have serious doubts. The type of European unity to be achieved and the countries to be included are subjects of controversy. This is one significant area where the Gaullist themes have not permeated the elites. As we noted, many respondents feel that de Gaulle speaks on behalf of Europe when at heart he is a nationalist and fear that he will undermine European unity.

Responses about the form of European union revealed considerable difference with de Gaulle. The great majority of respondents favors a form of integration with *some* degree of supranational control. Similarly, there is disagreement with de Gaulle's recent views of which countries should be included in a "European union": About 70 per cent of the respondents mention Great Britain and less than a third that many (22%) accept the Gaullist position of limiting European union to the Six. The purpose of European union is also perceived by the elites in a manner different from the traditional Gaullist line. Although, to be sure, many respondents see it as a means of military protection or to enhance European bargaining power vis-à-vis the rest of the world, the great bulk of them views European unity as an instrument for the "economic betterment of European peoples" or "to give Europeans the means and resources to solve economic, social, and political problems currently insoluble by nation-states alone."

Nuclear Policy

What is the likely future of the French *force de frappe?* As we have seen, most French respondents feel that the possession of a nuclear deterrent is not a prerequisite of a country's independence (52%), is not necessary for a nation's prestige in the world (54%) and is not even credible to France's enemies (51%). They are about evenly divided on the question of whether or not an independent deterrent is worth its cost; moreover, even if it constitutes a plurality only a third (34%) of these respondents think that the best defense against a military attack is national nuclear arms, and a still smaller percentage (22%) believes that the *force de frappe* would be kept as it is or strengthened if de Gaulle were to leave the political scene. This by no means indicates that these elites think that the French nuclear deterrent will be or should be abandoned. Indeed, only nine of our respondents (6%) suggested that the passing of de Gaulle will be followed by the abandonment of the *force de frappe*. And in overwhelming numbers they say that the best defense against a military threat entails nuclear arms— whether controlled by nation-states acting individually, by nation-states in alliance or an integrated European force. Quite clearly, however, French elites are not satisfied with the *force de frappe* and the Gaullist strategy.

If there were a choice, the majority of respondents would prefer a European force allied with the United States. The nature and extent of this alliance are moot. The present Gaullist stance in favor of ties along the lines of a "classic" alliance commands considerable support, provided that steps are taken toward creating a European deterrent. In effect this means the reform of NATO. Decisions to reform or not to reform NATO, the extent to which NATO is in fact restructured and the way in which these decisions are made will be instrumental in determining whether the "Europeans" will accept something more than a classic alliance with the United States or whether they will acquiesce to a national force. Another possibility of which we must take note—and this possibility is little more than a modification of the Europeanized deterrent force idea—is a pact between France and Great Britain for joint control of a nuclear arsenal.

Thus, as things stand now, French elite responses indicate the following scale of preferences:

1. independent European force (allied with the United States)
2. Franco-British nuclear force (allied with the United States)
3. a multilateral force (MLF) within NATO if that body is reformed; otherwise
4. an independent national nuclear force (allied with the United States) or
5. a national nuclear force totally independent of the United States.

The reform of NATO, therefore, is of critical significance. It will determine the direction of the shift of opponents to an independent French nuclear force and modify significantly the position of its proponents.[1]

NATO

The need to reform NATO is generally accepted by French elites. Only five per cent of these respondents reject NATO outright or claim that it cannot be relied on for the defense of Europe and France. Significantly enough, 41 per cent of the respondents favor strengthening *both* NATO and European unity, thus in effect taking an anti-Gaullist position. But to this must be added the fact that 34 per cent would rather work to strengthen European unity alone, as opposed to only three per cent who would work to strengthen NATO alone.

[1] Failure to reform NATO may well have left only two alternatives—a national force or a European one. The choice of proponents and opponents may be limited to these two alternatives. The third alternative—a Franco-British force—appears less and less likely.

Arguments by some governmental spokesmen and such experts as General Gallois notwithstanding, French elites seem reasonably confident that the United States will utilize its atomic arsenal to honor its NATO commitments. Of the 99 respondents willing to express themselves on this issue, 79 (or 54% of the entire sample) think it unlikely that America will someday abandon these commitments; and only a handful considers such a contingency either likely (1%) or likely under some conditions (7%). Moreover, over half of our respondents believe that the United States would use its nuclear deterrent to protect all or certain of its European allies (and, of course, France is included in both categories). Only four per cent express the opinion that America would use its deterrent *only* in response to an attack on the United States.

A Multilateral Force (MLF)

Though French elites continue to give a vote of confidence to a reformed NATO, they are not so enthusiastic about MLF. In fact, only a quarter (26%) of the respondents favors it, an equal number opposes it, and the rest are undecided or unwilling to respond. But, if such a force were to be created, then 41 per cent of the respondents would wish to see France participate in it. About half that number was either definitely (6%) or conditionally (14%) opposed to any French participation in MLF. There seems to be an inclination among these French elites, however, to accept the idea of an MLF only if its control were to be lodged in the hands of the United States, England and France. Thus support for MLF must be understood to mean no less than a desire to reform NATO in the direction of American-British-French control. In this sense, French participation in matters of global strategy, so often demanded implicitly or explicitly by de Gaulle, is shared by the French elites.

The Test-Ban Treaty

Gaullist indifference to the Limited Test-Ban Treaty initiated by the United States and the Soviet Union is not mirrored in the attitudes of French elites. Over half (51%) approve, 24 per cent are "indifferent," and 17 per cent disapprove. Thirty per cent feel that France should have been consulted while 49 per cent claim that it makes no difference. About two-thirds (66%) favor further arms control between the United States and the Soviet Union. Virtually the same percentage (60%) believes that France should be consulted in the event of any future agreements but, even if France were not consulted, 57 per cent of the respondents would still favor such agreement and only 27 per cent remain indifferent.

THE DIRECTION OF CHANGE

The single domestic event most likely to bring about a change in French foreign policy is the death of de Gaulle. What is likely to happen then?

The elite responses we have analyzed give us a broad basis upon which to speculate about the extent and direction of such changes. France will demand greater participation within NATO or, if such reforms are not granted, its replacement with a classic alliance.[2] France will continue to pay lip service to German reunification without doing anything to bring it about. France will continue to propound her "mission" in Africa and her interests in other parts of the world and, in certain cases, may prove to be just as much of an irritant to American policymakers as de Gaulle has been.

There are three major areas of policy, however, in which changes must be expected. With de Gaulle out of the picture, "European unity" so much favored by elites will have a *relance*, as the French put it. De Gaulle has given to the French a vision of national independence and greatness. The elites believe that this can be best accomplished in a united Europe. Elites and political leaders will push for a greater degree of European unity. Second, the national *force de frappe* will have to be reconsidered. Again, the elites believe that, after de Gaulle, the force will be "Europeanized." They also prefer, as we have seen, a European force to an independent or a NATO-controlled one. Therefore, unless conditions radically change, there is every reason to believe that there will be serious consideration of a European nuclear force. The only factor that might impede it would be a genuine Soviet-American agreement and a joint effort to oppose proliferation and work for disarmament. A strong case will be made for the participation of England in any European nuclear force, because British participation will offset German influence. Finally, it is unlikely that opposition to NATO or to MLF will be either so strong or so successful as has been the case under de Gaulle. The reform of NATO is an alternative to a European nuclear

[2] This seems to be in the process of taking place.

force; and a solid core of French elites (41%) prefers to work to strengthen *both* NATO and European unity. Indeed, they do not consider them to be incompatible.[3]

Future French governments are also likely to take a more constructive view toward disarmament talks and to participate in the effort made at Geneva. Many respondents feel that France's "mission" of disarmament and peace was being ignored by de Gaulle. But, however widespread the approval of the Test-Ban Treaty, it should not be interpreted to mean that, under present conditions, France will abandon her effort to test and improve her nuclear weapons. The general attitude will be more conciliatory and cooperative; but the nuclear vocation— European or, if the European effort fails, national—will not be easily abandoned unless there are severe economic difficulties.

It would be wrong to assume that, after de Gaulle, France will again return to the "Atlantic fold" as a docile member. France is more powerful now than in the first postwar decade, has a better sense of its role in the world, has tasted the fruits of independence and the poisons of the atomic era. There will be no return to the position of tutelage and dependence upon the United States. But, at the same time, there can be no full-fledged separation and independence from the Atlantic (as opposed to the European) world. To begin with, the demands for national independence will have to be qualified by an acceptance of that which France, in an act of revolt, rejected in 1954: European military integration.[4] Second, it is very likely that England will be allowed to "join" in the European alliance, politically, economically and militarily. Finally, even in its inevitable assumption of greater autonomy, European reliance upon the United States is very likely to continue in one form or another—through NATO or a classic alliance—unless, because of changes in or pressures on Soviet society, de Gaulle's great vision of a Europe from the Atlantic to the Urals becomes a reality. A possible Franco-Soviet pact may create radically new conditions. The growing military involvement of the United States in Southeast Asia coupled with the prospects of Sino-American confrontation may further alter drastically the international situation and the relations between the United States and its European allies.

[3] See, however, the preceding footnote on p. 112.
[4] Long after these lines were written, an article in *Politique Etrangère*, reportedly published with de Gaulle's approval, advocated in effect a European conventional military establishment; see *The New York Times*, 17 October 1965.

Part II
PATTERNS OF
GERMAN ELITE OPINION

CHAPTER **8**

The West German Elite Sample

It has become commonplace to point to Germany as a key area in world politics. Its history, location and resources make it a major object as well as subject of international politics. Perhaps in few other countries are domestic and foreign affairs, political and military issues, so closely and inextricably interwoven as in the West German Federal Republic. And, as numerous recent studies of its society and polity have stressed, public policy-making in the Federal Republic is left in the hands of a comparatively small minority of informed, involved and influential leaders—the elites who in the eyes of the overwhelming mass of the population "run" the country.

Between the end of May and mid-October 1964, four American university professors undertook extended interviews with 173 of these leaders. They included cabinet ministers, deputies, party leaders, high civil servants, leading businessmen and journalists, university professors,

119

bishops and trade union leaders—all of them individuals who by virtue of their reputed knowledge, involvement and influence in public life had been identified by a group of experts on Germany as members of that society's elite.

Mostly Protestant, of upper and upper middle class urban origin, university educated and veterans of one or both wars, our respondents differ in social background more or less significantly from that of the general adult population of the Federal Republic.

In associational ties our respondents also are highly atypical compared to the adult population. While at least one-third (including practically all of the business leaders and close to a third of the political and non-business association leaders) are known to be affiliated with business and industrial association, only one-half of one per cent of adult Germans belong to such groups. Although about 12 per cent of adult Germans belong to non-business associations, such as trade unions and farm organizations, comparatively few of our respondents do, and most of them are leaders of such groups. Close to one-half of our leaders, especially university professors and political leaders, are identified with one or more public policy associations, compared with about one per cent of German adults. About a fourth of our respondents (including three-fourths of the university professors) are members of professional groups, compared with two per cent of the adult population. About a tenth are associated with religious organizations as against one per cent of adult Germans.

About two-thirds of our respondents are members of a political party, compared to about two per cent of the entire electorate. About half belong to the Christian Democratic Union (CDU) or its Bavarian associate, the Christian Socialist Union (CSU), which together received 48 per cent of the vote in the 1965 federal election; another 13 per cent belong to the Free Democratic Party (FDP), which polled 10 per cent in 1965 and forms the governing coalition with the CDU/CSU. About a fifth of our respondents are identified with the Social Democratic Party (SPD), the opposition party which was supported by 39 per cent of the voters in 1965.

Somewhat more than half of our respondents had been associated with a political party in 1956 and somewhat less than half as early as 1946. Most of them were the political leaders in our 1964 sample, but in the case of CDU members they also included a very large number of the high civil servants and in the case of SPD members many non-business association leaders (mostly trade union leaders). About a fifth of our respondents had been anti-Nazis, and 10 per cent were known to have been members of the Nazi Party or one of its auxiliaries. A fourth had been associated with a political party even before the Nazi era, mostly with the SPD or the Catholic Center Party.

About half of our respondents had held their occupational elite position a decade or more and only ten per cent (mostly civil servants and mass media leaders) less than 5 years. Most political leaders and university professors had held top positions between 5 and 20 years, most business leaders between 10 and 20 years. Our data on recruitment and career patterns suggest that educational and political achievements are on the whole less important for obtaining the elite position than long and continuous service in the elite occupation.

Since we were interested not only in the manifest patterns of opinion on the various issues we discussed, but also in implicit orientation patterns that might throw light on the trend of German leadership opinion, each interviewer was asked to evaluate latent patterns which appeared to him to emerge in the course of an interview.

Most of our respondents appeared well informed in general and most seemed to the interviewers highly confident of their ability to evaluate the problems we raised. In fact, this sense of high competence at times appeared to exceed the actual extent of their information. Not surprisingly, mass media leaders in particular showed themselves well informed and indicated a high sense of competence about their ability to render opinions.

An overwhelming majority of our respondents, especially the military and political leaders, appeared in general to consider the issues we discussed with them extremely important but only a minority also seemed generally highly emotionally involved. This keen but impersonal interest displayed by most respondents varied considerably, of course, with particular issues and elites. Significantly, we found among mass media leaders the largest proportion of highly opinionated persons, as well as of particularly "open-minded" respondents.

Comparatively few of our respondents indicated a generally high sense of trust and efficacy toward other political actors, domestic or foreign. Political leaders proved to be exceptionally trusting and correspondingly low in anxiety. Most respondents appeared to be moderately suspicious about the motives of other actors, except on issues and relationships in their own particular area of specialization. Here the majority seemed less anxious and even highly trusting and displayed a high sense of personal efficacy.

A majority indicated only a moderate sense of actual and potential influence on political developments in general. The exception here again proved to be political leaders, a large proportion of whom seemed to feel both actually and potentially highly influential, not only in domestic but also in foreign affairs.

CHAPTER 9

West German Elites and Domestic Politics

PATTERNS OF POLITICAL CONSENSUS

Contemporary West German political intercourse and public policy-making processes appear to rest upon a broad, if diffuse, elite consensus supporting the political system. A majority (56%) of the leaders interviewed professes to be generally satisfied with the system, though only a comparatively small minority (18%) expresses enthusiasm. A somewhat larger minority (24%), including many mass media leaders, seems less than satisfied and even critical of certain aspects of the system, but in general the answers we received indicate no overt hostility toward or significant alienation from the West German political system.

Approval of the system nonetheless seems in a number of cases to include a certain evaluative reserve. Quite a few respondents indicate that this political system still has to prove its worth. In their comments many of these apply what might be termed the "Weimar Standard," that is, a comparison of current political structures and practices with those of the 1918-1933 era. While the present system is judged to be vastly better by most (though not all) respondents who make this comparison, not infrequently there is an inclination to qualify favorable evaluations by pointing out that the Bonn Republic has as yet not been confronted by a real test of its viability in a time of crisis. Also, respondents who are more critical of certain aspects of the present political system assert that it is difficult to evaluate a system which seems to them to be in a state of transition. It remains to be seen whether present political structures and practices are flexible enough to meet the challenge of dynamic technological developments for German society. Present estimates, therefore, must remain conditional.

To probe more deeply into attitudes toward the contemporary political system we asked our respondents to single out those of its features which they evaluate particularly positively or negatively (Table 9.1). Comments on positive features refer favorably to perceived elements of stability, such as the disappearance of small parties, governmental independence from interest group pressures, a balance among various regional and functional interests, and to a fair and efficient system of law (Rechtsstaat) and public administration. The democratic nature of the system is seen in the responsiveness of political leaders to public opinion; and a number of respondents single out public discussion of political issues as a particularly praiseworthy feature. They claim that the press, radio and television have developed into the most important and efficient guardians of German democracy, especially by mobilizing public opinion against governmental abuses (as in Der Spiegel case of 1962 and the wiretapping revelations of 1963). Mass media leaders tend to single out the democratic nature of the system for praise (38% mention it), while civil servants focus on institutional features (29%).

Comments on negative features show less consensus. While three-fourths of the answers focus on alleged structural defects in the present system, there is considerable disagreement over where such defects lie. Some single out the electoral system that others find particularly praiseworthy; some say that there is too little democracy, others too much; some claim that public officials pay too much attention to group interests, others say too little; some allege that the executive branch has too

Table 9.1

EVALUATION OF THE WEST GERMAN
POLITICAL SYSTEM

QUESTIONS: *What are the positive features of the present form of government?*
What are the negative features of the present form of government?

POSITIVE FEATURES

	Number of Responses*	Percentage
Democratic nature in general	79	46%
Institutions	52	30
Party system	31	18
Leadership	29	17
Stability	18	10
Other	53	31
Don't know	11	6
Not ascertained	16	9
Total	289	167%

NEGATIVE FEATURES

	Number of Responses*	Percentage
Federalism	58	34%
Institutions	50	29
Political apathy	26	15
Leadership	20	12
Other	63	36
Don't know	2	1
Not ascertained	30	17
Total	249	144%

* Multiple responses permitted.

little power, others that it has too much. In general, the focus and nature of such criticism seem to be conditioned by the occupational vantage point from which a respondent views the polity rather than by aspects of his social background.

Government ministers, civil servants and military leaders, on the one hand, complain about the alleged excessive influence and demagoguery of the mass media leaders and of too much outside pressure on executive departments. Leaders of the opposition party, university professors and mass media leaders, on the other hand, complain that government and administrative leaders are too indifferent to the wishes of the public and undercut democratic processes. Some go so far as to charge that present trends in this respect are rapidly transforming the Federal Republic into an authoritarian state (*Obrigkeitsstaat*). Bundestag deputies of all parties represented in the lower chamber complain that the Bundestag is too overworked with legislative details to control the executive and educate the public. Business leaders complain about the quality of the political leadership, asserting that ambitious opportunists rather than "the best qualified men" dominate political life and fill the benches of the Bundestag. The deputies themselves are blamed for the weak position of the chamber, especially because they choose to debate their differences outside rather than inside the Bundestag. Whereas political leaders praise the electoral and party systems as positive features of the present governmental system, non-political leaders criticize both. Some hold that the big parties are too anemic and spineless, others that the parties and pressure groups supporting them are far too successful in advancing particularist interests at the expense of the state and the national interest.

As Table 9.1 shows, more than a third of the comments on the negative features of the present system focus on a basic institutional structure, the relationship between the central government and the states (*Länder*) in the Federal Republic. Contemporary criticism of the educational system, which is controlled by the states, and recent disputes between the central and the state governments over the distribution of income from taxation may have drawn an unusual amount of attention to an arrangement which politicians and civil servants in the federal government hold to be a serious obstacle to progress. If the country is to meet the challenge of technological and socio-economic developments, it is said, both the fiscal powers of the states and their control over the educational system must be drastically reduced.

Finally, the alleged political apathy of the masses is singled out, particularly by university professors and mass media leaders, as an important negative feature of the West German governmental system. But it is apparent that those who complain about inadequate civic consciousness in the Federal Republic frequently have rather different ideas about what they mean by it. Some respondents phrase their criticism in terms of traditionalist conservative values, while others stress that most West Germans (particularly the young people) lack the sense of political involvement and of civic responsibility which are said to be essential for a sound democracy. Thus military leaders charge that a prevailing climate of materialism leads individuals and groups to put their selfish interests ahead of national interests, that a materialist outlook (*Wohlstandsdenken*) has replaced loyalty toward the state (*Staatsbewußtsein*) and patriotism. Intellectuals, such as university professors and mass media leaders by way of contrast, complain about the indifference of the masses toward public affairs and political developments in general. In both groups of critics the blame is usually placed on the political leadership, leading some mass media leaders to imply that therefore a realignment of political forces under new leaders is necessary to bind the masses more closely to the polity.

Such criticism and controversies do not, however, appear to reflect deep cleavages underlying a diffuse consensus in the polity. Most of our respondents appear to view the negative features they mention not as irreparable weaknesses in the system, but rather as shortcomings which need to be overcome to strengthen it. In other words, they speak as supporters and not as irreconcilable opponents of the system. Most of them appear to view desirable changes in terms of relatively minor policy issues rather than in terms of basic problems requiring a radical transformation of the system. As reflected in Table 9.2, the vast majority of our respondents does not see basic ideological or class cleavages dividing elite or mass opinion. At present, the legitimacy and, thus, the survival of the political system do not seem to be at issue.

Without significant distinctions among occupational elites and age cohorts, most of our respondents seem to perceive these cleavages as comparatively superficial differences. Comparatively few mention class (1%), ideological (12%) or generational (1%) differences, all of which have been at the root of political conflicts in the not too distant past. In fact, it seems to be the view of most of our leaders that the major present domestic conflicts do not even involve basically different sets of

Table 9.2

CLEAVAGES AND CONFLICTS IN WEST GERMAN POLITICS

QUESTION: *What are the most important cleavages and conflicts in German politics today?*

	Number of Responses*	Percentage
Domestic policy cleavages and conflicts		
Current domestic political issues	74	43%
Fundamental domestic political issues	47	27
Social welfare policy	32	18
Ideological issues	20	12
Other domestic policy cleavages	32	18
(Total domestic)	(205)	(118)
Foreign policy cleavages and conflicts		
Atlantic community problems (NATO)	54	31
Policy in Eastern Europe	37	21
European integration problems	25	14
Armament issues	11	6
(Total foreign)	(127)	(72)
None	11	6
Don't know	4	2
Not ascertained	2	1
Total	349	199%

* Multiple responses permitted

policies, but rather clashes between individual leaders and groups within a political system which all, or most of them, accept as the only legitimate arena for political action. Thus, different domestic and foreign policies are identified with various leading political actors who are said to be competing for participant positions in governmental decision-making. Domestic issues (such as tax reforms, pension rights, measures to boost the economy, even reunification) as well as foreign policy issues (such as European integration, Germany's role in the Atlantic Alliance and the relationship with Eastern Europe) are seen by the vast majority of our respondents as controversial, but not fundamentally divisive, political issues. In both domestic and foreign affairs the context for political action seems to allow German leaders only variations on the same theme—not an entirely new tune.

This image of political stability was further underscored when we inquired about "the most important differences between the major political parties." Fifty-nine per cent of our leaders say that such differences are superficial or do not exist at all. Among the civil servants, mass media leaders, and members of the Senior and Retiring Elite, three-fourths of the respondents give this reply. For 16 per cent, domestic policy issues (including the reunification problem) seem divisive, as are ideological issues for an equal number, including many of the trade union leaders interviewed. The comments which accompany these answers usually underscore belief in a broad consensus between the major parties. One of SPD Chairman Willy Brandt's closest associates blandly defined the difference as "some are in and the others are not." An important CDU leader said that it was difficult to find points of controversy with the SPD, quoting a current cabaret joke which held "the SPD in 1964 to be the best CDU we ever had." A number of respondents pointed out that basically the same domestic and foreign policy problems confront the major party leaders and alternative solutions either do not exist or differ only in degree. Therefore, it is inevitable that CDU and SPD should find themselves more or less in close agreement, though some of their leaders seek to deny it. A few respondents, particularly among the mass media leaders, regret the fact that the parties have lost their distinct profiles and no longer offer the voter a real choice between alternative policies. Most of the party leaders we interviewed, however, seem to be little troubled by such considerations.

Noting these contemporary images of political stability and· of widespread consensus about the legitimacy of the existing regime, we must face the question of the depth and permanence of these opinions. How solid do present political structures and practices appear to our respondents, how firm the societal basis upon which they rest? Do they see drastic alterations as a distinct possibility and, if so, under what conditions? Or do they believe that the present political roles and practices are so solidly established that even a severe crisis would not seriously affect them?

EXPECTED DEVELOPMENTS UNDER
PRESENT CONDITIONS

Unless they are specifically asked to consider the possibility of a major political crisis, almost all of our respondents appear to assume that there will be no major change in the present political system in the foreseeable future except perhaps in the relationship between the Federal government and the states. Elite opinion voiced in our interviews, as well as trends in mass opinion, suggests that the distribution of power in the Federal Republic may gradually be altered in favor of the central government. Despite the widespread criticism we noted earlier, however, the comments of our leaders do not reflect expectations of very radical changes in this sector.

One of our questions concerned expectations regarding another institutional relationship which was frequently mentioned as unsatisfactory. After having listened to rather emphatic complaints about the growing weakness of the popularly-elected lower house of the federal parliament, the Bundestag, it was somewhat surprising to learn that 69 per cent of our respondents expect the relationship between executive and parliament to remain unchanged, and only 31 per cent do not.

Another criterion for evaluating the stability of a political system is the influence of groups. In general, our respondents' perception of group influences in the political process also conveys a sense of future stability and continuity. Individual comments substantiate our quantitative findings that groups are seen as more or less balanced in influence (though by no means without influence) in a pluralistic polity. As one civil service leader put it, farm, trade union and business leaders all have far-reaching influence in policy-making, but none of these groups dominates the others nor is likely to do so in the future. Groups such as the Roman Catholic Church and the refugee organizations are believed by some respondents to have lost influence; and few attribute to them any substantial political influence. There are several outspoken opponents of the alleged dominance of interest associations over public policy-making (*Herrschaft der Verbände*). But such criticism is confined to a small minority. Most respondents indicate that they neither wish nor expect major changes in the pluralistic polity.

Finally, in examining perceptions of continuity and change under non-crisis conditions in the system, let us see how our respondents perceive the future evolution of the party system and its major components. In general it is assumed by most that the contemporary development toward just two major parties will continue. The Free Democrats, who dropped from 13 per cent of the votes in 1961 to less than 10 per cent in 1965, are not believed to have much of a future. The FDP is severely criticized by CDU and SPD politicians (even by military leaders) as an element of instability, as a conglomeration of opportunistic politicians, that is unlikely to survive as a political factor if present trends continue.

Most of our respondents appear to expect the Christian Democratic Union (CDU) to remain the chief government party for at least the next few years, if not for another decade. If the opposition, the Social Democratic Party (SPD), should come to power, however, comparatively few respondents expect this to result in significant changes in the political system. Specific comments reflect little or no anxiety on this score. Though one prominent CDU leader said it would be a "catastrophe," he subsequently went so far as to assert that it might be good for the development of German democracy—and for his party—if the CDU were to leave the government, and the SPD to take over. Some business-men express fear that latent radical elements may still exist in the SPD, but in general the transformation of that party into a popular mass party similar to the CDU seems to be accepted as genuine and permanent. Military men, business leaders, civil servants and others who in the past might have been far more anxious about an SPD government, seem to feel that they could live with it as readily as their British counterparts can with a Labour government—perhaps even more comfortably. As for the CDU—though of late controversies between some of its most promi-nent leaders have made headlines—most respondents do not think that it will become less cohesive in the next few years.

Our leaders thus appear to anticipate no major transformation of the political system from a change of incumbents in major policy posi-tions. Similarity in outlook and restraints imposed by the domestic and international political setting are expected to lead future government leaders to follow more or less identical patterns of political behavior.

To sum up, under present conditions the development of institu-tional structures and political activities is expected to follow stable evo-lutionary patterns. What seems less clear and certain to many of our respondents is what would happen if the political system should be con-fronted with a major crisis.

EXPECTED DEVELOPMENTS UNDER CRISIS CONDITIONS

As we already noted, a number of our respondents are reserved in their evaluation of the contemporary political system because to them it still has to prove itself in time of crisis. Under present conditions of economic prosperity and political stability the radicalization of political life seems a remote possibility. No one mentions leftwing radicals as one of the groups that has gained power in recent years and only nine respondents (5%) claim that rightwing elements have gained in strength. Although a number speak of the survival of a "Nazi mentality" among older Germans and, more vaguely, of unregenerated Nazis in high positions, comparatively few seem to attach much significance to possible vestiges of Nazism under present circumstances. All but 11 of 142 of our leaders responding to a question on this subject say that Nazism is dead. Asked whether a revival is possible, half of 152 expressing an opinion deny this (especially most civil servants and business leaders). Eighteen per cent declare that the possibility is minimal, but 29 per cent think that under certain conditions elements of Nazism might be revived in a radical nationalist movement or in some other modified form.

What might happen in case of a serious crisis was a muted theme until we brought up a number of questions designed to learn what kind of crisis our leaders could envision and what kind of reactions they anticipate in West Germany. Most of those respondents who can visualize a crisis (10% cannot) expect it to be economic in origin, caused either by external or domestic developments (such as technological unemployment). Less than a third mention or infer a domestic political crisis arising from military or political developments outside the Federal Republic, such as a war, increased international tensions, or an American-Soviet *détente* at "Germany's expense."

Confronted by the question of how the German people would respond to such a crisis, some of our leaders express considerable uncertainty about this reaction, and about the resilience of the present political system in meeting such a test. Here is the "great unknown factor" in the future of the political system, we are told; how the German people would react is "entirely an open question." More than one leader believes that no one can give us an answer to it, yet only a few respondents appear entirely uncertain themselves. Most, whether confident or anxious, seem to have more or less definite visions (Table 9.3).

Our respondents' expectations of the basic strength and weaknesses

Table 9.3

EVALUATION OF WEST GERMAN SOCIETY'S REACTION TO CRISIS

QUESTION: *How will German society react to a major upheaval in the world?*

	Number of Respondents	Percentage	Highest Elite Group by Response Category	
Confident				
Extreme cohesiveness or greater cohesiveness than at present	24	14%	Military:	28%
No change in cohesiveness	15	9	Political:	18%
Some (temporary) confusion and disarray	39	23	Military:	36%
Uncertain or don't know	19	11		
Anxious				
Extreme disarray	16	9	Mass Media:	19%
Left radicalization	21	12	Civil Service:	25%
Right radicalization	9	5	Mass Media:	10%
Left and right radicalization	19	11	University Professors:	24%
Not ascertained	11	6		
Total	173	100%		

of German society that will emerge in times of crisis are evidently based above all on their appraisal of latent elements in contemporary mass opinion. The innate strength of the German national character is mentioned most frequently, and the well-learned lesson of past crisis experiences (such as those of the Weimar Republic) next, by those who express confidence that West German society could surmount such a crisis. Both factors are cited particularly frequently by military men. Comparatively few respondents express confidence that enlightened leadership would prove the chief source of strength. Among the politicians, however, this factor is mentioned more frequently than any other, possibly due to the fact that their group image gives them greater confidence in the capacity of the political leadership than is shown by other elites. Qualified leadership would be available, it is said; it would rally mass opinion in support of the present political system and take adequate measures to check a crisis. More generally, the confident respondents assert that neither rightwing nor leftwing radical movements would in such a situation be able to command sufficient mass support to threaten seriously the democratic form of government. Contemporary Germans are said to be politically more mature than those of the 1930's: The older ones have learned their lesson through personal experiences, and the younger ones have been educated to cherish democracy.

Others are less confident. A substantial minority, including two-thirds of the mass media leaders commenting on this issue, expresses doubt about whether or not the democratic form of government could survive mass reactions to a serious economic crisis or to international developments seen as threatening "vital" German national interests or even the survival of the country. Two-thirds of these more or less anxious respondents single out failings in the contemporary national character as the major potential source of weakness in either event. Of the two perceived possibilities, an economic crisis seems by far the more likely to most, but especially to those anxious respondents belonging to the age group whose members had experienced the Depression of the 1930's in their formative years. Many of the anxious fear that mass unemployment would produce mass hysteria, possibly with catastrophic consequences for German democracy. To them it seems that most of their countrymen, regardless of age, lack the ideological substance that could give them the strength to face up to such an economic crisis with confidence and to rally behind democratic leaders in a surge of national unity. Seen as too accustomed to prosperity to accept potential economic deprivations and as wedded to a hedonistic materialism, West Germans are expected to turn against moderate, democratic leaders in an economic crisis and to support radical demagogues intent on destroying German democracy.

To sum up: The likelihood that the present political system might be shaken by a serious domestic crisis is apparently a remote possibility to most of our German leaders. The possibility of such a crisis and considerations of what might happen to the system if it occurred are not brought up by most of them until we deliberately inject this issue into the conversation. While a few reject the possibility, a large number professes either to be uncertain of what would happen or to be anxious. A substantial minority, however, expresses confidence that the system could readily surmount an economic or foreign policy crisis, the former possibility appearing more likely than the latter to most. Both the confident and the anxious single out national character as the most important source of strength or weakness in a crisis situation, the former (particularly military leaders) expressing the belief that it is a latent element of strength and the latter (particularly mass media leaders) seeing it as a latent source of weakness.

What we have called the "Weimar Standard" appears to be especially salient as a point of reference when it comes to considering a crisis. Among the anxious, in particular, the economic and political crises of that era appear to have etched themselves so deeply into their memory that they are highly prone to project them upon possible future crises in the present system. Respondents in the age cohorts most familiar with those past crises from personal experience are proportionally more confident than younger leaders. This suggests that, for the anxious, the Weimar Standard has primarily a symbolic meaning as a collective trauma. This trauma in the history of German democracy appears to have high saliency and symbolic content particularly among the mass media elite, and produces doubts and reservations about the resilience of the present system and the stability of pro-democratic opinion in the Federal Republic.

If these responses are in any sense representative of substantial elements of German elite or "opinion leadership" perspectives, it may be expected that many German leaders will remain highly sensitive to domestic developments that, in their view, might lead to a repetition of Weimar experiences. Another decade without crisis, or the successful weathering of one, may overcome these reservations and fears. As new political experiences replace Weimar memories, the resilience of the system and the stability of mass consensus may gradually be accepted even by those who are presently uncertain or anxious about them. For the immediate future, however, the large minority of anxious leaders is likely to oppose policy decisions which seem even remotely to threaten stability. In general the source of concern appears to be far more economic than international political developments affecting Germany. The extent to which fear of instability also affects German elite attitudes when it comes to the international environment is a matter we shall consider in the following chapter.

RESPONSE PATTERNS ON DOMESTIC ISSUES

Our examination of elite views on the present political system of the Federal Republic indicates patterns of broad, if diffuse, consensus which support the existing institutional structures and pluralist polity. On the whole, the elites' image of the future is one of continued political stability and domestic tranquility. The removal of one leader or the replacement of one set of leaders by another is not expected to produce far-reaching changes, not only because the confines of policy-making are believed to be too narrowly restricted to allow for major changes but also because incumbent and aspiring leaders are thought to be more or less in agreement on policy principles. No single political figure is the focus of elite attention; and fundamental class or ideological cleavages do not appear to divide the elites, nor are they believed by most of them to matter in the Federal Republic. At the same time, however, quite a few of the leaders we interviewed appear to feel that the present climate of pragmatic orientations toward political and social issues has deprived German society of ideological values which they believe to be necessary to provide a solid underpinning for the political system. Should domestic or international developments produce a severe crisis in Germany, in the opinion of some (particularly military) leaders, this void may be filled by a new spirit of idealism. Others, above all mass media leaders and members of the Middle Elite, fear that, on the contrary, lack of idealist enthusiasm for the democratic system may lead to its destruction should there be a major crisis.

In general, the pattern of manifest responses seems to indicate that German leaders are content with the present political system and feel more or less confident that their individual and group values can be satisfied within it. Important differences in orientations among age cohorts are not apparent (except on the crisis question) nor do different social or political background variables seem to shape opinion patterns significantly. Some variations, however, in political attitudes among different occupational elites are evident. Beyond such differences in orientation as might be expected in a pluralist polity, it seems that mass media leaders and, to a lesser extent, university professors are particularly critical of certain features of the present system. (Perhaps this is the mark of intellectuals in any modern society.) By way of contrast, respondents belonging to elites who are directly involved in policy-making—such as military leaders, civil servants and politicians—appear to be less critical and less concerned with changing elements of the system. Even leaders of the opposition Social Democratic Party seem on the whole more content with the system as it presently operates than many of the intellectuals.

References to a "Bonn Establishment" by some critics who perceive themselves as "outsiders" seem more or less substantiated by indications of a narrower and ostensibly more solid system-supporting consensus among the administrative (military and civil service) and political elites. Business leaders and leaders of non-business interest associations appear to be more peripheral to this consensual core in attitude, sharing the opinions of some of the members of the Bonn Establishment on certain policy issues and rejecting them, or remaining indifferent or undecided, on others. The group furthest removed from the consensual core seems to be the intellectuals, particularly mass media leaders, who feel it incumbent upon themselves to play the role of critics of the Establishment, though they accept the system in general.

CHAPTER 10

West Germany in World Politics

The Federal Republic's position in international affairs in recent years has presented an anomaly. On the one hand, this country of 54 million people is one of three or four of the largest economic powers in the world and in this respect exercises a major influence abroad. On the other hand, politically and militarily West Germany has played the role of a second- or even third-rate power, depending more on other states to determine its foreign policy and to provide for its security than on its own vast resources. The major source of this contradiction is the legacy of the lost war, which left Germany divided and its Western portions in a tenuous position between the superpowers in the postwar East-West conflict. The conduct of the Federal Republic's foreign policy has reflected the problems which are inherent in this situation. Closely tied to the West by military, political and economic ties, and one of the world's leading trading nations, the country has explicitly followed a course of intimate contacts with the Western and nonaligned states while maintaining a more or less hostile position toward the Communist countries. But the division of Germany and the continued growth of the Federal Republic's power potential pose the problem of whether the relatively static nature of its foreign policy can and will continue in a world of dynamic political, military and technological changes.

Our investigation sought to ascertain the views on this subject of those individuals in the Federal Republic who reputedly have the actual or potential influence to determine the future course of its foreign policy. How do they see and evaluate trends in international politics? What sort of policies do they expect or want their country to follow in this setting? What priorities do they assign to foreign policy goals? How much hope do they hold for the realization of these foreign policy goals? To what extent are they in agreement on these matters? How far does the consensus on domestic political issues carry over into foreign policy problems?

German leaders interviewed seem as a group more highly engaged on foreign policy than domestic issues. Almost half (41-50%) shift their position toward greater emotional involvement, firmer views, a tougher outlook and a lower sense of efficacy and trust. We also noted that on the whole respondents tend to be less logical and internally consistent in their discussion of foreign issues than domestic ones.

In general, fewer of our leaders seem to feel a sense of high actual or potential influence over foreign affairs than over domestic affairs. Our data do not permit us to say that this is a general phenomenon in all countries, and our manifest responses suggest that the gap in this respect may be greater among elites in the Federal Republic than in some other countries. There is however a considerable shift among those who feel actually and potentially influential in these two spheres. Fifty per cent of those who indicate a high sense of *actual* influence over domestic politics and an equal proportion who indicate a high sense of *potential* influence in this area do not appear to feel they have as great an influence over foreign affairs. At the same time, 73 per cent of those respondents who indicate a comparatively low sense of actual influence over domestic affairs seem to feel highly influential when it comes to foreign affairs and 23 per cent who seem to consider their potential influence to be low in the former area appear to believe it high in the latter. It may be of some significance that such a shift toward a higher sense of actual and/or potential influence is particularly pronounced among members of the business elite, the group which is particularly involved in the expansion of Germany's economic power in the world. Finally, we might note that a feeling that developments would inevitably take their course and that the influence of German leaders is, therefore, not very great is far more pronounced on issues of foreign policy than on domestic issues.

CONSENSUS AND CLEAVAGE ON FOREIGN POLICY GOALS

The most important goals of his government's foreign policy had been defined by Chancellor Ludwig Erhard in various statements between October 1963, when he took office, and the time we conducted our interviews. He declared that (1) the division of Germany is an intolerable situation and announced that efforts to achieve reunification through the self-determination of the German people are an integral part of (2) his government's efforts to seek an easing of international tensions. He said that his government (3) would not accept the Oder-Neisse Line as the boundary between Poland and Germany because it refuses "to relinquish . . . territories that are the native home of so many of our German brothers and sisters." The German people, according to Erhard (4) place "a particularly high value" on intimate friendship and cooperation with the United States and also seek (5) the "cultivation and extension" of close relations with France. His government wants (6) to help transform Europe into a partner of the United States that will be that nation's equal, but European unity must be based on close cooperation among all "free European countries" that wish to participate. Therefore, close relations with France have to go hand in hand with intimate and friendly relations with other European states, "above all Great Britain," and proposed measures to achieve greater European unity must be carefully evaluated in terms of their military, political and economic significance for the Federal Republic.

We found our German leaders to be in general agreement with these policy goals, though comparatively few are enthusiastic in their support (particularly businessmen). A small minority voices general or even vehement disapproval or asserts that the Erhard government "has no foreign policy." This point of view is particularly prevalent among university professors. The overwhelming majority, however, approves or has only mild reservations about some specific aspects of Erhard's policy. This general supportive consensus includes most of the supporters of the governing coalition as well as of the opposition party, as may be seen in Table 10.1.

Table 10.1

WEST GERMAN EVALUATION OF GOVERNMENT'S FOREIGN POLICY

QUESTION: *Are you satisfied with the government's foreign policy measures?*

	Number of Respondents	Per Cent of Total	Per Cent of Response by Partisan Identification			
			CDU/CSU	FDP	SPD	No Party
Enthusiastic	20	12%	21%	6%	—	16%
General approval	75	43	46	65	33%	52
Mild approval or disapproval	43	25	19	12	39	18
General and vehement disapproval	24	14	9	18	23	10
Don't know or indifferent	2	1	5	—	5	4
Not ascertained	9	5	—	—	—	—
Total	173	100%	100%	101%	100%	100%

A policy of intensive international cooperation seems, to practically all our respondents, mandatory for the Federal Republic; and it is supported with enthusiasm by over a third of them (particularly by military leaders). Political and military alignments with other nations are seen as the only possible approach to the satisfaction of German interests, though quite a number of respondents think that a more self-assertive pursuit of these interests is both desirable and reconcilable with such a policy. Comparatively few respondents seem to feel that domestic political developments, such as a change in policy-makers, might produce significant changes in German foreign policy. The prevalent view seems to be that any government will have relatively little room for maneuver and policy choices, simply because the international context does not permit it. Two-thirds of our respondents expect the present pattern of world politics, which they perceive to be a fairly stable bipolarity, to continue in the foreseeable future; even the one-third who anticipate a less stable, more multipolar international setting do not seem to feel that this would significantly change the specific context for German foreign policy-making. Therefore, all or at least most of the principal features of Erhard's foreign policy are expected to survive his government.

In sum, the same broad, if diffuse, elite consensus that we noted in our discussion of domestic politics appears to prevail also in the realm of foreign policy. Our respondents' perception of the present government's foreign policy goals corresponds to those enunciated by Erhard, reflecting a high degree of congruence between policy articulation and elite cognition. Though a few claim not to know the government's objectives, such statements appear to be mostly rhetorical rather than factual. It is at the level of policy particulars that our leaders perceive and articulate major points of disagreement over priorities and methods of German foreign policy. These focus on the three problem areas identified earlier as sources of cleavages in contemporary domestic politics: (1) Atlantic community (NATO) problems, particularly relations with the United States and France; (2) West German policies toward Eastern Europe (including the reunification issue, often identified as a domestic problem as well); and (3) problems connected with the integration of Europe.

THE WESTERN ALLIANCE AND ITS FUTURE

For the last fifteen years, political and military cooperation with the nations of the Western Alliance has been one of the anchor points of West German foreign policy. Initially a matter of controversy between government and opposition, the CDU and the FDP as well as the SPD have in recent years lost no opportunity to pledge their loyalty to the alliance. Leaders of all three parties have called attention to their country's faithful execution of NATO directives, to the Federal Republic's extensive financial and military contributions to the alliance and to the fact that it has been the only NATO member to give complete control over all its military forces to NATO. These themes were all stressed by the German leaders we interviewed. "We Germans obey NATO as we once obeyed our own military leaders—unquestioningly," as a business leader put it.

A multilateral, peacetime security arrangement is a novel experience for a people who in the past had relied primarily on their own national forces and had as their allies only temporary junior partners who accepted German leadership. The present arrangement makes the Federal Republic one of the junior partners in the Western Alliance, without nuclear weapons and subject to restrictions which do not apply to other members. But West German leaders describe this as an inevitable and necessary situation, dictated by both military and political considerations arising out of the division of Germany and the proximity of Soviet forces. Potentially, however, the Federal Republic may have the resources to play a far more major role in NATO—a role which its spokesmen claim they do not seek. The role of a junior partner, they say, follows from the continuing responsibility of the United States, Britain and France not only to provide for the protection of Berlin and West Germany but also to negotiate with their former fellow occupation power, the Soviet Union, for the reunification of Germany.

With but few exceptions, our respondents claim to accept and support the public position of West German leaders on NATO. Our interviews indicate, however, that the alliance is perceived and evaluated rather diffusely by German elites. Two views seem to emerge, one of which stresses the military and security aspects and the other more the political aspects of this Western Alliance. Which seems of primary importance to a respondent appears to depend primarily on his evaluation of Soviet intentions in general, and his country's need for military security against Russia and its allies in particular.

Three out of four leaders interviewed assert that their country's security is threatened by the Soviet Union and its allies and that this threat will last for a long time, if not indefinitely. Military men—the group which seemed least concerned about the political consequences of a domestic crisis—are particularly emphatic on this point. University professors, comprising a group which has been particularly anxious about their countrymen's reactions in a domestic crisis, seem least concerned about an external Communist threat. But when it comes to defining the nature of the external Communist threat, our respondents may be divided roughly equally between those who see it primarily in military terms and those who see this threat in the form of Communist political and economic activities directed against the Federal Republic. Here, even the military leaders are about evenly divided, whereas mass media leaders tend to stress the military threat.

Evaluations of NATO seem to relate to these different evaluations of the Communist threat. Those who are anxious about the possibility of an overt Soviet attack tend to appraise NATO primarily in terms of its military significance; those who focus on the non-military danger or who discount the external threat entirely tend to focus on its political meaning for German foreign policy.

But we must inject a qualification on this point. Only one out of three respondents categorically denies the existence of even a latent military threat. For the others the threat exists. The difference is that for the more anxious it seems to exist in a more acute form than for those who acknowledge it but who imply in their comments that present security arrangements are adequate to deter Soviet military power. The latent danger is not necessarily deliberate Soviet aggression, according to the prevalent view, but rather that an incident over Berlin or an uprising in the East German Democratic Republic (D.D.R.) might escalate into a limited war in Europe or even a world nuclear conflict. That the Federal Republic might become involved in a war that started elsewhere than in Germany seems beyond the perspective of practically all respondents.

Most respondents appear to fear the threat of a Soviet invasion with conventional forces rather than a nuclear conflict. Perhaps due to their experiences in the last war and perhaps also because of the arguments advanced for the rearmament of Germany in the 1950's, the greatest danger in the view of all respondents who perceive a Soviet military threat, actual or latent, is a non-nuclear attack. Because of its apparent superiority over the NATO powers in conventional land forces, the Soviet Union is thought likely to avoid the use of nuclear weapons and a possible nuclear exchange, relying on conventional superiority to attempt to seize the resources of West Germany more or less intact.

The best, if not the only, protection against both a conventional and a nuclear attack in the view of the majority of our respondents is a nuclear umbrella to deter such attacks, and ironclad guarantees that such nuclear weapons will be employed instantly if deterrence fails.

It is against this background of threat perceptions and security considerations that West German leadership opinion about NATO and about West Germany's relations with the United States, France and the countries of Eastern Europe must be evaluated. West Germans have on the whole not been entirely convinced in the past that the NATO alliance assures their security against a Soviet attack. But it must be added that confidence in NATO appears to have been increasing. While in 1959 only 18 per cent of respondents in a survey of West German mass opinion expressed a great deal of confidence in NATO's effectiveness, this figure had increased to 31 per cent by 1961.[1] However, another survey in September 1960 showed that only 19 per cent of a cross section of West German adults thought that a Soviet invasion could be prevented by NATO forces, as against 37 per cent who thought it was impossible and 44 per cent who were uncertain. Yet, two-thirds (67%) of the respondents in a 1963 poll thought that membership in NATO was more advantageous than disadvantageous for the Federal Republic and no more than 9 per cent were certain that it was disadvantageous.[2] The differences between the relatively small number who have confidence in NATO military capabilities and the much larger number who believe it advantageous for Western Germany to belong to NATO may reflect a distinction between the organization's military and political value for the Federal Republic and between NATO's perceived capacity to deter an attack and its ability to turn back an attack.

These distinctions are indicated in our discussion with West German leaders, as well as by other studies of German elites.[3] One-half of our respondents believe that an international defensive alliance with

---

[1] Data from Richard L. Merritt and Donald J. Puchala, eds., *Western European Perspectives on International Affairs: Public Opinion Studies and Evaluations* (New York: Frederick A. Praeger, Inc., 1967).
[2] Elisabeth Noelle and Erich Peter Neumann, *Jahrbuch der Öffentlichen Meinung 1958-1964* (Allensbach and Bonn: Verlag für Demoskopie, 1965), pp. 542, 539.
[3] A study of German leadership opinion found that in 1961 three-fourths of the leaders interviewed believed that NATO was strong enough to deter a Russian attack for at least the next five years, but that only a minority believed it strong enough to turn back an actual attack. Morton Gorden and Daniel Lerner, "The Setting for European Arms Control: Political and Strategic Choices of European Elites," *Journal of Conflict Resolution*, 9 (December 1965), 425.

nuclear powers, such as NATO, is the best way to provide for the defense of German interests and about an equal proportion express the belief that under present conditions the Federal Republic can rely completely on NATO to protect her security. On this point, most of the military leaders are very emphatic. Almost as many, however, and most particularly the political leaders, have some doubts about NATO's effectiveness as a military organization. Might a reform of the alliance make it more effective? Close to a third of the respondents say it needs no reform and a few assert that no reform could make it more effective. But almost half voice the belief that reforms might indeed make NATO a more effective alliance. Most of these, it must be added, seem to think of such reforms more in political than in military terms: European members might be given a greater voice in NATO policy-making and planning, for example, and cooperation within the alliance might be better coordinated. To judge by some of the comments which accompany these suggestions, quite a few German leaders feel that certain NATO nations, particularly the United States, Britain and France, have of late been neglecting their political responsibilities toward their German ally while the Federal Republic, for its part, has made considerable sacrifices to show its loyalty to the alliance.[4] Above all, a frequent complaint is that these three senior NATO partners could do a great deal more to further the cause of German reunification through negotiations with the Soviet Union and pressure on the German Democratic Republic (D.D.R.).

Yet, very few of the leaders we interviewed explicitly demand a greater voice for their country in NATO councils.[5] In part this may be political discretion toward other European members; in part, however, such apparent self-abnegation seems to be due to a feeling that NATO as such is less important than German relations with the United States. Only a tenth of our respondents (particularly political leaders) explicitly say so, but it seems apparent from other comments that for many of our leaders NATO is essentially a framework for a more or less bilateral political and defensive arrangement between the Federal Republic and the United States. Through NATO, six American divisions stationed in

[4] For example, some respondents point out that the Federal Republic faithfully obeyed NATO directives against the sale of certain strategic items to the U.S.S.R. whereas Britain felt no compunction about providing the Soviet Union with such goods.

[5] According to a still unpublished German study of 47 members of the Bundestag defense committee and 33 other deputies, 37 per cent thought in 1964 that the German government had an adequate voice in the formulation of NATO policy but 58 per cent desired greater influence in NATO, especially over personnel matters.

Germany give far more effective notice to the Soviet Union that American nuclear power protects the Federal Republic than does the formal treaty. Through NATO, the American forces in West Berlin constitute a more effective protection of that city's freedom than their size might indicate. Through NATO, the Federal Republic has greater means to influence American policy affecting Germany than might otherwise be the case. By demonstrating its loyalty to the alliance, so runs the argument of many of our German leaders, their country earns the right to claim American military and political support as the most faithful and dependable of America's NATO partners. Thus, to a large extent German leadership attitudes toward NATO appear to be conditioned by the emphasis and value which they place on close ties with the United States. This becomes particularly evident when we solicit our leaders' views on the multilateral force project.

The Multilateral Force

At the time we spoke to our German leaders the United States proposal for a multilateral polaris fleet of converted freighters had not as yet become the subject of French criticism or British modification proposals. Thus, when we injected the project into our conversations we had reference to the original plan to offer the non-nuclear NATO nations, including the Federal Republic, an opportunity to participate in target planning and firing of nuclear missiles capable of reaching the Soviet Union. In the United States, it will be recalled, the MLF project was seen as a way to still a presumed German desire for nuclear weapons and Intermediate Range Ballistic Missiles (IRBMs) to deter a Soviet attack.

When we asked our respondents what they thought of "the widely-discussed proposal of a multilateral nuclear force under NATO command," we encountered a sharp division of opinion toward the project. One-third are clearly in favor, and another 13 per cent are conditionally so. Support from members of what we have called the Bonn Establishment, military men and political leaders, is especially high. A third of our leaders, however, express their opposition with varying degrees of vehemence. Among these are two-thirds of the mass media elite—the group that we found on domestic issues tends to diverge most strongly from the views of the Establishment. Between these two camps are those who profess to be indifferent or unable to evaluate the issue—a comparatively small group (17%) in which civil servants and businessmen

businessmen predominate. Among age cohorts, the project appears to be especially salient for leaders under fifty, who divide more sharply than their elders and who are three to one in favor of MLF.

When we ask whether the Federal Republic should participate in such a force if it comes into being, however, only a fifth of our respondents remain opposed and very few (7%) still profess ignorance or indifference. A solid majority of two-thirds, including practically all the military men and even a majority of the mass media leaders, says "yes."

At first glance this shift in opinion may seem puzzling, but here as elsewhere the quantitative data alone do not tell the whole story. Judging by the qualifying comments which accompany these answers, it appears that the issue is in each instance perceived and evaluated differently by those leaders who switch their position from opposition or ambivalence about MLF to endorsement of German participation. Militarily, hardly anyone (including military leaders) seems to take the proposal very seriously. A multilateral polaris surface fleet seems hardly a substitute for the landbased IRBMs demanded by NATO commanders in Europe as a deterrent and defensive measure. Politically, too, there seem to be many objections based on perceived domestic as well as international implications. Our own and other data indicate that most German leaders do not consider NATO nuclear sharing either necessary or desirable, especially where it involves their own countrymen.[6] Nor is the proposal generally seen as a means for the European NATO nations, including the Federal Republic, to obtain significantly greater influence over when and where nuclear weapons are to be employed. Asked who should control the proposed multilateral fleet, 56 per cent of our respondents say the United States alone and only 39 per cent, the United States together with European and NATO powers.

If a supportive minority turns into a majority when we move from a general evaluation of the MLF proposal to a consideration of German participation, the reason appears to lie primarily in the desire of most German leaders interviewed to strengthen ties with the United States. If the United States government is determined to create an MLF, then the Federal Republic would for better or worse have to participate.

---

[6] Asked in 1961 whether they considered a revision of the MacMahon Act (to permit sharing of atomic information and technology) necessary for a sound Western defense policy, 60 per cent of German leaders responded negatively and only 35 per cent positively. This distribution represented an exact reversal of the replies to this question given by French and British leaders. See Daniel Lerner and Morton Gorden, "Strategic Thinking of the European Elites" (Massachusetts Institute of Technology, mimeographed, 1964).

"If necessary," declared Chancellor Erhard on 6 October 1964, "the Federal Republic is prepared to begin building the contemplated atomic fleet with the United States alone."

West Germans have come to accept the fact that they have a definite obligation in the defense of Europe,[7] and their leaders appear generally in agreement that NATO as presently constituted represents the best possible arrangement to provide for the security of the Federal Republic. In NATO and beyond NATO, however, the relationship with the United States appears to loom larger in the eyes of German leaders than the organization as such. To judge by the comments of our respondents, the future relationship between the Federal Republic and NATO depends principally on the evolution of West Germany's relationship with the United States and secondarily on other bilateral relationships—particularly with France and the Soviet Union. It seems that if the ties with the United States are weakened and the value of American military and political support becomes less significant for the leaders of the Federal Republic other arrangements which presently seem to conflict with Germany's NATO role will assume greater significance for them. Relieved of the necessity which they presently assume, that is, to prove their confidence in the United States through loyalty to the alliance, Germany's leaders may find it possible to be more flexible in their relationship with the United States as well as with France and the Soviet Union.

PRESENT GERMAN-AMERICAN RELATIONS

West German sentiments toward the United States have been characterized in recent years by far greater trust, respect and desire for friendship than have been shown toward any other nation.[8] Such

---

[7] Asked whether the Federal Republic had responsibilities for the defense of Western Europe, 68 per cent of a representative sample of West German adults said "yes" in 1964 (compared to 44 per cent in 1952) and only 10 per cent said "no" (27 per cent in 1952). See EMNID, *Informationen,* No. 27 (1964).

[8] For example USIA surveys of mass opinion in 1963 indicated that 76 per cent of West German respondents had good feelings about the United States, but only 49 per cent about Britain, 46 per cent about France and four per cent about the U.S.S.R. Only three per cent indicated bad feelings about the United States, while five per cent had bad feelings about Britain, ten per cent about France and 64 per cent about the U.S.S.R. (Data from Merritt and Puchala, *Western European Perspectives on International Affairs.*) In another poll, 90 per cent of respondents picked the United States in 1963 as the country with which the Federal Republic should have close relations, 71 per cent France, 65 per cent Great Britain and 27 per cent the U.S.S.R. (Noelle and Neumann, *Jahrbuch 1958-1964,* p. 533; cf. also pp. 547, 567).

feelings were also reflected in our interviews with German leaders. But beyond the level of sentiment, German relations with the United States appear to be of greater political importance to these leaders than any other international association. Among the foreign policies which are believed likely to survive the Erhard government, contemporary policies toward the United States are named more often than any other specific feature. Regardless of who should succeed Erhard or which party or combination of parties should take over the government, here is one international relationship which is expected to be preserved intact. More frequently than any other country or group of countries, the United States is singled out as having long-term common interests with the Federal Republic by all elites (Table 10.2).

But what are these common long-term interests? To judge by the pattern of responses in our interviews, they are for German leaders

Table 10.2

COUNTRIES SHARING LONG-TERM COMMON INTERESTS WITH WEST GERMANY

QUESTION: *With which of the following countries will Germany continue to share common interests for a long period?*

	Number of Responses*	Percentage
United States	125	72%
European Economic Community (EEC) countries	61	35
France	49	28
Great Britain	48	28
Western Europe	25	14
Other responses	105	61
Not ascertained	6	3
Total	419	241%

* Multiple responses permitted

primarily military. The United States is perceived as the guardian of German security against the Soviet threat which, as we noted, is seen by most of our respondents as a long-term, even indefinite, danger. According to a 1961 survey of European elites, in the view of 9 out of 10 German leaders the United States is the most powerful nation in the world and in the opinion of 5 out of 7 it will still be that at the end of the century.[9] Therefore, it seems logical in the view of German leaders that their country must assure itself of the benevolent guardianship of its security by the United States.

German-American relations, to judge by our interviews, are thus above all evaluated in terms of military considerations. German military security, even in the event that the country should acquire its own nuclear deterrent, is perceived as entirely dependent on the protection of American nuclear power by 7 out of 10 of our respondents. Here, for once, military and mass media leaders are not only in agreement, but lead all other elites in expressing this viewpoint. Practically all respondents in both groups consider West German security completely dependent on the United States. According to one mass media leader, the NATO Treaty as such is worth no more than the paper it was written on; its real significance for Germany is the implicit bilateral alliance with the United States. According to a prominent political leader the only "meaningful" relationship in NATO is "the Bonn-Washington Axis." Most express the firm belief that the United States will use its nuclear power to retaliate against any attack on the Federal Republic. The presence of American troops is seen as a guarantee of this. Therefore, a United States withdrawal from Europe is vehemently opposed by 6 out of 10 respondents and welcomed by none. Few, however, appear to fear such a contingency: Fifty-three per cent think it extremely unlikely, 18 per cent, unlikely, and only 13 per cent think it might happen under some conditions (such as a new isolationism in the United States or

---

[9] In comparison 8 out of 10 British leaders ranked the United States first in 1961 and 4 out of 7 by the end of the century; 7 out of 10 French leaders ranked the United States first in 1961 and 3 out of 5 by the end of the century. See Gorden and Lerner, "The Setting for European Arms Control," p. 425.

The average West German appears to estimate American power somewhat less favorably than his leaders. According to a 1964 opinion survey 54 per cent of West Germans considered the United States stronger than "the East," while 29 per cent considered both equally strong and 7 per cent thought the East stronger. This, however, represented an increase in popular estimates of American strength, for in 1958 only 33 per cent considered the United States stronger, while 30 per cent thought the East stronger, and 34 per cent believed both equally strong. See EMNID, *Informationen*, No. 36 (1964).

under an arrangement with the Soviet Union). Surely, so runs the argument, the United States cannot and will not withdraw its military protection, for American leaders must realize that such a move would bring about a Soviet conquest of all of Europe and, eventually, the United States.

The intensity of such a feeling of military dependency on the United States seems to relate to the degree of insecurity of a respondent. One out of four respondents, it will be recalled, fears that above all an international crisis involving Germany might threaten domestic stability. American deterrent power and protection seem to represent in this respect a safeguard for domestic stability if it serves to avert such international crises, particularly to mass media leaders. The American presence appears also to be welcomed by leaders who fear the ambitions of German radical nationalists as an assurance that German military power will be kept under safe American and NATO control.

To those respondents who focus on the external danger and perceive a Soviet threat as real and lasting, complete dependency on the United States seems unavoidable—at least under present conditions. The greater such anxiety, the greater, too, seems the eagerness of a respondent to deny that major differences might arise between the Federal Republic and the United States. This impression is particularly strong in the interviews we conducted in West Berlin, but by no means there alone.

Those who appear to be reconciled to this dependency on the United States often stress that West Germany is America's most reliable partner in the Western camp. One respondent, a leader of a refugee association, went so far as to say that the German press should avoid even mentioning possible American shortcomings or difficulties; the German public should have only the highest regard for and complete confidence in the United States. A mass media leader saw no reason why the United States should not dictate German foreign policy, so long as it does not try to get the Federal Republic involved in its own non-European ventures. A banker claimed to welcome increasing American investments in Germany on the grounds that these will provide further assurances that United States military power will not be withdrawn.

Practically without exception our German leaders sought to impress upon us the identity of German and American interests in world politics, though comparatively few seem fully aware of American interests in other parts of the world. These, insofar as they are referred to at all, seem to be perceived as sideshows to the major East-West arena of conflict in Central Europe. Numerous respondents in fact stress that Germans do not want to become involved in American activities in other areas of the world, above all not militarily. Extra-European interests of the United States in Vietnam, Korea and other areas of tension seem to be at best of marginal interest to most.

At the same time, quite a number of the leaders we interviewed seems to fear that the United States might fail to take sufficient account of German interests and simply take German allegiance for granted. Pressed to identify potential sources of friction between the two countries, over a third of our respondents refer to possible disputes which might arise over American neglect of German interests in relations with the Soviet Union. They appear to be haunted by a fear that the United States might slight German interests in efforts to achieve a *détente* with the U.S.S.R. or at least fail to support to the utmost German foreign policy goals relating to the preservation of the freedom of West Berlin, to claims for the recovery of the Oder-Neisse territory and, above all, to reunification.[10] One mass media leader went so far as to suggest that, if the United States seeks to prevent his countrymen from aiding an uprising in the D.D.R., relations might reach a breaking point.

But this is distinctly a minority point of view. Most of our respondents express confidence that the United States will support German foreign policy interests in the future. They seem to be reconciled, if not eager, to see their country remain a ward of the United States in return for continued American protection against the threat of Soviet military or political actions. Few indeed are those who express open resentment about their country's alleged status as an American "satellite" and its military dependence on the United States.

On the whole, German elites appear to be remarkably united in their views about German-American relations. Significant deviations appear neither among the occupational elites nor among the age cohorts. Some of the answers may be slanted a bit because the questions were put by American interviewers, but similar responses in surveys conducted by German interviewers appear in general to confirm our findings. For the purpose of conjectural analysis about the future course of

---

[10] That such fears were not confined to our respondents was evident in various opinion surveys between 1959 and 1962 which indicated that about one-quarter of West German adults believed that the United States might some day accept the permanent division of Germany in order to achieve a *détente* with the Soviet Union. (Noelle and Neumann, *Jahrbuch 1958-1964*, p. 558).

German-American relations, it seems fair to assume that what we were told reflects more or less accurately the opinions of German leaders.

THE FUTURE OF GERMAN-AMERICAN RELATIONS

The pattern of responses seems to us to indicate that under present conditions of high threat perception and high confidence in the ability and willingness of the United States to protect the Federal Republic and West Berlin against Soviet threats, most German leaders will be extremely eager to maintain a relationship based on an accepted senior-junior partnership association. Should the Soviet threat appear to become more acute, even more intimate ties with the United States might become an urgent matter for German leaders, overriding all other present associations with third parties. If a new crisis over West Berlin should develop or tensions in Central Europe increase for other reasons, they might seek a more explicit bilateral security arrangement with the United States. It seems more likely, however, given their perception of NATO as basically an American venture, that German leaders would in such a situation attempt to revive NATO as an effective multilateral defensive alliance and to strengthen their own country's position within this alliance.

Some German leaders would apparently like even now to forge closer political ties to the United States within the framework of an Atlantic community. If European political integration succeeds, such sentiments might wane. But if integration proceeds no further than a Gaullist "Europe of Fatherlands," while threat perception remains unchanged or even increases, such sentiments might become more numerous and intensive among German elites.

International political developments, however, such as a far-reaching American-Soviet *détente* or a major long-range shift of United States interests to other areas of the world, might reduce West Germany's value as an ally for the United States. So, too, might developments in military technology. Should this happen, German policy-makers would be confronted by a situation which most of them presently appear loath to contemplate. As some of our respondents state explicitly and others implicitly, the Federal Republic can ill afford an American withdrawal as long as it remains threatened by the Soviet Union. German policy-makers will probably make extreme efforts to avert such a development, but if they fail they will have to attempt to adjust to the situation.

One form of adjustment might be an effort to achieve an understanding of their own with the Soviet Union, but the price might be higher than present German leaders appear willing to pay. Another choice might be to accept French leadership of a European bloc of nations, perhaps in the hope that eventually Germany might become France's equal, if not superior, in such an arrangement. A third alternative might be an effort to achieve a European political union. Success would depend on the willingness of potential partners to enter into such an arrangement. German leaders might attempt to transform the Federal Republic into a powerful neutral power, balancing East against West, but this seems highly unlikely. Some seem to dream of a return to the days of Bismarck, but it is questionable whether this would be a realizable goal in the days of nuclear weapons and superpowers. Other forms of adjustment to a loosening of the German-American bonds may exist, but none that come to mind appears to be a desirable substitute for the present arrangement in the eyes of German leaders.

Even Germans who demand greater freedom of action for their country seem to feel basically that real independence from the United States is at least under present circumstances impossible. The paradox of the present situation is that the very intimacy of Germany's ties with the United States permits its leaders greater freedom of action than they would be likely to enjoy if these bonds were to be reduced or even severed.

The possibility that the Federal Republic might itself loosen the ties between the two countries seems unlikely in the light of present leadership opinion. At the moment, no alternative seems attractive enough to tempt German leaders to trade American support for some other arrangement. Even if the Federal Republic should forge more intimate ties with other countries, particularly in Europe, it seems likely that at least for the next decade intimate relations with the United States will remain a primary objective of German foreign policy-makers.

PRESENT GERMAN-FRENCH RELATIONS

In contrast to the number of our respondents (72%) who identified the United States as the country with which the Federal Republic shares long-term common interests, only 28 per cent named France explicitly. De Gaulle's press conference of July 1964, which preceded most of our interviews, may have contributed to this feeling: The General dramatically emphasized outstanding differences between the two countries, especially on relations with the United States and European integration. Our respondents incline to agree with his perceptions, though not with his evaluations. Again and again he is singled out as the chief obstacle to greater Western and European cooperation. Such appraisals of the French leader seem to have prevailed for some time among German elites, however, for even in a 1961 survey his policies were identified by 7 out of 10 German leaders as the greatest obstruction to "the fullest development of a sound Western policy in world affairs." [11]

Four out of ten respondents declare that the Federal Republic cannot rely on France as an ally, a point of view particularly prevalent among our intellectuals, and three out of ten consider France reliable only to a limited extent. The French, according to a business leader, perceive the Federal Republic as no more than a forward position for their own defense, not as an ally whose territory should be defended as if it were their own. The *force de frappe* is generally dismissed as of no military value, and three-fourths of our respondents do not consider it a useful political instrument for the pursuit of an independent French foreign policy. Not only is the French atomic force believed to lack credibility as a deterrent—on this point the military leaders are particularly emphatic—but some respondents even claim that it actually constitutes a danger for Germany. It might invite Soviet retaliation and, therefore, the sooner it disappears, the better. "We shall all sleep better," as a CDU leader put it.[12]

That this distrust and disparagement of the French ally in NATO and partner in the European Economic Community goes beyond the policies of the present government and the personality of its leader is suggested by the fact that a majority of our respondents does not think

[11] Data from Lerner and Gorden, "Strategic Thinking of the European Elites." In contrast 11 per cent singled out British policies and only 1 per cent, American policies. In Britain 58 per cent of the elites identified French policies as the principal obstacle and in France, only 18 per cent.

Mass opinion surveys in April and August 1964 indicated that a majority of those expressing an opinion believed that de Gaulle's policies would have unfavorable rather than favorable consequences for West Germans. See EMNID, *Informationen*, No. 40 (1964). In June 1964 only 4 per cent named de Gaulle as the foreign political leader in whom Germans had greatest confidence, while 42 per cent named President Johnson. See EMNID, *Informationen*, No. 31 (1964).

[12] The study of Bundestag deputies cited previously yielded identical results. Seven out of ten deputies considered the *force de frappe* antiquated, 6 out of 10 too expensive and only 15 per cent considered it justifiable on political and/or military grounds. Five out of ten did not believe the French atomic force would be employed to defend the Federal Republic.

that the demise of de Gaulle will affect German confidence (or the lack of it) in France.

Still, three out of ten respondents believe that the Federal Republic can definitely rely on France, and about two in ten believe that the *force de frappe* is necessary to protect French independence. As we noted earlier, 31 per cent of our leaders pointed to differences over the nature of their country's relationship with its allies in NATO as the principal conflict in contemporary domestic German politics. Widely publicized in the current press, this is the controversy between the so-called Atlanticists and Gaullists. Our respondents identify the Atlanticists with the Erhard government's policy of cooperation with all NATO partners, but particularly with the United States; this group is said to include most West German leaders that matter. The other group which, according to a Social Democratic leader, should really be called "secondary Gaullists," is said to favor far more intimate relations with France and Gaullist leadership of a "Europe of Fatherlands."

Identified particularly with former Defense Minister Franz Josef Strauss and his Bavarian CSU, but also with various nationalist and conservative groups, the German Gaullists seem to a fifth of our respondents likely to modify German foreign policy considerably should they come to power. Most of our respondents, however, do not expect that German foreign policy can be radically altered by any new policy-makers, be they Gaullists or Social Democrats. Accordingly, many respondents assert that the whole controversy is not to be taken too seriously. The German Gaullists are said to be far less firmly committed to the present French position than many of them claim. Most of their principal spokesmen are said to have chosen to oppose Erhard and Foreign Minister Schroeder for reasons of political expediency. To more than one respondent the controversy reduces itself to a power struggle in the CDU/CSU between a Roman Catholic and largely South German faction, identified with Strauss, and a North German Protestant faction, identified with Schroeder. One respondent went so far as to assert that if Schroeder should become a Gaullist, Strauss would at once become an Atlanticist.

The vast majority of our respondents gives answers which class them as Atlanticists who want friendship with France, but not at the expense of close relations with other European powers and with the United States. At most 15 per cent seem to be German secondary Gaullists. Among the most outspoken of the latter is a group of business leaders who see the French President as the principal proponent of a truly independent "Europe of Fatherlands." His policies are said to benefit all Europeans because he seeks to free them from "excessive" United States dominance. De Gaulle is not anti-American, we are told, nor does he wish to destroy NATO. On the contrary, his policy is intended to create a more permanent and stable alliance by providing for a greater political and military balance between the American and the European members.

In general, such responses leave the impression that the French leader offers his German admirers not so much an alternative to present security arrangements as a symbol of rebellion against American dominance over the Western Alliance. Our "Gaullists" emphatically reject what they describe as Germany's status as an American NATO satellite, and express strong sympathies for de Gaulle's efforts to free Europeans from such an extreme dependency relationship. They criticize alleged American inability to realize that the days of the "occupation mentality" are over and assert that Germans resent lectures from American leaders telling them what to do and how to behave in international affairs. American leaders are said to show a lack of finesse in their relations with the Germans and a singular inability to appreciate German sensitivities. Thus, German elite support for de Gaulle's foreign and military policy appears to be based in part on resentment and in part on evaluative political considerations relating to German domestic and foreign policies.

FUTURE RELATIONS WITH FRANCE

If the answers of our respondents indeed reflect German leadership opinion, it would seem that a bilateral Franco-German arrangement commands only slight support as an alternative to present NATO and American ties. After we had conducted our interviews, a number of prominent CDU leaders (including former Chancellor Adenauer) indicated certain sympathies for a closer relationship with France, but most observers interpreted these public utterances as new tactical moves in the power struggle between Gaullists and Atlanticists within the CDU of which we spoke earlier. More recently German Gaullism has found it increasingly difficult to endorse French policy.

What are the chances that sentiment for closer cooperation with a Gaullist France might in the future increase among West German leaders? Apart from domestic political realignments which might conceivably bring about a more pro-French course in foreign policy, the possibility of a change in leadership opinion seems to relate to three external factors.

The first of these is the future relationship between Germany and the United States. As long as German leaders fear a Soviet attack and rely on United States protection, it is unlikely that they will feel strongly drawn to a Gaullist France. If this threat perception should diminish and United States military power appear less significant, sentiments for greater cooperation with France might increase if German leaders saw in it an opportunity to gain a greater voice in international affairs. (As one respondent put it, Germany has little enough influence in the Western Alliance and would do well to pool what little it has with France rather than to try to negotiate bilaterally with the United States.) Similar consequences, as already mentioned, might be produced by a unilateral American move to loosen United States ties with Germany.

The second factor which may affect German opinion toward France is future Soviet policy. Heightened tension between Germany and the U.S.S.R., as we said, would increase the German leaders' sense of dependency on the United States and, consequently, diminish chances of cooperation with a Gaullist France. Reduced tensions, however, might increase such chances—a possibility of which Soviet leaders may not be entirely unaware and might encourage to weaken the American position. Alternatively, reduced tensions might make the United States less willing to support German revisionist demands in Central Europe and send West German leaders to Paris.

Lastly, German sentiments toward a Gaullist France will, of course, be strongly influenced by French policies toward Germany, the United States and the Communist countries. As many of our respondents indicate, German leaders feel uncertain about future political developments in France. Continued Gaullism, with or without the General, seems to some respondents likely to promote nationalist elements in France that basically oppose a close partnership with the Federal Republic and the German foreign policy goals in Eastern Europe discussed on page 169.

In short, present patterns of opinion among German leaders do not appear to favor a more intimate relationship with France at the expense of other international relationships, particularly the ties to the United States. Practically everybody expresses diffuse sympathies for France, but few appear willing to accept de Gaulle's interpretation of Franco-German friendship. Even most of the so-called German Gaullists appear to have reservations on that score, though they are glossed over in the domestic dispute with the Atlanticists. German Gaullism may in part be a projection of German wishes for greater independence in international politics, concealed behind a façade of Gaullist Europeanism. It may also represent an effort to introduce an element of controversy into domestic politics characterized by a lack of real differences. Some of the Gaullists as well as Atlanticists among our respondents seem to try to make a major issue out of the controversy, but other comments suggest that for the present at least these cleavages are not very fundamental.

We have mentioned international developments which might influence leadership opinion toward Gaullist France. Under present conditions, on the one hand, pro-Gaullist sentiments seem unlikely to increase and may even diminish if French and Russian actions should ally German leaders even more closely with the United States. On the other hand, a Russian-American *détente* interpreted as contrary to German interests, further disintegration of NATO and a more inviting French attitude might conceivably bring about an increase in pro-Gaullist sentiments or even transform "crypto-Gaullists" into genuine German Gaullists, that is, German nationalists.

German sentiments toward a non-Gaullist France are exceedingly difficult to predict. Many of our respondents indicate that their low estimate of French political and military power would not be affected by the disappearance of the Gaullist regime. Others say that a France under a popular front government might increase opposition to Franco-German cooperation. But by far the largest number seems to believe that the imperatives of European integration are bound to bring the two countries closer together regardless of who governs in Germany or France.

EUROPEAN INTEGRATION IN THEORY AND PRACTICE

Supranationalism as an ideal is accepted by practically all contemporary West German leaders. In 1961 a survey of European elites found that nearly every German interviewed considered the nation-state obsolete and looked forward to its final disappearance.[13] Past experiences appear to have convinced Germans that their interests can best be satisfied through organic political associations with other countries, particu-

---

[13] French and British leaders were not nearly as unanimous on these points. See Lerner and Gorden, "Strategic Thinking of the European Elites" for relevant data.

larly with the countries of the Western Alliance. In a sense, this is not particularly surprising, for Germans—unlike the French and British— have had nothing to lose and much to gain by participating whole-heartedly in the efforts of the last two decades to promote European integration. The policy of the Adenauer government yielded political and economic dividends in this respect; and European integration as a general goal of German foreign policy has ceased to be a matter of intense controversy, as it was in the early years of the Federal Republic.

The leaders we interviewed all agree that German foreign policy, generally speaking, seeks further limitations on national sovereignty and the overwhelming majority endorses this objective. The extent of their enthusiasm on this score corresponds to that of mass opinion (Table 10.3). European integration is also singled out as one of the primary objectives of the Erhard government's foreign policy; and while a comparatively small number (14%) consider it a major source of contemporary domestic controversy, they describe such differences as relating to the nature and form of integration, rather than fundamental cleavages over the principle as such. In short, both German elites and mass opinion endorse the general principle of a supranational political union.

Ideally, many German leaders would apparently like NATO to become the framework for a North Atlantic supranational political association. In 1961 six out of ten German leaders interviewed believed that an Atlantic community that would include North America would be the most effective form of association. Many of our own respondents indicate that this appears to them to be the ideal way to overcome strains in the alliance, assure Germany of indefinite American protection and expand the Europe of the Six into an acceptable political association.

This, however, is clearly a remote ideal. In discussing the possibilities of a supranational political association, our respondents consider only its possibilities in Europe, excluding an Atlantic association from consideration. Their observations on the nature and composition of a strictly European association reflect a considerable gap between the general consensus on its desirability and perceptions of its form.

Table 10.4 indicates but fails to reflect fully the numerous combinations of states proposed for inclusion in a European political association. Occupational interests, religious ideologies and political sympathies appear to influence our respondents' thoughts more than do any concrete visions of a European community. Proponents of a union limited to the six EEC countries, and this includes some civil servants

Table 10.3

WEST GERMAN ELITE AND MASS VIEWS ABOUT INCREASED EUROPEAN INTEGRATION

QUESTION FOR ELITES (Summer 1964): *Most people agree that since World War II the general trend in Western Europe has been toward limiting national sovereignties in favor of international associations. To what extent do you consider efforts in this direction to be sensible?*

	Number	Percentage
Enthusiastically in favor	79	46%
Generally or conditionally in favor	77	45
Indifferent; undecided; not ascertained	9	5
Generally or conditionally against	8	5
Vehemently against	0	0
Total	173	101%

QUESTION FOR GENERAL PUBLIC (asked of 1,523 respondents in West Germany in March 1962): *Are you in favor of or against the idea of European unification? Strongly in favor (against) or only moderately so?**

	Percentage
Strongly in favor	50%
Moderately in favor	31
No reply	15
Moderately against	3
Strongly against	1
Total	100%

* Data from Gallup International, "Public Opinion and the European Community," *Journal of Common Market Studies*, 2 (November 1963), 102.

whose positions involve them deeply in the activities of the Common Market, fear that the inclusion of other countries might wreck the entire enterprise. Other civil servants as well as university professors, trade unionists and Protestant leaders insist that the EFTA countries have to

Table 10.4

WEST GERMAN PERCEPTIONS OF MEMBERSHIP IN A EUROPEAN POLITICAL UNION

	Number of Respondents	Percentage
European Economic Community (EEC) countries	18	10%
EEC countries and Great Britain	14	8
EEC and European Free Trade Association (EFTA) countries	38	22
Community of Europe (CE) countries	19	11
All Western European countries	12	7
All European countries with "Western" orientation	11	6
Other combinations of Western European countries	19	11
Combinations including Eastern European countries	31	18
Don't know	2	1
Not ascertained	9	5
Total	173	99%

be included to balance the Roman Catholic countries now dominant in the EEC. Those who speak of including even the Communist states—some repeat de Gaulle's reference to a Europe "from the Atlantic to the Urals"—apparently hope that it will provide the framework for the reunification of Germany.

Disregarding combinations (such as the inclusion of Eastern Europe) which even those who advance them do not seem to take very seriously we may say that most of our respondents think in terms of an association composed of the EEC and EFTA countries. When we ask what form such a political association should take, roughly half opt for a federation, while most of the others prefer at least for a start a looser form of association, either a confederation (24%) or some sort of mixed system that would leave the participating states a measure of independence (23%). The Gaullist version of a "Europe of Fatherlands" finds very few supporters, and the opposite extreme, a European unitary state, none.[14] To quite a few respondents these versions do not seem to conflict. They describe the development of a European political community as an evolutionary development from economic to political union and from confederation to federation. The example of the emergence of the German Empire of 1871 from the German Customs Union (*Zollverein*) is often cited as an example, though no one mentions that it took "blood and iron" to create the *Reich*.

When we inquire about the primary purpose of a European union, three points of view emerge which seem to reflect the professional orientation of various respondents. (1) One out of five respondents expresses what seems to be the West German businessman's reasons for desiring a united Europe, stressing above all the economic advantages. (2) A third of our leaders advances what appears to be the German politician's reasons for wanting a united Europe. Broader in focus than the businessman's perspective, this point of view stresses that jointly the participating countries would command the resources they lack individually to meet the economic, social and political problems facing them all. (3) Finally, about another third of our respondents looks beyond Europe in giving reasons for unification. To them a united Europe promises to be above all more capable of pursuing common interests in international politics. This point of view is shared by members of elites which on other issues are found in opposite camps—administrative leaders (civil servants and military men) and mass media leaders. Specific military and political arguments stressing that a united Europe would be able to deal more effectively with one or the other or both superpowers are rarely brought up. Other studies of German elites, however, suggest that such considerations also play a role in stimulating the German wish for European unity.[15]

Though their notions of the form and extent of European unity thus differ a good deal, most of our respondents seem to feel that European unification is bound to happen sooner or later. More than on any other issue we discussed with them they appear to believe that the trend of developments cannot be reversed. One-half of our leaders—particu-

[14] In a 1961 survey of elite opinion, 51 per cent of West German leaders opted for a federation and 45 per cent for a confederation, roughly corresponding to our own findings. See Lerner and Gorden, "Strategic Thinking of European Elites."

[15] In 1961, 82 per cent of German leaders interviewed saw the present European community as a counterpoise to the Soviet Union (compared with 43 per cent of British and 69 per cent of French leaders), but only 23 per cent saw it as a counterpoise to the United States (compared with 38 per cent of British and 60 per cent of French leaders). See Gorden and Lerner, "The Setting for European Arms Control," p. 430.

Table 10.5

WEST GERMAN EXPECTATIONS ABOUT THE ACHIEVEMENT OF EUROPEAN INTEGRATION

QUESTION: *Is European integration likely to be achieved within the next ten years?*

	Number of Respondents	Percentage
Definitely will be achieved	14	8%
Very good chance that it will be achieved	23	13
Moderate chance that it will be achieved	36	21
Depends	17	10
Probably will not be achieved in the next ten years	26	15
Definitely will not be achieved in the next ten years	29	17
Will never be achieved	0	0
Don't know	13	8
Not ascertained	15	9
Total	173	101%

larly military men, interestingly enough—reflect a high sense of inevitability about the process of European integration in their responses. But to many it seems that unity remains for the time being more or less an ideal rather than a concrete prospect. As indicated in Table 10.5, relatively few feel certain that it will come in the next decade and not many more think there is at least a good chance. In part these doubts and uncertainties seem to relate to the form which is conceived for such a union and the countries that are to be included.[16] The firmer the association and the larger the membership that is envisaged, it seems, the greater the pessimism about early unity. Another source for pessi-

[16] Mass opinion on the question of whether or not Western Europe would be united in the lifetime of the respondent reflects a similar uncertainty, but a much higher level of pro-European optimism. Between 1955 and 1961 opinion surveys indicated that about one-third of respondents were certain, one-third uncertain, and one-third had no such hope. See Noelle and Neumann, *Jahrbuch 1958-1964*, p. 545.

mism, however, appears to be contemporary developments within the existing community of the Common Market countries. Here the ideal seems to clash with the real.

The contemporary Common Market setting for German efforts to promote European political integration does not seem to augur well for its early realization in the view of many of our respondents. Communist strength in Italy and France gives rise to doubts not only as to whether political unity is possible, but as to whether it is even desirable under present conditions. The question of whether or not efforts to promote German reunification might not be hindered by attempts to integrate non-Communist Europe appears to be another reason for uncertainty.[17] But above all, French intransigence is cited again and again as a chief obstacle to political integration.

De Gaulle's veto of Great Britain's bid for membership in the Common Market seemed a blow to the cause of European unity. Opinion polls reflecting German reactions indicate that for most Germans who are concerned, close cooperation with France is less important than British membership in the EEC.[18] French demands for a common EEC tariff policy are said by leaders interviewed by us to be contrary to the interests of the Federal Republic since West Germany depends heavily on trade with non-EEC nations. French insistence at the time of our interviews that Germans yield on a policy of common agricultural prices for the community and de Gaulle's policies in NATO are said by numerous respondents to undermine the unity of the community. To practically all the leaders we spoke with, the Gaullist vision of a "Europe of Fatherlands" as a counterpoise to the United States does not match their

[17] Asked in 1961 whether they thought that their country's obligations in the European community would hamper reunification, 34 per cent of German leaders said yes, 66 per cent no. Asked whether the Federal Republic should postpone its aim to reunify Germany in order to strengthen and consolidate the EEC, 53 per cent said no and only 37 per cent yes. (Data from Lerner and Gorden, "Strategic Thinking of European Elites.") In a 1963 survey of mass opinion 65 per cent of the respondents listed German reunification as their wish for the future, only 28 per cent European unification. A 1964 poll showed that 41 per cent believed reunification to be the most important issue facing Western Germany and only 3 per cent European unity and expansion of the Common Market. (Noelle and Neumann, *Jahrbuch 1958-1964,* pp. 242, 251.)

[18] An opinion poll at the time (February 1963) indicated that only 10 per cent of respondents endorsed de Gaulle's veto, while 55 per cent disapproved. Thirty-six per cent were ready to loosen ties to France in order to gain the inclusion of Britain in the EEC, and only 24 per cent considered close cooperation with France more important than British membership in the EEC. (Noelle and Neumann, *Jahrbuch 1958-1964,* pp. 544-45.)

image of the purpose and value of the community. Above all, it is clear, they are not prepared to sacrifice American protection against a Soviet attack at the altar of Franco-German friendship.[19] French proposals for closer collaboration seem to imply weakening both the ties to the United States and ties to other present and potential members of the European community. Very few of our German leaders are willing to accept de Gaulle's invitation. To most the price seems too high and the potential yield not very attractive.

Their country's membership in the present European community is for most German leaders above all a political matter.[20] Thus, when our respondents single out the countries of the EEC as second only to the United States in having long-term common interests with the Federal Republic, it appears that they think more in terms of joint political than common economic interests. To judge by our interviews, Brussels (the seat of the High Authority of the EEC) has come to an increasing extent to rival Bonn as an important decision-making center in the eyes of German leaders. The impact of economic integration as well as extensive coverage of the activities of the community by the German news media have increasingly focused the German voters' attention on the EEC and its potential for the future as well as its present limitations.[21] To an ever-growing extent West German domestic as well as external politics have become enmeshed with those of its five partners. These developments, it seems, lead many of our respondents to feel that the present supranational structures are inadequate and to call attention to the provision in the Treaty of Rome which calls for the creation of a political community to which the member nations are to surrender some or all of their sovereign rights. The prospects for the activation of this provision, however, appear for the time being very scant to our respondents.

[19] Ninety-two per cent of the members of the Bundestag defense committee and other deputies questioned in the unpublished study cited earlier did not believe in 1964 that a united Europe would be strong enough to do without the protection of the United States.

[20] In 1961 almost two-thirds of German leaders interviewed believed that political interests involved in this issue were of greater significance than economic. (Data from Lerner and Gorden, "Strategic Thinking of European Elites.")

[21] While in 1957 opinion polls indicated that most West Germans had not even heard of the EEC, by 1960 two-thirds of the respondents in a survey were aware of its existence, and it seems likely that this proportion has continued to increase. (Data from Noelle and Neumann, *Jahrbuch 1958-1964*, pp. 544-45.) In another series of opinion surveys between 1962 and 1964, the great majority of West Germans questioned thought that the EEC was more advantageous than disadvantageous for them. See EMNID, *Informationen*, No. 23 (1964).

The general feeling of the German elite members interviewed by us seems to be that the process of European integration has come to a halt and that in the coming decade the rapid development of economic unity in the 1950's is not likely to be followed by similar advances in the political field. If, as one university professor put it, "Germans have lost their taste for integration," it seems that more than the natural growing pains of the economic community are responsible.[22] The ideal, as we have seen, remains, but in the view of German leaders it cannot be realized without effective political integration. Businessmen and politicians insist that the European "bureaucrats" in Brussels have to be placed under the control of an effective political authority if integration is to proceed. Interest group leaders and parliamentary deputies demand a European parliament with extensive powers over the High Authority. The German government is said to have no real plans for further integration because it has to face the fact that "under present circumstances" (meaning de Gaulle) it is impossible. The Rome Treaty was a fact which we must accept, a business leader told us, "but there is bound to be trouble."

Trouble there has been and more may develop if political integration proves impossible in the coming decade. German leaders evidently do not wish to follow de Gaulle's invitation to reverse the process and reassert the sovereign rights they are prepared to turn over to a European community. At the same time, they obviously do not wish to accept French dominance of the community or to endanger their ties with the United States. Nor are they prepared to sacrifice their demand for reunification for the sake of European political unity. The diffuse consensus supporting the ideal may be undermined, if not shattered, if these latent conflicts should be activated by French or Soviet actions.

Three developments might conceivably induce Germans to reconsider the ties which have already been forged through various European associations, particularly the Common Market. (1) A Communist government or a popular front regime in Italy and/or France would seriously bring into question the value of the community. (2) In the absence

[22] The German psychologist Walter Jaide in a recent study detected among young Germans a weariness with "the old Europe with its frozen cleavages and divisions," a weariness which contrasted sharply with the enthusiasm for European unity that prevailed in the postwar years. See Walter Jaide, *Das Verhältnis der Jugend zur Politik: Empirische Untersuchungen zur politischen Anteilnahme und Meinungsbildung junger Menschen der Geburtsjahrgänge* 1940-1946, 2nd ed. (Neuwied and Berlin: Luchterhand, 1964), p. 127.

of a supreme European political authority, an economic crisis in the EEC countries, such as an inflation in Italy, might induce the German government to resort to measures that would protect the German economy and political system but which would conflict with its commitments to the EEC. (3) Finally, developments in Eastern Europe which suggest to the Germans that reunification might be possible at the cost of European ties might seriously strain their allegiances to European unity.

The diffuseness of the general consensus supporting a policy striving for European unity is underscored by the fact that the pattern of responses indicates no sharp cleavages between either age cohorts or occupational elites. We have called attention to certain differences between majorities among the elites on specific responses, but it is not possible to associate a distinct point of view toward European unification to any group. Nor do biographical characteristics, such as religion or age, appear to correlate with a particular pattern of responses.

LOOKING EASTWARD

Earlier we noted that policy toward the East seems to our respondents to be one of the most important sources of domestic controversy and potential friction with the United States. From the point of view of German leaders the whole complex of relations with the Communist states transcends the realm of foreign relations since it also involves problems which are seen as domestic issues—the freedom of West Berlin and the reunification of Germany. Here anxieties about the stability of the domestic political system become involved with anxieties about external threats, and the feeling of dependence on the United States with fears of a Soviet-American *détente*. On no other issue we discussed with our German leaders does the broad elite consensus of which we have spoken seem as shallow as on this one. Yet, even here, disagreements do not appear profound enough to threaten this consensus seriously, at least in present circumstances.

The emotions which we aroused by questions about German reunification, the D.D.R. and the Oder-Neisse Line seem to be the principal explanation for the greater sense of elite involvement with foreign policy issues than with domestic issues. Many of the German leaders interviewed display a considerably greater degree of toughmindedness and rigidity of opinion on matters relating to relations with the Communist states of Eastern Europe than on others. On the basis of the nature and quality of their responses and comments in this area we can say that about two out of five respondents feel particularly highly involved. It is in the East that our respondents seem to see the source of the greatest problems and uncertainties facing the Federal Republic and of latently explosive issues that might give rise to grave domestic and foreign policy problems for the Federal Republic. Some seem to feel that German leaders are more or less helpless about the situation which confronts them here and that their country is but the object of international developments. Others, however, appear to see just here opportunities for Germans to take greater initiative in influencing the trend of international politics and to alter the environment for German foreign policy.

In general, two points of view appear to prevail: First, there are the tough anti-Communists, particularly military men, civil servants and politicians—the core of what we have previously referred to as the Bonn Establishment. Their greatest concern appears to be the possibility of an American-Soviet *détente* which they describe as a threat to the security of the Federal Republic and to its foreign policy objectives in Eastern Europe. Professing not to trust any Communist—German or foreign— they insist that the only way to deal with questions affecting German reunification, the Oder-Neisse Line and relations with the Communist countries of Eastern Europe is from positions of military and political strength. (*"Hart auf hart,"* as one respondent put it.) They see little profit and considerable danger in closer relations with the D.D.R. and the smaller Communist countries, and they firmly embrace the so-called Hallstein Doctrine which calls for severance of diplomatic relations with any country that recognizes the D.D.R. On the whole pessimistic about early reunification, their principal hope in this respect appears to be that the Soviet bloc will eventually disintegrate or, at least, weaken to a point where a strong and united West can dictate terms to the Soviet Union. Some express the hope that the Sino-Soviet conflict may accelerate this development if it compels the Russian leaders to yield in Europe in order to gain strength in Asia.

The Sino-Soviet conflict plays a part in the thinking of the second group as well, though here opportunities it may present are interpreted differently. More amorphous than the first, this group includes the mass media leaders and university professors—in short, members of elites which we already earlier identified as peripheral in orientation to the views of the Bonn Establishment. They denounce the Hallstein Doctrine as an anachronism and favor rather than fear a Soviet-American *détente,* holding that a *détente* will diminish tensions in Central Europe which they see as a threat to domestic and international stability. To them the irreconcilable position of the tough anti-Communists seems to hold grave risks in this respect, and while they appear to be by no means pro-Communist, they feel that the interests of Germany and of world peace will best be served by some sort of accommodation with the Communist countries, including the D.D.R. Some of them look to the Sino-Soviet conflict to help reduce tensions in Central Europe and, thus, in the long run, to promote reunification.[23] Others, more pessimistic on the chances of reunification, assert that German and Western interests will be best served by abandoning the official demand for "unity in peace and freedom" within the borders of 1937 as a sacred principle governing relations with the Communist countries.

In terms of domestic partisan politics, some leaders (particularly CDU supporters) assert that these differences in outlook are the principal cleavage between the major parties. Our own findings seem to indicate that such differences of opinion cross party lines. As in the case of the Atlanticist-Gaullist controversy in the CDU, supporters of the SPD are counted both among the "hards" and the "softs," the tough and the conciliatory. Nor do these differences sharply divide age or occupational groupings. Supporters of both points of view are to be found in practically all elites, although in varying proportions.

GERMAN REUNIFICATION

At the core of the controversy is the reunification issue. Every major German political leader belongs to the "Association for an Indivisible Germany" (*Kuratorium unteilbares Deutschland*) and stands pledged to his utmost for reunification. In foreign relations, friends are distinguished from foes by the degree of their professed commitment to

---

[23] Two-thirds of the Bundestag deputies surveyed in the unpublished German study cited earlier believed in 1964 that Soviet-Chinese differences were serious enough to compel the Russians to shift their activities to the East and expected that this would lead to a long-range reduction of tensions in the West.

the restoration of German unity. Allied leaders who fail to provide periodic assurances that they desire a united Germany are eyed suspiciously and foreign statesmen who visit the Federal Republic are expected to appeal for German unity before they depart. Mass opinion polls have suggested that West Germans in increasing numbers consider reunification the single most important problem demanding the attention of their government. Domestic economic questions, the preservation of peace, the furtherance of European unity and disarmament appear to be of far smaller significance to them.

But if, officially, reunification is an article of faith which every German leader thinks he must profess lest he bring upon himself the wrath of public opinion, it seems that it is a creed that, out of the public view, is held less firmly. Talking to us in the privacy of their offices and homes, 57 per cent of our respondents indeed claim to be enthusiastic supporters of reunification, but 22 per cent are far less emphatic and 21 per cent appear ambivalent about desiring reunification (favoring or opposing it conditionally). Party membership and age seem to be irrelevant in this distribution of opinions. Among occupational elites civil servants and non-business association leaders claim to be fervent supporters of reunification to a somewhat larger extent than do other groups.

The range of sentiment which we encountered varies from highly emotional tirades to expressions of grave doubts as to whether or not it is realistic and wise in present circumstances to insist on reunification. Some fervent supporters told us that this is a subject which involves the heart more than the mind and, therefore, cannot be considered dispassionately by Germans. Those on the other side of the Elbe are "our people" and the land "our land." A divided Germany, they declare, is an "unnatural" state of affairs which cannot and must not last. Americans must realize that the situation threatens domestic stability and world peace, because Germans will never accept this intolerable condition.

Quite a number of respondents are unexpectedly blunt, however, in repudiating what one politician called the nonsensical ritualistic official formula of "unity in peace and freedom." The best way to advance German interests, particularly in Eastern Europe, is to stop acting like madmen, according to a university professor. Germans cannot expect to move closer to reunification, at least as long as they couple their demand for German unity with demands for the *status quo ante bellum* in Eastern Europe. A high military leader touched upon a possible conflict between the desire for reunification and the wish for European unity when he said that the basic question is, "Who is closer to us, the Communist German in the D.D.R. or the anti-Communist Frenchman?" Another respondent fears that the present political system might not survive reunification with an area which for over thirty years has known only dictatorship and by now has been thoroughly Communized.

A rather sober realism seems to win out over emotionalism when it comes to estimating the likelihood of reunification. There, even most of those respondents who declare it their passionate wish appear to doubt whether Germany will be united in their lifetime. Only one out of ten claims to expect it within the next 25 years, while four out of ten have serious doubts, and three out of ten consider it highly unlikely or entirely out of the question.[24] The younger age groups are neither more nor less optimistic than the older. Among occupational groups only the civil servants include a disproportionately large number of individuals who claim to be certain that reunification will take place within 25 years.

As quite a number of respondents points out, much as one might desire reunification, there is no getting away from the fact that international political developments do not favor it. The Soviet Union would never agree to it, according to some of the most pessimistic respondents, except under conditions which would be equally unacceptable to the West Germans and their NATO allies. Given a choice between reunification and NATO a majority of Germans seem to prefer to forego reunification rather than give up membership in the alliance. Neutralization in exchange for reunification, the only solution which has ever been suggested by the Soviet Union, appears unacceptable to a majority among German leaders and masses alike. Besides, as one mass media leader pointed out, it seems doubtful that even the Federal Republic's Western allies—particularly France—would wish to see the balance of power in Europe drastically altered through the reemergence of a unified Germany.

[24] A corresponding, though perhaps not as pronounced, trend seems to have been developing in mass opinion in recent years. While majorities in various opinion surveys have been rejecting the suggestion that the division of Germany must be accepted as an inevitable situation, there has been a significant increase in the number of pessimists who consider reunification impossible "without war" in the foreseeable future. Constituting only 22 per cent of respondents in 1957 surveys, this group had increased to 45 per cent by 1961. Forty-six per cent still expected peaceful reunification within a few years. See Noelle and Neumann, *Jahrbuch 1958-1964,* pp. 481, 483, and 491.

RELATIONS WITH THE GERMAN DEMOCRATIC REPUBLIC

Even sharper differences of opinion emerge when we touch upon a related official taboo, recognition of the German Democratic Republic (D.D.R.). In 1964 one out of five adult West Germans was a refugee from what officially is still referred to as the Soviet Zone of Occupation, and about an equal proportion of our leaders were born in that area. One out of four West Germans had friends and relations in the D.D.R. and sent packages and letters to them.[25] At the official level, trade and other contacts have been extensive, but these contacts are carefully characterized as "intra-German" relations with the Soviet Zone, and the Federal government has gone to extreme lengths to deny even *de facto* recognition to the D.D.R. or to allow other states to do so. To recognize the D.D.R. as a sovereign state, official West German spokesmen have asserted, would be to accept the division of Germany and to recognize a regime which is illegitimate.

When we bluntly asked our respondents whether recognition might help reduce international tensions, 30 per cent answered that it would not and 24 per cent that it would be likely to increase tensions. Members of the Bonn Establishment—civil servants, military leaders and politicians—are practically unanimous in denying that international tensions might be eased. Any concession in this direction would be interpreted as a sign of weakness by the Communists, we are told. To recognize the D.D.R. would be a betrayal of the East German people and would be interpreted as such by West Germans. The repercussions might shake the world. There would be a tremendous outcry against any government that granted recognition, and it would be swept out of office by the public wrath. Not only in West Germany, but also in the East, recognition might have grave consequences, for the desperate population might rise in revolt to nullify the act. Then West Germans would not again stand idly by—as in 1953.

In view of the way we put this question about a taboo endorsed by the vast majority of the West German masses,[26] these replies do not

[25] Data from Institut für Demoskopie, *Die Neubürger* (Allensbach and Bonn: Verlag für Demoskopie, 1964), and EMNID, *Informationen*, No. 24 (1964). For earlier data, see Karl W. Deutsch and Lewis J. Edinger, *Germany Rejoins the Powers* (Stanford, Calif.: Stanford University Press, 1959), p. 178.

[26] An opinion survey in January 1964 had shown West Germans to oppose recognition by a majority of seven to one. Data from Institut für Demoskopie, *Die Neubürger*, Table 62. I am indebted to Frau Prof. Dr. Elisabeth Noelle Neumann for providing me with a copy of this study in draft form.

come as a particular surprise. More startling is the fact that 22 per cent of our respondents think that recognition might ease tensions and 13 per cent are evasive. Mass media leaders and university professors—our intellectuals—once again stand out among those who voice an anti-Establishment position, but a number of Protestant religious leaders and businessmen join them on this issue. Some argue that recognition might actually help to reunify the country by demonstrating the willingness of the West German government to come to terms with the D.D.R. leaders. More take the position that, since reunification is impossible in any case given present circumstances, a truly patriotic German policy should aim at helping the population of the D.D.R. through official contacts with their government.

The latter thesis has become a matter of public debate among German leaders since we conducted our interviews and may become increasingly important in the future. It might therefore be of interest to examine it in somewhat more detail. Adopting in particular ideas advanced by the philosopher Karl Jaspers, the proponents of at least *de facto* recognition hold that efforts to liberalize the D.D.R. regime must take precedence over questionable and possibly dangerous attempts to force the Communist countries to agree to German reunification. The official policy of bitter antagonism toward the D.D.R. and the refusal of the government to allow any but minimal contacts between the two parts of Germany is said to aggravate the isolation of the East German population and to strengthen the position of the Ulbricht regime. The mass media leaders and university professors who defend this thesis emphatically claim that the present policy aids Ulbricht in maintaining a dictatorship which is the most oppressive in all of Eastern Europe and prevents elements in the D.D.R. which might liberalize the regime from gaining influence. To insist on the unconditional surrender of the D.D.R. government in the name of "unity in freedom" is said to enable its leaders to obtain Soviet support for the preservation of their iron rule. They can exploit the tensions in Central Europe which the official position of the Federal government is helping to maintain. A less rigid policy of non-recognition or even *de facto* recognition of the D.D.R., in this view, might reduce these tensions, loosen the grip of the Communist dictatorship and smooth the way for its liberalization through increased contacts between the two parts of Germany. Not only would this serve to ease the condition of the population of the D.D.R., but it would provide opportunities to encourage popular pressure on the regime to become more liberal, as well as to reassure the Soviet Union and other Communist states who presently support Ulbricht unconditionally.

Proponents and opponents of recognition are found in about equal proportions among all groups, and Gaullists and Atlanticists are found on both sides of the argument. The only relatively clear division on this issue, as on reunification, is the cleavage between the members of the Bonn Establishment and the intellectuals.

RELATIONS WITH EASTERN EUROPE

As the reunification issue is intimately related with recognition of the D.D.R., so the problem of the Federal Republic's future relations with the Soviet Union and the smaller European Communist nations— particularly Poland—is associated by our respondents with both other issues. For example, the tough anti-Communists argue that recognition of the D.D.R. would crush the alleged hopes for liberation on the part of other European people living under Communist rule. Proponents of a *détente*, however, hold that closer relations with all Communist governments might also improve the conditions of Germans in the D.D.R. and its leaders' efforts to maintain an iron dictatorship on the strength of high tensions in Central Europe.[27]

Eight out of ten of our respondents expect relations between the Federal Republic and the countries of Communist Eastern Europe to improve appreciably during the next years. (None expects them to get worse.) About half of these anticipate primarily closer economic ties; the others believe that political and cultural relations will grow more intimate. But another official taboo stands in the way of improved relations, as our respondents acknowledge: acceptance of the Oder-Neisse Line as the border between divided Germany and Poland. Supported by mass opinion, the Federal government has adamantly insisted that the borders of 1937 are sacrosanct.[28]

Four out of ten of our respondents, above all university professors,

---

[27] Many respondents attach especially great importance to the role of the D.D.R. chief Walter Ulbricht as an obstacle to better relations with the Communist nations. His departure may be interpreted by some German leaders as a signal for a new policy toward the D.D.R. and Eastern Europe.

[28] A study in Hamburg in 1961 found that over half of a cross section of adult citizens would not be willing to allow an open advocate of recognition of the Oder-Neisse Line to be heard in public. Wolfgang Hartenstein and Günter Schubert, *Mitlaufen oder Mitbestimmen: Untersuchung zum demokratischen Bewußtsein und zur politischen Tradition* (Frankfurt/Main: Europäische Verlagsanstalt, 1961), pp. 61-64.

come out in opposition to the official position, holding that acceptance of the Oder-Neisse Line would help to ease tensions in Central Europe and further the cause of German reunification. On the other side, a minority of three out of ten claims it would make no difference but only one out of ten, particularly civil servants, says that it might make matters worse. This shift in the distribution of opinion, in comparison with the reunification issue and recognition of the D.D.R., in favor of a more conciliatory attitude may be indicative of a general trend also reflected in mass opinion surveys.[29]

The ten per cent who form the hard core of toughminded anti-Communists can see nothing gained and conceivably an important ace in hand lost if the Federal Republic should accept the Oder-Neisse Line. Some, perhaps projecting, assert that the Poles would not believe the sincerity of such a concession. Some argue that this would only be taken as a sign of weakness by Communist states who respect only power. One cannot appease Communists, and demands for more concessions are bound to follow—to the detriment of the Germans and the West. Here, even those who expect more intimate relations with the East Europeans seem to have a closed mind, refusing to concede on emotional grounds what quite a number of them admits might be desirable for purely rational reasons. Others advance formal legal objections, arguing that the Federal Republic cannot recognize a non-existent border with Poland; the issue cannot be settled until Germany is reunified. As in the case of the question about recognition of the D.D.R., the argument that acceptance would threaten political stability in the Federal Republic is advanced particularly by those who argue that tensions in Central Europe would increase. Rightwing nationalists would exploit mass dissatisfaction to denounce as traitors the democratic leaders who accepted the Oder-Neisse Line, it is claimed, just as the Weimar leaders who signed the Treaty of Versailles had been attacked.

The proponents of a *détente*, increased in numbers on this issue, hold that acceptance would ease tensions by improving the image of the Federal Republic in Eastern Europe and, perhaps, draw Poland closer to the West. Some agree with the tough anti-Communists that acceptance

[29] While in 1959 over two-thirds of the respondents in an opinion survey refused to accept the Oder-Neisse border and only 12 per cent were willing to accept it; by 1962 opposition had dropped to 50 per cent, while 26 per cent were willing to accept the border. (Noelle and Neumann, *Jahrbuch 1958-1964*, p. 505.) Among the former residents of these regions, only a quarter were certain in 1964 that they would go back if the areas were to be returned to Germany; the rest were uncertain whether they would return (33%) or certain they would not (36%). Data from Institut für Demoskopie, *Die Neubürger*, Table 54.

is indeed a valuable ace in hand, but hold that it will quickly lose its value if it is not used soon. Others, de Gaulle for example, may steal the ace before it can be played. A very prevalent argument, on which business leaders and Protestant clergymen join the intellectuals eager for improved relations, is that the Oder-Neisse territories are in fact already Polish—abandoned by their original population—and, therefore, little or nothing can be gained by refusing to recognize the situation formally. The whole issue is absurd in view of the labor shortage in Western Germany: Few of the "expellees" would want to return and leave behind the fleshpots of the Federal Republic. Nor could the economy spare them, according to a military leader.

The pattern of opinions which we have indicated suggests that, on matters affecting relations with the Soviet Union and other Communist states of Eastern Europe, most of the leaders interviewed are wary of a *détente* between the Soviet Union and their Western allies. On the whole, they do not seem to have much faith in signs of liberalization and polycentrism in the Soviet bloc. In particular they see closer economic relations as a boost to Communist strength and profess to see no reason why the West should assist the Soviet bloc to overcome its internal difficulties. Many assert that at any moment the Communist camp may reconsolidate its forces and renew the conflict with the West with heightened vigor, a matter of particular concern to Germans. Anxiety about their external security and about Communist subversion, strong emotions about German reunification and the D.D.R. and fears that the United States may overlook German interests in striving for an easing of international tensions—all seem to lead a majority to be extremely cautious in relations with the Communist countries. "No experiments," the slogan under which Adenauer waged his political campaigns in the past, appears to be the general point of view.

A minority, however, and particularly mass media leaders and university professors, appears to feel that this is a standpat position which surrenders all initiative on matters affecting German interests to other powers. They assert that the Federal Republic must exploit liberalization and polycentrism in the Soviet bloc in order to break through the Iron Curtain along the Elbe and gain friends in Eastern Europe. Not all would agree with the mass media leader who said that "We must camp on the Russians' doorstep until they agree to reunification"—a form of "sit-in." But not solely intellectuals seem to seek a *détente* that would allow West Germans to become politically and economically more active in the Communist countries. A number of businessmen interviewed appear eager to enter new markets in Eastern Europe, though others express serious doubts that a basis for extensive trade exists or that ties with the Common Market countries would permit it. The Sino-Soviet conflict also appears to encourage hopes for a *détente* in Central Europe. In fact, more than one German leader suggests that much might be gained if the West seeks to come to an agreement with Russia against China—a settlement which might also profit the Germans.

Among the leaders we interviewed those who emphatically favor a *détente* appear to be still a minority. Quite a few others, however, seem to be ambivalent and likely to accept if not endorse an East-West *rapprochement* which does not appear to threaten German security and foreclose the possibility of eventual reunification. In May 1964, a public opinion poll conducted at our request asked a cross section of West Germans whether they thought an easing of tensions to be in their interests: 74 per cent believe it is, while only 7 per cent think it is not. Put in these general terms, a similar question might well yield an equally large endorsement of a *détente* among German elites.

As we move from the general to particulars, however, elite support for tension-reducing measures is likely to diminish. Improved economic and cultural relations with the Communist countries of Eastern Europe may well be supported by a majority of German leaders under present conditions and barring unforeseen incidents. Improved political relations is another matter, for here such problems as recognition of the D.D.R. and the Oder-Neisse Line enter the picture. Judging from the opinions revealed in our interviews, most German leaders are as yet not prepared to renounce the Hallstein Doctrine openly, though there are some indications that they may accept its gradual erosion. Recognition of the D.D.R. by the Federal Republic or acceptance of its recognition by any West German allies seems for the time being quite unlikely. Very gradual and cautious moves in the direction of Eastern Europe seem likely, but a dramatic reorientation of present policies, as certain Western observers fear, seems out of the question.

THE IMPLICATIONS OF WEST GERMAN ELITE ATTITUDES TO FOREIGN POLICY ISSUES

We opened this chapter with the observation that while the German Federal Republic today is potentially one of the most powerful nations in the world it plays in fact the role of a second- or third-rate power in world politics. We asked whether the views of German leaders reflect a desire to change this situation and suggest that in the future German leaders will try to play a more significant part in international affairs. Judging by the pattern of responses to our questions bearing on this issue, the answer seems to be "no." Apparently to an even greater extent than the average West German, the leaders we interviewed seem to feel that their country will never again be able to play the part of a major world power. However, they appear to feel that this does not mean that Germans should, therefore, try as much as possible to keep out of international politics and simply concentrate their energies on maintaining and expanding their standard of living.[30] This seems neither possible nor desirable to the elite members we spoke to, above all because the geopolitical position of their country, its inescapable involvement in international politics, the division of the former Reich and the precarious position of its former capital city will not allow it.

Our survey of German elite opinion indicates a broad consensus supporting a foreign policy of close political and military cooperation with other Western nations, above all with the United States, and a widespread suspicion of the Communist countries. Most are concerned about at least a latent danger of Soviet aggression and look to NATO and, particularly, to American military power to safeguard their security through deterrence powerful enough to prevent such aggression. The perceived need to be assured of such deterrent power and the convictions that neither national nor European military capacities will ever be adequate enough to dispense with American protection appear to convince the vast majority of our German leaders that the Federal Republic has little choice but to accept American dominance of the Western Alliance and to adjust German foreign policy objectives to those of the United States.

This primary commitment, however, denies to German foreign policy the flexibility and independence of action which many of our leaders seem to desire to a greater extent than at present. It also gives rise to a certain ambivalence in perceived German foreign policy objectives. On the one hand the overwhelming majority of German leaders wants to maintain intimate ties with the United States; on the other these leaders fear that American foreign policy may seek a *détente* with

---

[30] In a 1964 opinion poll 33 per cent of West Germans opted for staying out of big power politics and concentrating on domestic welfare; 43 per cent rejected this suggestion, and 24 per cent were uncertain. (Institut für Demoskopie, *Pressedienst*, October 1964).

the Soviet Union at the expense of "German interests." On the one hand they want a close association with France; on the other they reject de Gaulle's policies, and they lack confidence in France as an ally. And on the one hand they insist that the peaceful reunification of Germany must be a guiding principle of the Republic's foreign policy and reject recognition of the D.D.R.; on the other they are not prepared to consider a settlement with the Communist states that might further the cause of reunification.

Not only a sense of dependence on the United States but the lack of any negotiable objects for political bargains appear to German leaders to tie the hands of their foreign policy-makers. Present German leaders, at least, seem not prepared to trade membership in NATO for reunification or to renounce participation in a multilateral nuclear force desired by the United States to achieve better relations with the Communist countries.[31] Perceiving their country more as an object than a subject in international politics and its foreign policy-makers more as passive than active participants, most of our leaders seem to believe that at best events largely beyond their control might produce conditions which would allow Germans greater initiative. Intensification of the Sino-Soviet conflict or of Franco-American differences seems to some to promise such possibilities, while others appear to hope that the emergence of more liberal leaders in the Soviet bloc might create new opportunities for German foreign policy in Eastern Europe.

In discussing foreign policy issues, as on domestic matters, elite opinion appears to be united by a broad consensus which limits what German policy-makers can and cannot do at the present time. On policy particulars here, too, differences emerge which can be associated with occupational elites rather than with age cohorts. As in domestic affairs, these cleavages of opinion roughly divide members of what we have identified as the Bonn Establishment from intellectuals associated with the mass media and the universities. Other elite members, such as businessmen and leaders of non-business interest associations (particularly trade unionists and Protestant ministers), again oscillate in their views

---

[31] The average German seems more willing to consider such bargains. In an April 1962 poll 42 per cent were ready to forego nuclear weapons for the German armed forces if it would help to make the Russians more agreeable to reunification and only 27 per cent were not. (Noelle and Neumann, *Jahrbuch 1958-1964*, p. 486.) In February 1964, 42 per cent thought neutrality between East and West was to be preferred to friendship with the United States, 49 per cent believed the latter was the more desirable course. See EMNID, *Informationen*, No. 13 (1964).

between these two principal camps. Both the proponents and opponents of the Establishment's foreign policies seem at times highly inconsistent in their arguments and guided more by emotional than rational considerations. Domestic differences and considerations, moreover, seem to influence more or less strongly views about foreign policy issues—particularly those relating to reunification.

Generally, we might delineate the patterns of opinion which emerged on foreign policy issues as shown in Table 10.6.

In the eyes of its critics the Bonn Establishment's foreign policy lacks clear and consistent goals when it comes to translating diffuse objectives into specific policies in its relations with the United States, France, and Eastern Europe. At the same time it is charged that many of the objectives of contemporary German foreign policy are too rigid and outdated. This is particularly the complaint of those respondents who advocate a more flexible course on matters relating to the D.D.R. and relations with the countries of Eastern Europe, as well as those who have been identified as German Gaullists. They want greater flexibility and more initiative in German foreign policy.

A number of business and political leaders claims that the government is prone to yield too readily to unstable elements, such as refugee and mass media leaders, whose "erratic" objectives are said to be dangerously "irrational" and "emotional." In their opinion it would be best

Table 10.6

PATTERNS OF WEST GERMAN ELITE OPINION ON FOREIGN POLICY ISSUES

| | | Attitudes Relating to the Western Alliance | |
		Atlanticists	Gaullists
Attitudes Relating to Relations with Eastern Europe	Anti-détente	Majority of Political and Administrative Elites	Minority of Mass Media and Business Elites
	Pro-détente	Majority of Mass Media and University Professors; Minority of Business, Non-Business and Political Elites	Small Minority of Business and Mass Media Elites

to follow a highly consistent approach that will reassure the country's allies as well as safeguard domestic stability.

A few of the critics of Germany's contemporary foreign policy predict that within a decade a more dynamic leadership is bound to replace the Establishment. Younger men, now in their twenties and thirties and not yet members of the dominant elites, will be willing to take greater risks and attempt drastic changes in foreign policy. Here the wish may be father to the thought. Our study at least could detect no trends indicating such major changes. In the view of most of our respondents, regardless of age, major policy changes are not to be expected because the external setting and elite consensus severely limit German leaders' freedom of action—now and in the foreseeable future. The feeling that matters will inevitably take their course and that Germans can do little or nothing to influence them appears to dominate their outlook.

CHAPTER 11

Arms Control, Disarmament and the "German Problem"

For close to half a century the "German Problem" has been intimately associated with arms control and disarmament efforts in international politics. The Treaty of Versailles and various other international agreements in the interbellum period sought and failed to eliminate Germany's military potential as a source of international conflict. The agreements of the victorious allies to keep Germany indefinitely disarmed after World War II also broke down within a few years. Once more, Central Europe became a principal focus of international tensions and once again efforts were made to keep a rearmed Germany under control.

A rearmed East Germany was kept under close Soviet control through the presence of large contingents of Soviet troops and its inclusion in the Warsaw Treaty Organization. For their part the Western powers sought through extensive and complicated treaty arrangements to keep expanding West German military power under control. The entire military establishment was incorporated into NATO and, under the Western European Union (WEU) Treaty, the Federal Republic was forbidden to *produce* nuclear, bacteriological or chemical weapons, as well as guided missiles, submarines and larger warships, except with the approval of two-thirds of the WEU members. Since 1955, when these arrangements were made, however, a number of restrictions have been modified. Moreover, the Federal Republic by 1964 possessed not only the second largest military establishment in NATO but the potential capacity to produce missiles and nuclear weapons. Its forces were already equipped with the means to deliver nuclear weapons and there was talk of a further expansion of a capacity to strike directly at the Soviet Union in case of attack.

Proposals to reduce tensions in Central Europe and to curb expanding German military power had been made by Communist as well as Western leaders for years, but none of these had proved even remotely acceptable to both camps. The Western powers, including the Federal Republic, categorically rejected proposals for the withdrawal of foreign troops, a nuclear free zone or the neutralization of Germany, ideas advanced particularly by Polish leaders. The Communist countries, for their part, vehemently objected to Western proposals that included provisions allowing Western or even all of a reunited Germany to belong to NATO. Above all, they opposed any move to give West Germans access to nuclear weapons.

This possibility, however, seemed not entirely out of the question when we conducted our interviews in 1964. The French government dropped hints that it might not be averse to the creation of a European nuclear force more or less autonomous of NATO, while the MLF plan of the United States proposed to give West Germans access to nuclear weapons in a rather different form. Both proposals were advertised by their sponsors as means to control expanding German military power and, particularly, to prevent the direct acquisition of nuclear weapons by the Federal Republic.

The German Problem had also been linked to efforts to promote worldwide disarmament, especially by the government of the Federal Republic. Supported by its Western allies, it had insisted that disarmament and German security and reunification could not be considered separately. This had been stressed just before we conducted our interviews when the Bundestag debated ratification of the Soviet-American

Test-Ban Treaty. The chief objection voiced against the treaty, subsequently ratified, was that it downgraded German reunification because the German Democratic Republic was permitted to adhere to it.

Armament rather than disarmament had been the major preoccupation of the German Federal government and effective deterrence of Soviet aggression, rather than arms control, the principal argument of its spokesmen regarding international stability and world peace. The Federal Republic had not directly participated in any of the postwar disarmament conferences nor had it apparently sought to play an active role in this area. Extreme caution and a pronounced suspicion toward arms control and disarmament appeared to underlie rather vague endorsements of both.

THE MEANING AND SIGNIFICANCE OF ARMS CONTROL AND DISARMAMENT FOR GERMAN LEADERS

Our discussion of arms control and disarmament indicates that the former means very little to German leaders, and the latter stimulates little interest. We devoted a considerable part of our discussion of "common problems" of the Western Alliance to questions designed to reveal how German leaders evaluate the risks and opportunities of international arms control and disarmament. Persistent questioning drew forth replies, but the quality of these answers seems on the whole to bear out the position of a leading member of the Federal government, who said that "we do not follow such matters very closely here." They are seen largely as rather abstract and technical problems, of interest only to military experts.

Though the German leaders we interviewed are reputed to be particularly knowledgeable about and interested in these problems, the interviewers' evaluations of their latent attitudes indicate that they are on the whole decidedly less well informed and feel less involved and less influential on these than on any other cluster of issues we discussed with them. In particular, our elite members reveal a considerably lower sense of efficacy and trust toward other actors than in the discussion of foreign policy, European and, especially, domestic problems (Table 11.1). On the whole, quantitative data on such implicit attitudinal shifts seem to support our general impression that many, if not most, of our respondents are particularly uncertain when it comes to discussing arms issues. Those who do seem to feel an exceptionally great amount of actual and/or potential influence over developments in other areas—

Table 11.1

WEST GERMAN RESPONDENTS RANKING HIGH ON LATENT ATTITUDES

Ratio of number of respondents ranked "Very High (+3)" or "High (+2)" to the total number of respondents ranked on a seven point scale from "Very High (+3)" to "Very Low (−3)." *

LATENT ATTITUDES	ISSUES DISCUSSED			
	Domestic Affairs	Foreign Affairs	European Integration	Arms Control
Information Dimension:				
Extent of information	.78	.81	.82	.36
Breadth of focus	.69	.75	.74	.55
Sense of competence to discuss issues	.87	.87	.87	.46
Involvement Dimension:				
Perception of significance of issues (saliency)	.69	.78	.74	.47
Emotional involvement (affect)	.49	.60	.48	.29
Firmness of views on issues (cloture)	.41	.52	.50	.35
Sensitivity to other relevant actors	.38	.38	.32	.16
Sense of efficacy and trust toward other relevant actors	.36	.26	.35	.15
Toughmindedness on issues	.27	.38	.19	.23
Influence Dimension:				
Sense of actual influence	.45	.31	.24	.09
Sense of potential influence	.51	.31	.31	.08

* See pp. 9-10 and 121-22.

particularly domestic affairs—to a very large extent appear to consider their influence over developments relating to arms issues not nearly so great. Most seem to feel that here matters are more or less out of their hands. Emotions appear to be far less highly involved; and many of the respondents who indicated high affective involvement when we discussed domestic, or European, or other foreign policy questions now seem to care far less. Almost all respondents who showed an exceptionally high trust toward other actors on other issues now seem far more anxious. Also, two-thirds of those who did not appear to be especially toughminded in the discussion of other matters become exceptionally toughminded when we turn to arms issues. The smallest shift in attitudes relates to firmness of opinion (cloture). Here, it seems, we are dealing with a hard core of opinionated individuals, numbering about a third of our respondents, who are particularly closed-minded on every issue. Even some of these leaders, however, are less opinionated on arms questions.

These patterns of orientation appear to reflect more or less faithfully the contemporary climate of opinion in West Germany on arms control and disarmament. Except for a small minority consisting largely of military leaders and intellectuals (but also some politicians and religious leaders), West Germans appear to take little interest in these matters. According to a recent study nine out of ten Bundestag deputies concerned with defense matters thought in 1964 that West Germans were all too indifferent to military and political problems relating to the external security of their country.[1] The average West German, for his part, did not see his leaders as particularly interested either. When a West German opinion survey organization questioned a representative sample of West Germans in the summer of 1964, 38 per cent said that the Russians did most of the talking about disarmament, 26 per cent the Americans, but only 4 per cent named their own government and only 6 per cent the major German parties.

It seems that the passions and controversy which rearmament and nuclear testing aroused in the 1950's have yielded to a mood of apathy, indifference and cynicism about disarmament. Nor have the government or the parties particularly encouraged public interest.[2] Discussion of arms and disarmament questions seems to be limited to a very small interested public, which writes and reads occasional articles on these matters and participates in small conferences organized by the German Foreign Policy Association, Protestant clergymen and some other attentive groups.

[1] See the survey cited in note 5 on page 146.
[2] The Federal Republic has neither an Arms Control and Disarmament Agency nor any other special office specifically concerned with these matters. Only recently was a special position in the Ministry of Foreign Affairs established (on the initiative of some Bundestag deputies), which is to be held by a comparatively minor official concerned with disarmament problems.

To judge by our interviews, only when arms issues appear to transcend the realm of technical discussions among experts and seem clearly to involve German political and security interests do they arouse greater attention among German leaders. It is for this reason that the views of German leaders about the proliferation of nuclear weapons, about a general East-West disarmament agreement and about specific arms control proposals can only be understood in terms of the opinion patterns on domestic and foreign policy issues described previously. The relevance of arms control and disarmament for German leaders appears to depend on the extent to which they perceive any relationship between internal and external German politics. Such issues become relevant when they are seen as affecting domestic political developments, as in the dispute between Gaullists and Atlanticists, and arouse interest when they appear to involve relations with the United States, NATO and the countries of Communist and/or non-Communist Europe.

In our interviews the extent to which such connections are made in the minds of respondents appears to vary with individuals as well as questions. To most respondents, questions about a German nuclear force, for example, appear to be of little interest because they relate to a matter which is evidently not taken very seriously. Questions about general disarmament proposals and techniques of enforcement also seem to elicit only perfunctory and even bored answers. Other questions appear to be associated with domestic and foreign policy problems that are of concern to respondents and provoke correspondingly greater interest and livelier comments. This appears to be particularly the case when we come to talk about arms control proposals to reduce tensions in Central Europe.

In general, however, it seems that only a small minority of our respondents perceives an intimate connection between international arms control and disarmament on the one hand, and their own and their country's interests on the other. This minority consists largely of mass media and military leaders; in noting their responses we are in a sense observing a dialogue between a few German leaders who are more deeply interested and involved than most.

Latent aspects of the arms control and disarmament problems, however, which in 1964 seemed to be of only academic interest to most of our respondents, may in the future become more manifest to German leaders. For example, nuclear dispersion within and outside NATO and the relationship between deterrence and arms control may become of considerably greater concern to more German leaders once they appear to involve German security, reunification and European unity. Most of his countrymen, according to one of the highest German military leaders, are unfortunately still unaware of these relationships; he considers it his mission to arouse interest.

GERMAN FINGERS ON NUCLEAR TRIGGERS

The suggestion that the Federal Republic might acquire nuclear weapons in any form or fashion draws forth only strongly negative reactions. Only one out of 159 respondents with opinions explicitly includes his country among those that should possess such weapons and at best only one out of ten would even entertain the idea that it might. German elite sentiment against the production of nuclear weapons by their country appears also to be overwhelming and seems to have increased in recent years.[3] Moreover, in the opinion of nine out of ten defense experts of the West German Bundestag, the Western European Union would not permit it even if the Federal government requested permission.[4] The possibility that their country might have the potential capacity to manufacture nuclear weapons in secret, however, seems to be a disturbing thought for some respondents who recall the secret rearmament of Germany in the 1920's.

Three issues that we raised were all interpreted to pose in different forms the question of whether or not Germans should obtain access to nuclear weapons. First, should Germans acquire their own national nuclear force? Second, should the non-Communist European countries join in creating a supranational nuclear force outside NATO? Third, should a multilateral nuclear force be created within NATO, and should Germans participate if it were to be established? The first two possibilities are categorically rejected by practically all of our respondents; the third, as we reported earlier, provokes rather ambivalent sentiments.

Nine out of ten respondents consider a national nuclear force neither necessary to maintain any country's independence or prestige, nor worth the expense of such a venture. As we noted earlier, almost all of our respondents consider the French *force de frappe* a militarily and

---

[3] In 1956 seven out of ten leaders opposed the manufacture of hydrogen bombs by their country; in 1961 this had increased to nine out of ten. Gorden and Lerner, "The Setting for European Arms Control," p. 428.
[4] Data from the survey of Bundestag deputies cited earlier.

politically useless and prohibitively expensive enterprise. A few allow that it might serve to boost French morale or provide France with greater influence in international affairs, but most of them maintain that these considerations do not apply to their country.

In rejecting the notion that such a national nuclear force might be necessary to assure the independence of their country, our German leaders advance three arguments. First, while a national nuclear force might conceivably allow countries such as the United States or the Soviet Union to be more independent, the Federal Republic does not seek such independence but, on the contrary, seeks the establishment of a supranational political community to which it can surrender its sovereignty. A second argument is that a country can maintain its independence just as well, or even better, without a national nuclear force. An SPD leader argued that the cost of such a force might diminish a country's independence by weakening its economy and depriving it of resources which might be used to further its interests abroad. Finally, real independence is said to be in any case impossible in the contemporary world and, therefore, the argument that a national nuclear force provides it is a myth.

In reply to our question of whether or not a national nuclear force might increase the prestige of the Federal Republic, we are told that the country does not and should not seek to gain prestige in this fashion. One out of ten even argues that, in the light of Germany's past history of militarism, a national nuclear force would in fact serve to lower its present international prestige and negate the gains of recent years. Others assert that Germany could increase its prestige more effectively by non-military, particularly economic, means.

Asked whether such a force would be credible to the country's enemies, eight out of ten leaders say "no." The Federal Republic is said to be far too vulnerable to attack to convince a potential opponent of the credibility of a national nuclear force. Most of those who think it would be credible say that that would be just the trouble. It would increase fear and distrust toward the Federal Republic—in the West as well as in the Communist countries—and, possibly, invite a preventive attack.

Finally, a national nuclear force is rejected on the grounds that it would constitute a threat to domestic peace and stability. According to a university professor it would stimulate atavistic, primitive desires which at present are only latent dangers to German democracy. A mass

media leader asserted that such a national nuclear force would constitute an enormous danger to Germany as well as to other nations.

When we suggest that European nations might join in creating a
nuclear force independent of NATO, eight out of ten respondents reject
this notion—five out of ten even vehemently. As for the rest practically
none strongly supports the suggestion; some favor it conditionally.

An independent European force is seen as inviting reduced American commitments, a possibility which few of the German leaders we
interviewed care to contemplate. Even a united Europe could not dispense with American deterrent power in the view of nine out of ten
Bundestag defense experts.[5] Most of the conditional supporters of an
independent European nuclear force hedge on this question and speak
of an autonomous rather than independent force. Citing President Kennedy and other American leaders to support their arguments, they claim
that a greater balance of European and American forces within NATO
would strengthen the alliance.[6]

But what about a NATO nuclear force in which Americans as well
as Germans participate? The United States has asserted that its proposal
for a multilateral polaris surface fleet (MLF) would give Germans and
other European NATO allies a chance to participate in a NATO deterrent force and, therefore, influence over decisions as to where and when
nuclear weapons are to be employed. Opinion surveys have indicated
that most West Germans want the European countries to obtain more of
a voice in such decisions[7] but the MLF does not strike most of the
leaders we interviewed as a very effective way to obtain it. One-third
nonetheless endorse the project, though very few with enthusiasm, while
about an equal number opposes it more or less vehemently. But as noted
earlier, a majority of our respondents is willing to go along if MLF

[5] Data from the previously cited German study of Bundestag deputies.
[6] In contemporary public discussions this argument is associated with a dumbbell or
elliptical concept of a reorganized alliance that would consist of two power centers.
Conceivably, we were told, such an arrangement might serve as an alternative or
successor to a multilateral force that includes the United States. If Europeans have
at least an option to form their own force within NATO, their waning loyalty to the
alliance will revive, according to this thesis, because they will feel less dominated
by the United States. To deny them this option will ultimately lead to the disintegration of the alliance. Some respondents, however, claim that NATO is in any case
moribund, making the establishment of a European nuclear force an absolute necessity. In general, these are the arguments of the so-called German Gaullists.
[7] In November 1963, 56 per cent of a sample of West German adults wanted the
European NATO countries to obtain influence over the use of NATO nuclear deterrent forces; 21 per cent were willing to leave such decisions to the President of the
United States. (Noelle and Neumann, *Jahrbuch 1958-1964,* p. 541.)

Table 11.2

WEST GERMAN ATTITUDES TOWARD A MULTILATERAL NUCLEAR FORCE UNDER NATO

QUESTION: *What do you think of the widely-discussed proposal of a multilateral nuclear force under NATO command? Should Germany participate in such a NATO nuclear force, if such a force were created?*

	MLF under NATO		West German Participation	
	Number of Respondents	Percentage	Number of Respondents	Percentage
Favor enthusiastically	16	9% ⎱	93	54%
Favor generally	42	24 ⎰		
Favor conditionally	22	13	20	12
Indifferent; undecided	8	5	3	2
Opposed conditionally	5	3	8	5
Opposed generally	37	21 ⎱	27	16
Opposed vehemently	21	12 ⎰		
Don't know	20	12	9	5
Not ascertained	2	1	13	8
Total	173	100%	173	102%

should become a reality largely, it seems, because the United States appears to want it (Table 11.2).[8]

Generally, the proposal appears to be poorly understood and to give rise to rather ambivalent sentiments. As a military factor it is not taken very seriously and opinion is divided over whether MLF would prevent nuclear proliferation or accelerate it. Many support it as a means to prevent the further development of national nuclear forces among the NATO nations and the creation of an independent European force, as well as a means to strengthen the NATO alliance and German ties to the United States. The project is, however, also seen as a not too subtle American attempt to block the creation of a European force and to perpetuate United States dominance over NATO. A mass media leader

[8] See pp. 147-49.

described the plan as window dressing designed to perpetuate Germany's position as a satellite of the United States and to deny it effective control over nuclear weapons. Still others are uneasy about the proposal, or reject it entirely, because in their view it will sooner or later give Germans just such control over nuclear missiles. According to a university professor, the Federal Republic is too vulnerable and contains "too many hot heads" to take that chance. A Social Democratic leader feared that MLF would lead to proliferation of nuclear weapons. A prominent business leader called the MLF proposal "complete nonsense," part of a "childish game" to satisfy the cravings of some Germans for greater international prestige. Others believe that it will increase tensions in Central Europe and prevent a *rapprochement* with the Communist countries. German participation in MLF is also perceived, however, as an opportunity to give Germans a better bargaining position vis-à-vis these countries.

On the whole, as mentioned earlier, the MLF proposal is not seen as giving Germans significantly greater access to nuclear weapons or European NATO nations greater influence over the deterrent forces of the alliance. The possibility of German participation is accepted more or less reluctantly, it seems, not only because the United States sponsors the project but also because it appears to be the least objectionable way to meet demands for greater European influence in NATO and perhaps prevent direct German access to nuclear weapons. About six out of ten of our respondents want the United States to control the polaris fleet should it actually come into being; four out of ten want the European NATO nations to share such control.

Thus it appears that the German leaders we interviewed are inclined to favor greater European participation over decisions affecting the disposition and potential employment of nuclear deterrent forces but are nonetheless unenthusiastic about the prospect that this might also place nuclear weapons in German hands. Moreover, a majority of our respondents seems to be inclined to leave well enough alone and allow the United States to continue to safeguard German security against Soviet aggression through its nuclear deterrent power. Neither a national nor a European nuclear force seems to almost all of them an acceptable alternative. However, our respondents split roughly evenly for and against another effort to establish a European NATO army composed of conventional forces dependent entirely on American nuclear power, such as proposed for the stillborn European Defense Community

(EDC) in the early 1950's. Those who oppose it tend to assert that too much water has flowed over the dam in the years since 1954 to make another try. Proponents, particularly university professors, are ready to support an EDC if it should serve to keep nuclear weapons out of German hands.[9]

There appear to be no significant divisions among age groups, occupational elites or political groupings in the overwhelming rejection of a national or independent European nuclear force. On the proposal to create a multilateral polaris fleet within NATO, the Bonn Establishment —particularly military men and politicians—stands opposed to most of the mass media leaders, as was noted earlier. Younger leaders under fifty overwhelmingly support the project, in contrast to their seniors. Such differences disappear, however, on the question of whether or not the Federal Republic should participate if the fleet comes into being. The belief that intimate ties with the United States are all-important appears to overcome the reservations of most of those who oppose the project in principle.

The responses and comments of our respondents indicate that the possibility that Germans might possess their own nuclear weapons—or even produce them—is unwelcome to German leaders. But it also seems rather remote to them. Second, it seems likely that an American-sponsored multilateral NATO nuclear force would be accepted without enthusiasm by German leaders who would not wish to forego participation in such a venture. Whether such a project will assuage or increase their overwhelming opposition to German nuclear weapons our data do not reveal. In the opinion of quite a number of our respondents such a project may well arouse latent desires in Germany for greater access to nuclear missiles than MLF seems to offer. In that case, they fear, the consequences for domestic and international stability would be catastrophic. But note that these are but the fears of a small minority of intellectuals. The Bonn Establishment seems to contemplate the prospect of a multilateral NATO force with far less concern. Political and administrative leaders are disposed to see considerable political advantages for their country if it were to participate in such an enterprise, and they appear willing to accept whatever risks it might involve.

[9] A 1961 survey of German elites found as many as seven out of ten leaders willing to make another attempt to create a European Defense Community within NATO. See Gorden and Lerner, "The Setting for European Arms Control," pp. 427-29.

PERCEPTIONS AND EVALUATION OF GENERAL INTERNATIONAL DISARMAMENT AND ARMS CONTROL AGREEMENTS

Seen as a more or less abstract ideal, international disarmament is readily endorsed by West Germans and their leaders. Our interviews, as well as a mass opinion survey during the same period, indicate that only a comparatively small minority views disarmament talks as a waste of time (Table 11.3). Nine out of ten of our respondents endorse efforts to prevent nuclear proliferation; and another survey, in 1961, found that six out of ten German leaders thought it more important to push disarmament than to strengthen the deterrent power of the West.[10]

But while disarmament discussions might seem to them a worthy enterprise, a majority of West Germans, leaders and masses alike, evaluates the chances of success pessimistically—at least under prevailing international conditions (Table 11.4). On this score, it is particularly the military men and civil servants among our respondents who express grave doubts. Whereas university professors insist that the world simply must find a way to ease international tensions through disarmament, these pessimists maintain that one has to be realistic about such matters and, realistically, world conditions doom any efforts to negotiate disarmament agreements with the Communist nations. International tensions, in their opinion, arise from fundamental political differences between East and West. Negotiations over ways and means to reduce such tensions through disarmament and arms control arrangements will therefore never succeed until drastically different international conditions allow such negotiations to move from fruitless, propagandistic debates over details into the realm of more promising, broad-gauged political negotiations. Some respondents hold out no hope whatever for disarmament talks, pointing to the failure of disarmament negotiations in the past and asserting that such agreements in any event never keep up with the development of new weapons systems.

This gap between general endorsement of the ideal of disarmament and hopes for the success of negotiations appears to be due largely to the widespread sense of anxiety about the threat of Communism to German security which we noted earlier and the corresponding feeling

---

[10] Three out of ten believed greater priority should be given to strengthening the Western deterrent forces. Data from Lerner and Gorden, "Strategic Thinking of European Elites."

Table 11.3

WEST GERMAN ATTITUDES ON THE PROSPECTS FOR DISARMAMENT

ELITE QUESTION: *Do you think it is possible to ease international tension by disarmament, or is the whole question of disarmament and arms control a mere utopia not worth discussing?*

MASS QUESTION: *People are talking nowadays about disarmament and arms limitation. What is your personal opinion on this matter?* *

	Elite Attitudes		Mass Attitudes
	Number of Respondents	Percentage	Percentage
Positive attitude	131	76%	53%
Negative attitude	39	23	17
(Not at the present time)	(17)	(10)	
(Utopian)	(22)	(13)	
Ambiguous/ambivalent attitude	—	—	10
Don't know	0	0	20
Not ascertained	3	2	—
Total	173	101%	100%

* Data from EMNID, *Informationen*, No. 39 (1964).

that only a strong Western deterrent can provide adequate safeguards against this danger. From this perspective, most of the German leaders interviewed appear either to discount efforts to promote international disarmament and arms control or to feel vaguely anxious that negotiations with the Soviet Union might produce disadvantageous results for Germany.[11] This impression becomes even stronger when we ask our respondents to consider more specific arms control and disarmament

[11] One qualification should be added. A number of respondents expresses the hope that the Sino-Soviet conflict might make the U.S.S.R. more amenable to disarmament negotiations with the West. In the study of Bundestag deputies cited earlier, 65 per cent anticipated that this conflict would promote an easing of tensions between the Soviet Union and the Western powers and 21 per cent thought that this should lead to greater efforts to negotiate disarmament agreements.

Table 11.4

WEST GERMAN ESTIMATES OF LIKELY SUCCESS OF DISARMAMENT AGREEMENTS

ELITE QUESTON: *Do you consider it likely that a general agreement on international disarmament, covering both conventional and nuclear weapons, will be reached in the next few years?* *

MASS QUESTION: *Do you think that in the foreseeable future there is a real chance that arms limitation in East and West will come about?* †

| | Elite Opinion | | Mass Opinion |
	1959	1961	1964
Yes	44%	39%	39%
No	41	53	44
Don't know	16	8	17
Total	101%	100%	100%

* Data from Morton Gorden and Daniel Lerner, "The Setting for European Arms Control: Political and Strategic Choices of European Elites," *Journal of Conflict Resolution*, 9 (December 1965), 424.
† Data from a survey (N = 1,833) of the Institut für angewandte Sozialwissenschaft (ifas), Bad Godesberg, Summer 1964.

proposals. Insofar as these relate to general and geographically undefined proposals to ease international tensions, they tend to be only diffusely perceived and evaluated. Proposals relating specifically to Central Europe, however, appear to have greater relevance for our respondents. They appear to stimulate more concrete considerations and, as we shall shortly see, provoke more specific expressions of opinion (Table 11.5).

One out of four leaders professes to be unfamiliar with any proposal and four out of ten feel unable to support any. Civil servants, businessmen and leaders of non-business interest associations in particular indicate that they know little or nothing about such matters and feel unable to evaluate such proposals; military men, mass media leaders and politicians feel more competent to pass judgment. Military men either reject all proposals (36%) or endorse only general worldwide disarma-

Table 11.5

WEST GERMAN PERCEPTION AND EVALUATION OF ARMS CONTROL PROPOSALS

QUESTION: *Of which arms control and disarmament plans have you heard most?*

Which of the various arms control and disarmament plans would you favor?

	Perception		Positive Evaluation	
	Number of Responses*	Percentage	Number of Responses*	Percentage
All or most plans	18	10%	5	3%
General, complete disarmament	20	12	17	10
Freeze in production of nuclear weapons	15	9	10	6
Destruction or reduction of nuclear weapons or stockpiles	9	5	10	6
Denuclearization of Central Europe	57	33	18	10
Troop withdrawal in Central Europe	25	14	6	3
Neutralization of Central Europe	23	13	6	3
Inspection of weapons	39	23	31	18
Ban on atomic testing	9	5	4	2
Other plans	19	11	8	5
No plans; none in particular	7	4	32	18
Don't know	44	25	44	25
Not ascertained	10	6	13	8
Total	295	170%	204	117%

* Multiple responses permitted

ment plans, such as a freeze on nuclear weapons production (21%). Political leaders are less negative: Only two out of ten reject all proposals, but most of the others confine their endorsement also to worldwide proposals, including complete international disarmament (18%) and inspection of weapons (18%). The mass media leaders are divided in their evaluation of disarmament and arms control plans. While four out of ten consider no plan worth supporting, five out of ten see some merit in one or more proposals.

A sense of remoteness from matters that are considered rather hypothetical and abstract is also reflected in opinions on the execution of agreements. Practically all of our respondents reply affirmatively when we ask whether an East-West agreement should provide for an inspection system, but one-third are unable to be more specific when we press them to name the kind of agreement they would favor. Some say such questions are a matter for the experts, others that no inspection system can be effective, as Germany's secret rearmament in the Weimar era had shown. Of the remaining two-thirds who express a definite preference on inspection systems, roughly half favor inspection by the participating countries, half inspection by an international agency or by neutral observers. As to whether such inspection should be on-site or not, four out of ten favor on-site inspection, two out of ten remote aerial or electronic inspection (Table 11.6).

To ascertain the acceptability of future agreements by German leaders we asked our respondents to evaluate the Soviet-American Test-Ban Treaty that had been recently ratified by the Bundestag. Practically all of them approve of it. Thirty-six per cent express enthusiasm, 47 per cent indicate less fervent approval, and only 15 per cent seem to be ambivalent. There are no noticeable cleavages on this issue among the elites, but many respondents also appear to attach little importance to the Test-Ban Treaty. A note of cynicism is evident in some of the comments. A business leader called it a mere "propaganda stunt." About one-half of our respondents (particularly politicians) feel that the Federal Republic should have been consulted before the agreement was concluded—if only as a matter of courtesy. Just as many, however, say that it makes no difference to them that Germany was not consulted. In the future, however, most of our respondents want the Federal Republic to be consulted, though close to a majority say they would support an agreement even if it were not (Table 11.7).

Here two different sentiments appear to influence opinions. On

Table 11.6
TYPES OF INSPECTION SYSTEMS FAVORED
BY WEST GERMAN LEADERS

QUESTION: *In your opinion, what kind of inspection would be most feasible?* *

| | Type of Inspection | | | |
	On-Site	Aerial	Electronic	Total
Inspecting Agency				
Pact nations	20%	8%	1%	29%
International agency	12	8	2	22
Neutral observers	13	2	0	15
Total	45%	18%	3%	66%

* Multiple responses permitted; the distribution shown in this table represents the responses of 46 per cent of the total number of respondents.

the one hand, many respondents seem concerned about the image which is projected. They evidently do not want to appear categorically opposed to any Soviet-American arms agreement nor to have their country seem to stand in the way. (Non-American interviewers might, perhaps, have gotten somewhat different responses.) On the other hand, however, quite a number seems to fear that German interests might be slighted in future agreements. This is particularly true of politicians and civil servants who suggest that the United States should have consulted the Federal government on the Test-Ban Treaty. A sense of injured national pride and a certain anxiety appear to play a role here. The average German seems less concerned than his leaders. According to an opinion survey conducted at the same time as our interviews, 57 per cent of a cross section of West Germans thought it quite possible that the United States and the Soviet Union would reach an arms agreement without consulting the Federal Republic very much, but only 22 per cent of these respondents believed that this would be bad for their country. Regardless of political affiliation, most thought it would cause Germany no harm.[12]

Although vaguely defined and apparently diffusely perceived, un-

[12] Data from Institut für angewandte Sozialwissenschaft survey, Summer 1964.

Table 11.7

PRIOR CONSULTATION WITH THE FEDERAL REPUBLIC ON ARMS CONTROL AGREEMENTS

QUESTION: *Should Germany be consulted in negotiations for further arms control agreements of this kind* [Limited Test-Ban Treaty]?

Would you favor further arms control agreements even if the country is not consulted?

	Should Germany be Consulted?		Support if not Consulted	
	Number of Respondents	Percentage	Number of Respondents	Percentage
Yes, definitely	84	49%	75	43%
Yes, preferably/probably	18	10	24	14
Yes, conditionally	28	16	21	12
Indifferent; undecided	13	8	0	0
No, conditionally	2	1	0	0
Preferably/probably not	10	6	6	3
Definitely not	3	2	25	14
Don't know	2	1	1	1
Not ascertained	13	8	21	12
Total	173	101%	173	99%

specific future Soviet-American arms agreements are endorsed overwhelmingly and with identical degrees of enthusiasm by West German elite and mass opinion (Table 11.8). Biographical background variables, such as age and political identification, appear to play no role in the extent of endorsement of future agreements, but occupational elite position seems of some relevance. The administrative elite of the Bonn Establishment—military men and civil servants—tends to be more reserved and ambivalent about its support than are other leaders. To the contrary, those previously identified with groups peripheral in attitude to the Bonn Establishment—mass media leaders, university professors and businessmen—endorse future Soviet-American arms agreements in particularly large numbers.

Table 11.8

WEST GERMAN ATTITUDES TOWARD FUTURE SOVIET-AMERICAN ARMS AGREEMENTS

ELITE QUESTION: *Would you favor further arms control agreements between the United States and the Soviet Union?*

MASS QUESTION: *If America and Russia were to agree on a limitation of armaments, would you find that very good, good, not so good, or bad?* *

Elite Attitudes	Number of Respondents	Percentage	Mass Attitudes	Percentage
Strongly favor	76	44%	Very good	45%
Generally favor	63	36	Good	35
Favor conditionally	20	12		
Indifferent; undecided	1	1	—	
Oppose conditionally	1	1	Not so good	6
Oppose generally	1	1		
Oppose vehemently	2	1	Bad	2
Don't know	1	1		12
Not ascertained	8	5	—	
Total	173	102%		100%

* Data from a survey (N = 1,833) of the Institut für angewandte Sozialwissenschaft (ifas), Bad Godesberg, Summer 1964.

ARMS CONTROL IN CENTRAL EUROPE

As soon as we move from a consideration of arms control and disarmament agreements in general to proposals affecting Germany and Central Europe in particular, German leadership opinion becomes more sharply focused. Thus, it appears that a Soviet-American agreement that might threaten the security of West Berlin would arouse strong opposition. The leaders we interviewed are practically unanimous in rejecting it. Two-thirds of them do not consider it possible that the United States will conclude an agreement of this sort; one-third, however, do not rule out such a "deal"—reflecting once again the concern which any suggestion that the political status quo might not persist seems to arouse among a substantial number of German leaders. As was noted in discussing opinions on reunification and relations with the Communist countries, however, there is, particularly among the intellectuals peripheral in attitudinal orientation to the Bonn Establishment, a considerable minority with no such anxieties and which favors a change in the status quo in the form of a *détente* in Central Europe. This again becomes evident when we probe more deeply into attitudes about arms control proposals relating specifically to Central Europe: denuclearization, withdrawal of foreign troops and the complete neutralization of the area. These are the proposals most familiar to our respondents as well as the ones about which they hold the most definite opinions.

It develops that, although all three of these proposals are overwhelmingly rejected when evaluated along with other plans (See Table 11.5), they are not quite as categorically and overwhelmingly opposed when our respondents focus explicitly on their military and political implications for West Germany: While only one out of ten endorses a nuclear free zone as a general arms control measure, three out of ten think it would help to ease the threat of war in Central Europe; while only one out of ten approves of the withdrawal of foreign troops, two out of ten believe it might help to ease tension in Central Europe; and while hardly any of our German leaders generally favor the complete neutralization of the area, two out of ten consider it at least a possibility worth considering as they give more thought to it. Neither the withdrawal of foreign troops nor complete neutralization is unconditionally endorsed by more than a few respondents, but about 14 per cent think that under certain conditions both might be possible—in fact, that one might gradually lead to the other. Six out of ten leaders, however, are opposed to a nuclear free zone, primarily on the grounds that it would increase the threat of a conventional attack by superior Communist forces, and seven out of ten reject more or less vehemently the possible withdrawal of foreign troops and the complete neutralization of Central Europe.

Thus, consensus on the desirability of arms control and disarmament agreements appears to be less extensive when it comes to proposals directly affecting Central Europe. Opinion is divided in roughly the same proportions and between the same groups which also disagree on the resilience of the domestic system in times of crisis and the desirability of a general political *détente* in Central Europe. Opposition to proposals to alter the military status quo in this case, too, concentrates around the civil servants and military men, while intellectuals once again tend in disproportionately large numbers to oppose the stand of the administrative elite. In this instance mass media leaders are more divided in their views, but university professors support all three arms control proposals to an exceptional degree, though usually with reservations.

Proposals to create a nuclear-free zone in Central Europe, such as the second Rapacki Plan, are the least unpopular. Here, university professors are joined by mass media leaders, trade unionists and a few Social Democratic politicians on the argument that this would have the dual advantage of assuring that German soldiers will not come into the possession of nuclear weapons and furthering improved relations with the Communist countries. On the assumption that the Federal Republic will continue to enjoy the benefit of American deterrent forces, German and allied conventional forces in the country are considered adequate to deal with minor incidents. In case of a nuclear encounter it is said to make no difference whether there are such weapons available in the Federal Republic, whereas their removal from Central Europe would reduce the danger of such a clash. Opponents, as noted, hold, however, that the superiority of the Communist countries in conventional forces requires the possession of nuclear weapons by Western forces stationed in the Federal Republic.

The complete withdrawal of all foreign troops is not as popular and what support it receives is mostly qualified.[13] Here the comments of those who are not entirely disinclined to support such an agreement reveal a good deal of ambivalence, suggesting difficulties in reconciling the wish for the continued engagement of American and other NATO forces in Germany—above all, West Berlin—with a desire to obtain the withdrawal of Soviet troops from the D.D.R. Some suggest that a thinning-out of foreign troops in Central Europe might at the same time permit the retention of deterrent trip-wire allied forces at the Elbe and in West Berlin while weakening the position of the dictatorship in the D.D.R.

The suggestion that the Federal Republic dispense entirely with NATO guarantees in exchange for the complete neutralization of Central

---

[13] In 1961, about four out of ten German leaders (37%) endorsed such a disengagement, six out of ten (57%) opposed it. See Gorden and Lerner, "The Setting for European Arms Control," p. 426.

Europe receives the largely qualified support of those leaders who see it as an essential step toward the reunification of Germany. They argue that a Soviet offer to neutralize a united Germany along Swiss, Austrian and Swedish lines might be hard to resist, provided the country is allowed to retain strong defensive forces and is protected by strong and effective international security guarantees. To judge by other surveys and studies of German opinion on this question, such neutrality sentiment has considerably diminished in the last decade. The thesis that Germany is too vulnerable and too rich a prize to be neutralized appears to be supported by most West Germans; and even most of the remaining neutralists appear to have serious doubts that their proposals can be realized in the foreseeable future.

IMPLICATIONS OF RESPONSE PATTERNS ON ARMS CONTROL AND DISARMAMENT ISSUES

The nature and quality of German elite opinion on arms issues suggest that the Federal government's official position on nuclear proliferation, arms control and disarmament matters is supported by a general elite consensus. With the partial exception of the government's wholehearted commitment to participation in the MLF, the leaders we interviewed on the whole support the armament policies of the Erhard government. The government's largely noncommittal endorsement of worldwide disarmament and cautious, wary position on arms control proposals affecting Central Europe seem to strike a judicious balance between the elements clamoring for a *détente* and those opposing any move likely to diminish Western involvement in Germany. With the exception of a comparatively small minority, the leaders we interviewed appear to be quite willing to let their government continue its policies of aloofness on general disarmament and *immobilisme* on arms control in Central Europe.

The comparatively very small minority which appears to have reservations about current government policies may be divided into two groups. There are first of all the categorical opponents of German nuclear armament in any form or fashion, who even oppose participation in a multilateral NATO fleet. University professors and mass media leaders in particular express strong fears that such a development might very well have catastrophic consequences for domestic and international stability. They are entirely willing to leave the nuclear protection of their country exclusively in the hands of the United States and consider the contemporary Soviet-American standoff the best assurance of German security and domestic and international stability.

Second, an even smaller group intimates rather cautiously that for political and strategic reasons West Germans should be allowed greater direct influence over the employment of nuclear deterrent forces in NATO. Military leaders, in particular, suggest that German forces armed with nuclear weapons would be better equipped to deter a Soviet attack or, if deterrence failed, to repel it. Such weapons would permit the lost art of war to be recovered, in the words of a top German general, by providing the German defensive forces with greater flexibility to counter the threat of escalation through the application of graduated deterrents ranging from conventional to nuclear forces. A military expert of one of the largest West German newspapers, to the contrary, advanced the Gaullist argument that, with nuclear weapons in German hands, they as well as their prospective opponents could be more certain that American massive retaliation would be the instant response to any Soviet military action against West Berlin and the Federal Republic. A number of respondents in this group claims that nuclear sharing in NATO is absolutely essential if the alliance is to be saved from disintegration, because present American discriminatory practices in this respect undermine the loyalty of its European members. A military leader asserted that Germans will be less tempted to circumvent present restrictions if these are modified to permit them to acquire, though not produce, nuclear weapons and missiles. Finally, a number of leaders indicates that they think that the possession of nuclear weapons would boost West German political power and allow the Federal Republic greater flexibility in dealing with its allies as well as with the Communist countries. Even though "drugstore bombs" would constitute only a minuscule fraction of the nuclear might of the superpowers, as one of the highest German military leaders said, they would allow their possessors a great deal more influence in international affairs than non-nuclear powers have.

But these, as we said, are opinions expressed by only a very small minority. Our own findings as well as other elite and opinion surveys indicate that between these two camps stands the vast, more or less indifferent, majority of West Germans, neither craving nuclear weapons nor categorically rejecting participation in a NATO nuclear force.

German elite opinion on arms control and disarmament agreements reflects a broad consensus on their general desirability in the abstract, but considerable cleavages when it comes to evaluating proposals concerning arms control in Central Europe. The leaders we interviewed appear to be comparatively ignorant and indifferent about general proposals, to consider their own influence over developments in this area close to nonexistent and to find apparent technical details difficult to fathom. Insofar as they are at all interested in general disarmament plans, they tend to consider negotiations about arms limitations a pretty futile activity which seems to put the cart before the horse. Such agreements are said to require a degree of mutual trust such as does not exist in the world of the mid-1960's. A radically different international political climate is said to be an essential prerequisite not only because agreements of this sort do not reduce tensions and create trust, but also because they can only follow in the wake of much improved political relationships between East and West. In this sense, procedural questions about arms control and disarmament agreements seem unimportant to most of our respondents and substantive political issues all-important.

Proposals relating to Central European arms control appear to trigger a sense of greater relevance and involvement and create greater disagreement. Here, as on the issue of nuclear weapons acquisition, military leaders and intellectuals (especially university professors) tend to take opposing positions. In this instance, however, the intellectuals are dissatisfied with prevailing conditions, and the military leaders express concern about dangerous instability if the status quo should be altered. Essentially, opposing opinions in both instances appear to relate primarily to different perceptions of the needs and opportunities of German foreign policy in Central Europe.

The quality and nature of these patterns of elite opinion suggest that under present conditions the great majority of German leaders is not likely either to support or to oppose worldwide disarmament and arms control proposals very strongly. They are likely to avoid, if possible, any move that would make them appear to stand in the way of such general agreements. Political and security considerations, however, apparently constitute rather rigid limitations to their consent when such proposals relate to Central European arms control. Any proposals seen as threatening the security of West Berlin or of the Federal Republic itself are likely to encounter strong opposition and may well mobilize elite opinion, which at present is largely indifferent about Soviet-American arms negotiations. Therefore, we may expect that any West German government will seek to prevent and, failing that, to delay as long as possible any agreement which is seen by German leaders as directly weakening the protective deterrent power of the West. Proposals that avoid the rather indistinct threshold between latent and active elite anxiety on this issue are difficult to identify and the force of opposition that might develop cannot be predicted with any degree of accuracy. In 1964, among the leaders we interviewed, proposals to create a nuclear-free zone in Central Europe appeared to encounter the least opposition. If such a plan were to be combined with convincing evidence that American strategic deterrent power would continue to be effective in Germany it might conceivably prove to be acceptable, not to all but perhaps to a majority of German leaders. And if past experiences are an indication, mass opinion would follow the lead of elite opinion.

Part III

A COMPARISON OF FRENCH AND GERMAN ELITES IN THE EUROPEAN POLITICAL ENVIRONMENT

CHAPTER 12

The Questions and the Evidence

The elites of France and Germany have considerable influence over the policies of their countries, but they—much like individual statesmen—can only exercise this influence within the framework of given conditions and on-going processes which they cannot wholly control. France and Germany are distinct national economies and political decision systems, and both are part of a larger though looser system of Western Europe. In summarizing much of our research, the following sections will deal with the French and West German elites and their foreign policy attitudes in the perspective of this larger system and its possible future.

THE BASIC QUESTIONS

Our research aimed at a single basic question: What arms control and disarmament measures might be acceptable to Western Europeans in 1966, in 1971, and in 1976? More broadly put, what is likely to be

Europe's attitude during this period to either arms competition or arms control? What particular policies in these respects would be most popular in Western Europe, and which ones would be least so?

This single basic question implied four more detailed questions. The first: What is Europe now, in 1966, and where is it headed for the 1971 to 1976 period? Is it going to be a Europe of nation-states, with common functional arrangements on matters of only marginal importance to the concerns of its citizens? Or will it be partly but to some extent substantially integrated, with some major policy decisions made by common institutions rather than by the sovereign governments of each of the major Western European nations? Or will it be predominantly integrated economically and politically? Will it become in most ways, therefore, a common body politic speaking with a single voice and developing common institutions for a wide range of decisions?

Second, do Europeans in general approve or disapprove of arms control? Do they welcome the relaxation of tensions between America and Russia and between the East and West, or do they fear such a relaxation? Do Europeans think they will be better off if America and Russia are more hostile to each other, because this might increase European bargaining power and make it less likely that America and Russia might make some compromise at the expense of European interests, or do Europeans feel that, if the big powers can reduce tensions somewhat and negotiate some reductions in arms levels or underground nuclear tests, Europe will be better off?

The third question: What specific arms control measures are likely to be most acceptable to Western Europeans, and which arms control measures are likely to be least acceptable?

And, fourth, what are the strength, the location, and the time aspects of political support for specific policies, such as those policies of France and its President de Gaulle vis-à-vis the NATO alliance and the United States? Is this mainly a matter of President de Gaulle's unique personality, or is he expressing deep-seated attitudes shared by many Frenchmen? What is the European attitude to the nuclear striking force of France, the *force de frappe,* and the proposals that other European countries should also have national nuclear striking forces? What in particular is the attitude of Europeans, both in Germany and elsewhere, to the idea of nuclear weapons for Germany, either directly, for instance, through purchase by the German government for the German military establishment, or less directly through the abrogation of the Paris Agreements of 1954 and therefore eventually through the German manufacture of nuclear weapons? What is the attitude of Europeans to a multilateral nuclear force, either limited to Western European countries alone or including the United States?

How can one answer questions such as these, and how can one get evidence that is more than just one scholar's whim or preference? Let it be emphasized that ultimately the diagnosis of the doctor, the verdict of the judge, and the judgment of the political scientist all are made in the light of many considerations not all of which can be made fully explicit. A doctor who has seen many sick people, a judge who has listened to many plausible but not always trustworthy witnesses, a political scientist who has some experience in the course of the years of his professional work as to how deceptive evidence can be—each of these is likely to do better in his appraisal of reality than one who only looks at what the figures and pieces of paper in front of him are saying.

FIVE CONVERGING STREAMS OF EVIDENCE

Nevertheless, though it must be interpreted with judgment, evidence speaks with its own voice and deserves to be taken seriously in its own right. We have tried to develop five lines of mutually independent evidence from elite interviews, from mass opinion polls, from content analysis of the press, from a survey of arms control proposals, and from aggregative statistics of actual behavior.

The first of these streams of evidence is from elite interviews. In order to concentrate on the heart of the problem, as well as for reasons of time, money and manpower, we have limited our project to just two countries, Germany and France. If there is a European policy or an arms control policy on which France and Germany can agree, the Netherlands is very unlikely to veto or torpedo it. If the French and the Germans can agree, a policy would be very likely to work in Europe, and if they cannot agree, it is quite unlikely to work.

We developed a sample of elite leaders by combining the methods of position and reputation. How we did this is described in Chapter 1. The elite interviews, however, although they involved a good deal of work, were by no means the only source of evidence.

We also surveyed relevant mass opinion polls, going back for about fifteen years. In many cases the same question had been asked every year of samples of voters, ranging from between one thousand to two thousand respondents, and we knew, therefore, what people would say in answer to such questions as: What is the most important problem for people in your country today to be concerned with? Or, what are your feelings about France? About Germany? And, to what extent would you trust France—or trust Germany—as an ally in case of war? On many such questions it was possible to compare how mass opinion had changed over time, and how it agreed with or differed from elite views in the early 1960's.

We also carried on two content analysis projects, one for a large number of newspapers and periodicals in four countries—France, West Germany, Great Britain and the United States—by coders using their judgmental categories and hand-coding techniques, and the other one in greater depth for four leading newspapers in France, West Germany, Great Britain and the United States, by computer. The results of such content analysis of printed materials are, of course, independent from those of elite interviews and mass opinion polls, but we wanted to find out whether the same trends would be revealed. To show such trends over time, we analyzed newspapers reactions to ten specific arms control and disarmament events dating from 1946 to 1963. The more detailed analysis of the "prestige" newspapers for 1953 and 1963 permitted us to ask such questions as: Did the number of symbols of, or references to, Europe go up, go down, or stay unchanged, and did interest in arms control—in European unification—increase or decrease over time?

Another study analyzed data from a survey of arms control and/or disarmament proposals bearing directly on Europe and made by governments, responsible officials or important public figures in France, Germany, Britain, the United States or the Soviet Union or Poland during the years 1945-1964.

Finally we got a very large number of aggregate data about actual behavior. What is happening, not to editorials about trade, but to actual trade? What is happening, not to speeches about universities, but to the numbers of young Germans and young Frenchmen actually crossing the border to study in the other country? What is happening to travel? What is happening to migration? What is happening to the exchange of mail? Are the French and the Germans not only saying they like each other more, but are they writing more letters to each other? These data are available from the statistics published by the countries concerned or by various international organizations. Since they are aggregated for each country as a whole, they do not tell us which groups of the population do most of the international trading, traveling, letter writing or studying abroad. But they did tell us whether these transactions had increased or declined, relative to other transactions or to the same transactions in other years or with other countries.

Using all these five streams of evidence, we then tried to make our judgments. A few of the points that came out of the combined use of the five types of evidence can be briefly summarized.

ELITE ATTITUDES AND THE FRAMEWORK OF MASS OPINION AND ACTUAL BEHAVIOR

This confrontation of evidence showed clearly that elite politics are carried on in a framework of the attitudes and the actual behavior of countries and of populations. The flow of such transactions as foreign trade, mail, travel and even the decisions of students to study abroad all represent the actions, choices and habits of large numbers of people. They are indications of that "plebiscite of everyday living" in which Ernst Renan saw the essence of nationality and in which we still see a fundamental aspect of political and social integration. The evidence of such transactions also throws some light on the old question whether people act in the way in which they talk, that is, whether expressions of attitudes indicate anything about actual behavior.

The next chapter will focus on the aggregate statistics of the actual behavior of West Europeans, and particularly of the French and the Germans, in order to discover something about the larger framework of reality in which their elites have been operating and which has expressed at least in part the consequences of their actions.

CHAPTER 13

The Halting of European Structural Integration: The Evidence of Transactions

The first point to emerge from this analysis was this: European integration has slowed since the mid-1950's, and it has stopped or reached a plateau since 1957-58. In the 1957-58 period, Europe reached the highest level of structural integration that it has ever had. Most of this high level was reached by 1954, but there were slow advances until 1957-58. Although it is clear that Europe is much more highly integrated now than it was between the wars or on the eve of World War I, it is equally clear that since 1957-58 there have been no further structural or fundamental gains.

Content analysis of editorials in *Le Monde* and the *Frankfurter Allgemeine Zeitung* in 1953 and 1963 shows no significant increase in the frequency of symbols of Europe, Europeans or European integration. Elite interviews show that, of among the 141 French and 158 German leaders who stated their views on this question only minorities—19 per cent in France and 46 per cent in Germany—see even a "moderate chance" that European integration will be achieved "within the next ten years," whereas 49 per cent in France and 35 per cent in Germany say that this probably or definitely will not happen. On the level of mass opinion, there was between 1957 and 1962 some evidence of an increase in the importance of an image of a united Europe, and an increase in the similarity of political perceptions in France and Germany, but there was no decrease in the dissimilarity of French and German political preferences and values.

THE EVIDENCE OF INTERNATIONAL TRANSACTIONS

The most substantial evidence, however, comes from aggregate statistics of actual behavior. Such behavior is expressed in the flow of transactions in the Europe of the Six, and particularly between Germany and France, and shown in the statistics of international trade, mail, travel and the exchange of students. There are, to be sure, absolute increases after 1958 in trade, travel, postal correspondence and the exchange of students, but all this can be accounted for by the effects of prosperity and the general increase in the level of these activities in the 1950's and early 1960's. There have been no increases in integration in regard to all these transactions beyond what one would expect from mere random probability and increase in prosperity in the countries concerned. Such general prosperity, however, was not unique to Europe in the late 1950's and early 1960's. Japan, Turkey, Austria—all of which are not in the Common Market—were similarly prosperous in the 1950's and showed similar increases in national income and foreign trade, without becoming more closely integrated with other countries.

In Europe, there have been no increases—and there have been some marked decreases—in the observable preferences of the Six, and particularly of France and Germany, for dealing with one another rather than with other countries. The structural integration of European trade, in terms of mutual preferences for accepting one another's exports, seems to have reached its peak in 1948-51. In regard to mail flow, tourist travel and student exchanges, the peak of mutual preference was reached in each case in, or about, 1955-57. In none of these fields has there been any substantial progress toward greater structural integration since that time.

THE METHOD OF ANALYSIS

The statistical computations on which these findings are based must be given elsewhere.[1] Here it can only be said that they are based on the Index of Relative Acceptance—the RA index—which measures the percentage by which the volume of actual transactions (such as, for instance, trade) between two countries exceeds or falls short of the hypothetical amount that would be proportional to the overall share of each of these two countries in the total flow of transactions among all countries in the world. This index thus measures by how many more or fewer per cent these two countries deal with one another than they could be expected to do according to random probability and the mere size of their total foreign trade. The RA index separates, therefore, the actual results of preferential behavior and structural integration from the mere effects of the size and prosperity of countries.

The RA index seeks to give a realistic measure of the extent to which the distribution of foreign trade among two or more countries deviates from the level which could be expected from the mere size of the total foreign trade of each. It thus measures the aggregate effects of geography, special economic interests, established credit channels, congenial culture patterns and consumer tastes, as well as the effects—intended or unintentional—of public policy, all of which may combine to produce the deviation. In fact, the RA index works well in identifying closely knit regions of economic collaboration, such as the United States and Canada, Britain and Australia; and the five Scandinavian countries. It also identifies existing or former colonial empires, and even such less strongly integrated collectivities as the countries of the Arab League.

High positive RA indices have been found to apply to trade not only between small countries, where they could be produced by a shift of relatively small absolute amounts of trade, but they also hold for very large flows of trade among major countries, such as the United States and Canada, that seem to be economically fairly well integrated by this test. Canadian-American trade tends to be larger than trade between Germany and France, and its positive RA indices usually are much higher.

[1] Data are given in Donald J. Puchala, "European Political Integration: Progress and Prospects" (New Haven: Yale University, Political Science Research Library, mimeographed, 1966).

SOME RESULTS FOR WESTERN EUROPE

In examining the data for several years and a good many countries, it appears that the effects of geography and natural resources on the total flow of trade are somewhat weaker, and the effects of economic and cultural institutions and political practices somewhat stronger, than often has been believed. Moreover, in repeating our RA analysis for several different years, geographic and linguistic conditions change relatively little, and it should be possible to appraise the effects of social and political change on the observable degree of integration in various world regions.

The RA index for a region such as the Six of Western Europe can then be compared with the RA index for other regions for the same year; and it can also be compared with the RA index for its own region for earlier years, so as to test whether the structural integration of that region has increased or diminished in regard to that particular class of transaction flows. Some comparisons of this type for the period 1890-1963 are shown in Table 13.1.

An analysis of the changes over time in this measure of integration among the Six suggests that the integrative effects of the specific policies of the 1950's may have been rather limited. If the average trend of 1890 to 1938 had simply continued in regard to the structural integration among the Six, their level of integration in 1963, as measured by the RA index, would have been fairly close to what it actually turned out to be in that year. In this respect, the combined effects of World War II, Hitler's New Order, the Marshall Plan, and more than a decade of efforts at European unification after 1950 all seem to have added up to just about as much as another 24 years of mixed European history of the 1890-1938 type might have accomplished. This is less, it should be noted, than what the quarter century between 1913 and 1938 did in fact accomplish. If the RA index of structural integration among the Six had continued to grow in the 25 years after 1938 at the same rate as it did from the eve of World War I to the eve of World War II, the index in 1963 would have reached 94 per cent, far above the 77 per cent it actually did.

As regards the first type of comparisons, those among different groups of countries, it appears that Western Europe has been significantly integrated in terms of RA index values at least since 1890, and

221

Table 13.1

REGIONAL RELATIVE ACCEPTANCE SCORES
FOR INTERNATIONAL TRADE, 1890-1963

Year	The Six	Anglo-America*	Scandinavia	Canada-United States	United States-Canada
1890	.40	.63	11.89	3.73	3.25
1913	.30	.63	6.26	3.59	4.39
1928	.57	.36	5.30	1.81	3.13
1938	.62	.40	2.69	2.15	3.46
1948	1.07	.10	3.06	2.1	1.9
1954	.79	.45	2.73	2.85	2.93
1957	.82	.48	2.28	3.2	2.2
1959	.83	.49	2.99	2.7	2.3
1963	.77	.53	3.89	2.6	2.5

* The "Anglo-American region" includes Britain, Canada, Ireland and the United States, that is, all English-speaking countries in the North Atlantic area. For a discussion of other aspects of this four-country group, see Karl W. Deutsch, *et al., Political Community and the North Atlantic Area* (Princeton: Princeton University Press, 1957), reprinted in part in *International Political Communities: An Anthology* (New York: Doubleday Anchor Books, 1966), pp. 1-91.

Sources: 1890, 1913, 1928, 1938—I. Richard Savage and Karl W. Deutsch, "A Statistical Model of the Gross Analysis of Transaction Flows," *Econometrica*, 28 (1960), 551-72.

1954, 1959—*Ibid.*; Hayward R. Alker, Jr. and Donald J. Puchala, "Trends in Economic Partnership in the North Atlantic Area," in *Quantitative International Politics*, J. David Singer, ed. (New York: The Free Press, 1966); Karl W. Deutsch and I. Richard Savage, *Regionalism, Trade and the International Community* (forthcoming).

1948, 1957, 1963—Alker and Puchala in Singer, *Quantitative International Politics*.

probably much longer. In 1890 and 1913, economic integration among the Six, as measured by the RA index, was less than that among the English-speaking countries of the North Atlantic area, that is, the United States, Britain, Canada and Ireland. In 1928, and thereafter, however, integration was stronger among the Six than it was among those four English-speaking countries. Nevertheless, integration among the Six was at all times much weaker than it was among the Scandinavian countries, or between the United States and Canada.

The second type of comparison of different RA indices, those across time, are summarized in Table 13.2, A-D, for four types of international transactions: trade, mail, travel and the exchange of students, from one country to another, or from any one of the Six countries to any other in that region.

The series in Tables 13.1 and 13.2 show that integration between France and Germany, as well as for the group of the Six as a whole, has remained consistently and substantially higher after World War II than it was from 1890 to 1938. During the pre-World War II period, there was little, if any, significant direct integration between France and Germany, but there was always some integration for the whole group of the Six. After World War II, integration increased substantially not only for the entire area, but also directly between Germany and France.

These data clearly suggest, however, that *since* 1955-1957 the structural unification of a Europe of the Six has *halted*. There have been general increases in the level of transactions among the Six, but no more than can be accounted for by the effects of the boom and of the general recovery and increased activity in the 1950's. There have been few increases—and there have been some decreases—in the observable preferences of the Six, and particularly of France and Germany—for dealing with one another rather than with other countries.

Even in regard to the pre-World War II degree of trade integration, the postwar gains for the Six as a whole are relatively modest. As Tables 13.1 and 13.3 show, the RA index for exports from France to the Six in 1963 was roughly where it had been in 1928. The RA index for trade exports from the six EEC countries retained within the EEC area roughly doubled from 0.30 to 0.60 during the 15 years from 1913 to 1928, but then rose only by another one-half, from 0.62 to 0.81, during the 29 years from 1928 to 1957, and then remained substantially unchanged at that level during the 6 years from 1957 to 1963.

The data in Table 13.3 also show that the overall halting of structural integration in regard to trade after 1957 was not limited to Germany and France, and cannot be ascribed to the policy of France, or indeed of any single country. Structural integration between France and Germany increased and so did integration between France and Italy, but integration between Germany and Italy, for instance, as measured by the RA index, was slightly lower in 1963 than it had been in 1957.

It should be remembered that these RA indices are not statistical artifacts. They are based on the analysis of very large amounts of trade, involving large numbers of transactions. They show considerable stability and fairly stable trends over several decades, and they pinpoint effectively other areas of long-established or incipient economic integration, through the voluntary formation of communities, such as in the case of Scandinavia or through current or relatively recent colonial relation-

Table 13.2

INDICES OF RELATIVE ACCEPTANCE OF INTERNATIONAL TRANSACTION FLOWS, 1925-1963

A.

Period	Year	From France							
		To Germany				To The Six			
		Trade	Mail	Travel	Students	Trade	Mail	Travel	Students
I	1925				-.9	.6			
	1928	0.0							
	1929		-.5	-.5					
	1937		-.5						
II	1948	* 1.0				* .7			
	1950			-.5				.1	
	1952				.1				.9
	1954	.5				.4			
III	1955		* .7	* -.3			* .9		
	1957	.6			* 1.5	.5		0.0	* 1.2
IV	1960				.9				.7
	1961		.1				.5		
	1962			-.4				* .2	
	1963	.7				.6			

B. From Germany

Period	Year	To France				To The Six			
		Trade	Mail	Travel	Students	Trade	Mail	Travel	Students
I	1925				.3				
	1928	0.0				.5			
	1929			-.9					
	1937		-.6						
II	1948	* 3.8				* 3.0			
	1950			-.7				-.5	
	1952				.1				0.0
	1954	.3				.9			
III	1955		.2	* -.3		.8	.3	* 0.0	
	1957	.4			* .5				* .2
IV	1960				.3				.1
	1961		* .7				* .4		
	1962			-.5				-.3	
	1963	.7				.8			

* Indicates peak of series; if same peak was reached several times, the earliest peak is marked.

225

Table 13.2 (Continued)

C.

Period	Year	To France				To Germany				To The Six			
		Trade	Mail	Travel	Students	Trade	Mail	Travel	Students	Trade	Mail	Travel	Students
I	1925	.3				.3				.6			
	1928												
	1929												
	1937												
II	1948	1.0				.6				* 1.1			
	1950			−.4				−.4				−.1	
	1952				.3				.2				.2
	1954	.3				* .9				.8			
III	1955	.4		* −.2	* .6	.8	* .6	* −.3	* .9	.8	* .6	* 0.0	* .5
	1957	.4	.4			.8				.8			
IV	1960				.4				.5				.3
	1961		* 1.3				.3				.6		
	1962			−.3				−.3				−.1	
	1963	.7				.9				.8			

D.

Summary: Percentage of Peaks in Each Period

Period		Years with data	Entries	Peaks	% Peaks
France-Germany	I 1925-1937	4	8	0	0
and vice-versa	II 1948-1954	4	8	2	25
	III 1955-1957	2	8	5	63
	IV 1960-1963	4	8	1	13
France-The Six,	I 1925-1937	0	0	0	0
Germany-The Six,	II 1948-1954	4	20	5	25
and vice-versa;	III 1955-1957	2	20	12	60
and The Six	IV 1960-1963	4	20	3	15
TOTAL	I 1925-1937	4	8	0	0
	II 1948-1954	4	28	7	25
	III 1955-1957	2	28	17	61
	IV 1960-1963	4	28	4	14

Source: Donald J. Puchala, "European Political Integration: Progress and Prospects" (New Haven: Yale University, Political Science Research Library, mimeographed, 1966), Tables I-IV, VII-X.

ships. In a sense, the RA indices serve as a yardstick for comparing the structural integration of EEC countries in regard to trade and other transactions, or acts of communication, with the degree of such integration in other well-known cases of partial or incipient community formation. It is in comparison with these other cases, then, that we can say that the structural integration of the economic and social fabric of the six EEC countries has virtually stood still since 1957.

It is perhaps necessary to stress this point, because the evidence of the RA indices modifies to a large degree the surface image presented by the conventional growth indices of intra-EEC trade. Such trade, as is well known, has grown considerably between 1957 and 1963, and it has grown a good deal faster than the trade between the EEC countries and the rest of the world. The point is, however, that precisely this amount of growth of intra-EEC trade was expectable from the mere fact of greater prosperity in the EEC countries than in much of the rest of the world, *without any structural change in intra-EEC relations.*[2]

This appears to have occurred in Western Europe between 1957 and 1963. During these years, while the institutions of the European Economic Community presided over a major economic boom, increases in intra-EEC trade were just of the size to be expected from such a boom, without any additional intra-EEC trade increase that would suggest an underlying structural change. This absence between 1957 and 1963 of evidence for any such structural changes toward greater European integration is the more notable since there is clear evidence of just such structural changes toward European integration during the

---

[2] An example may be useful here. If the total share in world trade of each of two countries, A and B, should double, while the average trade of the rest of the world remained unchanged, and if their mutual trade were proportional to their respective shares in world trade, as would be the case under assumptions of random probability, then the flow of trade from A to B would double once in proportion to the doubling of the share of world exports originating from A, and it would double once again in proportion to the doubling of the share of world exports accepted as imports by B. Thus, the total flow of trade from A to B would increase *fourfold* as the result of pure "prosperity effects," with no structural change whatever in mutual trade preferences between the two countries, and on the basis of no other assumptions than those of random probability. The favorable expectations aroused by EEC, of course, may have increased the propensity to invest and made the prosperity of Western Europe greater and longer than it would have been otherwise. Much of this psychological impact, however, occurred before 1958. Thereafter, as the West European rates of economic growth slowed down in the early 1960's, a particularly strong growth of intra-European trade would have led to higher RA indices for 1963. No such increase in the RA index for the EEC region occurred. Whether such an increase will be found for the 1963-1966 period remains to be seen.

long preceding period from 1913 to 1955-57—a period which spanned times of prosperity as well as of recession.

FORMAL INTEGRATION vs. ACTUAL BEHAVIOR

The spectacular increase in the number of formal European agreements and organizations must be evaluated in this perspective. The number of such organizations increased rapidly until 1958, and particularly quickly between 1955 and 1958, but thereafter the trend to 1963 flattened out. The development of such European treaties and institutions since the mid-1950's has not been matched by any corresponding deeper integration of actual behavior.

To be sure, a large number of new European organizations could conceivably be founded in some future year and change the present slowed-down trend; but it would be easier to found new formal organizations than to increase substantially the integration in the daily actions and habits of millions of people. Formal organizations represent promises of future behavior. It takes the actions, habits and commitments of states and populations to give them substance and endurance.

Much then may depend on whether there is any strong desire among the elites and masses of France and Germany to increase quickly the level of practical actions and commitments for European integration well beyond its present level. The evidence on these points has been presented in detail in other sections of this study. Summing up its weight, however, it can be said that there is no evidence of any such strong popular or elite pressure to increase Western European integration in any way drastically beyond its present level. Moderate steps may prove both feasible and acceptable, or even mildly popular, from time to time, but there is little present evidence of serious impatience or enthusiasm. The nearly 16 per cent of the popular vote in the first round of the French presidential election in late 1965, polled by the only major candidate with an unequivocally pro-European and pro-United States appeal, Jean Lecanuet, represents too small a section of French mass opinion to promise any early and drastic changes in this respect.

As far as they go, the transaction data do not suggest that any substantial increase in European integration should be expected by 1970 or 1975, even among the Six, if there should be a mere continuation of the practices and methods of the 1950's and the early 1960's.

The most likely pattern for the next ten years, therefore, will be a Europe of national states, linked by marked but moderate preferences for mutual transactions, in contrast to transactions with countries outside Europe, and with little growth—and possibly some decline—in the intensity of those preferences as expressed in actual behavior of the populations and business communities of the European countries.

A CRUCIAL CASE: THE PARTIAL FRENCH RETREAT FROM FOREIGN TRADE

Arguments of this kind apply with particular strength to France. The French government has carried out its obligations under the EEC treaties as loyally as any other EEC member. The French economy and the French population, however, have had a greater psychological distance to cover and have had to undergo a greater change of attitudes toward freer trade; and thus far they have retained somewhat more national self-preoccupation, and have accepted in their actions somewhat less of the limited European integration than have those of Germany, Italy and the Benelux countries.

Between 1928 and 1963, the ratio of French foreign trade to French national income declined by one-third, from 46 to 28 per cent, while the corresponding ratio for Germany shifted only from 36 to 38 per cent over the same 35-year period despite the drastic changes in territory, population and economic resources from the Weimar to the Bonn Republic.

In this drastically reduced dependence on foreign trade it was France, not Germany, that underwent a major transformation (Table 13.4). The foreign trade sector within the French national economy in 1928 was substantially larger than was the corresponding sector in Germany, but by 1963 this relationship had become reversed. From 1913 to 1938, France ranked ahead of Germany and Italy in the relative size of her foreign trade sector; from 1954 on, France has ranked at the bottom among the Six in this respect.[3] Germany substantially has recovered her 1913 and 1928 proportion of foreign trade to national income. Italy did so by 1957, and has since then markedly increased her foreign trade sector. It is only the French foreign trade sector that seems to have

[3] Data from the EEC Statistical Office, based on higher estimates of national income for 1913 and 1928, show French foreign trade to national income ratios of 38.7 and 38.2 per cent for 1913 and 1928. The decline occurred almost entirely in trade with third countries, while trade with EEC partners remained at 10.7 and 10.2 per cent in 1928 and 1963.

Table 13.3

THE RELATIVE ACCEPTANCE OF INTERNATIONAL TRADE IN THE NORTH ATLANTIC AREA
1928, 1948, 1954, 1957, 1959, 1963

To:	U.K.	U.S.	Canada	Ireland	Region 1	Germany	France	Bel-Lux.	Netherlands	Italy	Region 2	Switzerland	Region 3	Rest of World
From:														
U.K.														
1928		-.5	-.0	4.7	-.1	-.4	-.3	-.1	-.2	-.4	-.3	-.4	.1	.3
1948		-.8	-.2	3.8	-.5	-.4	-.6	-.3	-.2	-.7	-.4	-.4	.4	.4
1954		-.6	-.1	5.1	-.4	-.5	-.5	-.4	-.1	-.3	-.4	-.4	.7	.3
1957		-.5	.0	6.0	-.2	-.6	-.6	-.3	-.1	-.4	-.4	-.4	.6	.3
1959		-.4	.0	4.8	-.2	-.5	-.5	-.5	-.1	-.3	-.4	-.2	.5	.3
1963		-.4	-.1	4.6	-.2	-.3	-.3	-.3	-.1	-.3	-.3	-.2	.6	.2
U.S.														
1928	-.2		3.1	-.7	.3	-.2	-.3	-.4	.1	-.0	-.2	-.9	-.2	.0
1948	-.7		1.9	-.6	-.1	1.5	-.3	-.2	-.3	.6	.1	-.2	-.4	-.1
1954	-.6		2.9	-.7	-.4	-.4	-.5	-.4	-.3	-.3	-.4	-.3	-.7	.1
1957	-.6		2.2	-.8	.3	-.4	-.5	-.4	-.4	-.1	-.4	-.3	-.6	.2
1959	-.6		2.3	-.7	.4	-.6	-.7	-.5	-.3	-.3	-.5	-.5	-.6	.2
1963	-.5		2.5	-.7	.4	-.6	-.6	-.5	-.3	-.4	-.5	-.5	-.6	.3
Canada														
1928	.8	1.8		-.6	1.1	-.7	-.8	-.3	.1	-.4	-.6	-.9	-.6	-.5
1948	.8	2.1		-.6	1.4	-.9	-.7	-.7	-.5	-.6	-.7	-.6	-.8	-.6
1954	.3	2.8		-.6	1.7	-.6	-.8	-.6	-.8	-.8	-.7	-.6	-.8	-.7
1957	.4	3.2		-.6	1.9	-.6	-.8	-.6	-.6	-.6	-.6	-.7	-.7	-.7
1959	.4	2.7		-.7	1.7	-.7	-.8	-.7	-.7	-.8	-.7	-.7	-.7	-.7
1963	.6	2.6		-.8	1.7	-.7	-.8	-.7	-.7	-.8	-.8	-.8	-.7	-.4
Ireland														
1928	4.3	-.9	-.9		1.8	-.9	-.9	-.9	-1.0	-1.0	-.9	-.8	-1.0	-.9
1948	4.9	-.9	-.9		1.5	-1.0	-.9	-.3	.2	-.9	-.6	-.9	-.9	-.9
1954	6.3	-.9	-.9		1.7	-.7	-.9	-.6	-.8	-.9	-.8	-.9	-.8	-.8
1957	6.5	-.8	-.9		1.8	-.6	-.7	-.6	-.8	-.8	-.7	-.9	-.8	-.8
1959	5.9	-.5	-.8		1.6	-.7	-.8	-.8	-.8	-.8	-.7	-.9	-.8	-.7
1963	7.1	-.5	-.6		1.9	-.7	-.7	-.8	-.8	-.8	-.7	-.8	-.9	-.7

Key: Region 1 = Anglo-American Region (UK, US, Canada, Ireland)
Region 2 = Current EEC Members (the Six: Germany, France, Italy, Netherlands, Belgium-Luxembourg)
Region 3 = Scandinavia (Denmark, Sweden, Norway, Finland, Iceland)
Rest of World is a composite "region" accounting for all remaining world trade.

Source: Table 2 in Hayward R. Alker, Jr., and Donald J. Puchala, "Trends in Economic Partnership in the North Atlantic Area," in *Quantitative International Politics*, J. David Singer, ed. (New York: Free Press, 1966).

Table 13.3 (Continued)

From:	To:	U.K.	U.S.	Canada	Ireland	Region 1	Germany	France	Bel-Lux.	Netherlands	Italy	Region 2	Switzerland	Region 3	Rest of World
Region 1	1928	.1	.0	1.6	1.5	.4	-.3	-.4	-.3	-.2	-.3	-.3	-.7	-.2	.0
	1948	-.3	.1	1.2	.7	.1	-.6	-.4	-.3	-.3	.0	-.2	-.3	-.2	-.1
	1954	-.3	.5	1.8	1.2	.5	-.5	-.6	-.4	-.3	-.4	-.4	-.4	-.2	-.1
	1957	-.3	.7	1.5	1.0	.5	-.5	-.6	-.4	-.3	-.3	-.4	-.4	-.3	-.1
	1959	-.3	.7	1.5	.9	.5	-.6	-.6	-.5	-.3	-.4	-.5	-.4	-.3	-.1
	1963	-.2	.6	1.7	.7	.5	-.5	-.5	-.5	-.3	-.4	-.5	-.4	-.3	.2
Germany	1928	-.5	-.5	-.9	-.8	-.6		.0	.2	1.7	.4	.5	1.8	1.4	.2
	1948	.1	-.7	-.9	-.9	-.4		3.8	4.0	2.7	.4	3.0	2.9	1.5	-.9
	1954	-.7	-.6	-.9	-.4	-.7		.3	1.2	1.2	.9	.9	2.2	1.6	-.1
	1957	-.7	-.5	-.8	-.5	-.6		.4	1.1	1.4	.7	.8	2.9	1.3	-.1
	1959	-.7	-.5	-.8	-.5	-.6		.6	.8	1.2	.7	.8	2.2	1.2	-.1
	1963	-.6	-.5	-.8	-.4	-.6		.7	.8	1.0	.6	.8		.8	-.2
France	1928	-.2	-.6	-.7	-.9	-.4	-.0		3.9	-.3	.3	.6	2.8	-.5	.0
	1948	-.4	-.8	-.9	-.9	-.7	1.0		1.6	.4	-.6	.7	1.5	.2	.3
	1954	-.5	-.8	-.9	-.8	-.6	.5		1.2	-.4	.3	.4	1.5	-.1	.4
	1957	-.5	-.6	-.9	-.6	-.6	.6		1.5	-.2	.3	.5	2.1	-.2	.2
	1959	-.6	-.5	-.8	-.7	-.6	.5		1.1	-.3	.5	.5	1.3	-.3	.3
	1963	-.5	-.7	-.9	-.6	-.6	.7		1.4	-.3	.6	.6	1.9	-.4	.0
Bel-Lux	1928	-.1	-.4	-.7	-.5	-.3	.3	1.2		3.0	-.3	.9	.6	-.0	-.3
	1948	-.4	-.6	-.8	-.3	-.6	.8	.7		4.0	-.3	1.3	2.2	.9	-.3
	1954	-.5	-.8	-.8	-.3	-.5	.7	.9		4.1	-.1	1.4	.8	.5	-.3
	1957	-.5	-.4	-.6	-.2	-.5	.4	1.0		5.3	-.4	1.4	.9	.3	-.4
	1959	-.5	-.2	-.8	-.3	-.4	.6	.9		4.9	-.1	1.3	.6	.1	-.4
	1963	-.5	-.5	-.8	-.5	-.5	.7	1.0		3.0	-.2	1.0	.1	-.3	-.2
Netherlands	1928	.2	-.7	-.8	-.6	-.3	1.2	.0	1.9		-.4	.8	.2	.4	-.3
	1948	.1	-.8	-.9	-.1	-.4	.5	.6	3.9		-.1	1.2	1.2	1.3	-.3
	1954	-.1	-.6	-.9	-.1	-.4	1.8	-.2	3.4		-.3	1.1	.5	1.0	-.3
	1957	.0	-.6	-.9	-.2	-.4	1.6	-.1	4.1		-.2	1.2	.7	1.0	-.4
	1959	-.0	-.7	-.9	-.1	-.5	1.6	.1	3.6		-.1	1.3	.4	.8	-.4
	1963	-.1	-.8	-.9	-.3	-.5	1.4	.2	2.7		.3	.9	.0	.2	-.2

From:	To:	U.K.	U.S.	Canada	Ireland	Region 1	Germany	France	Bel-Lux.	Netherlands	Italy	Region 2	Switzerland	Region 3	Rest of World
Italy	1928	-.5	-.2	-.9	-.8	-.4	.3	.6	-.4	-.7		-.1	3.4	-.6	.3
	1948	-.3	-.5	-.9	-.8	-.4	-.1	.1	-.1	-.3		-.1	2.7	.5	.2
	1954	-.3	-.5	-.9	-.7	-.5	1.0	.2	-.2	-.3		.3	3.8	.1	-.1
	1957	-.4	-.3	-.8	-.7	-.5	1.0	.2	-.2	-.4		.3	4.1	-.2	-.1
	1959	-.3	-.3	-.8	-.8	-.4	1.0	.3	-.2	-.3		.4	3.2	-.1	.0
	1963	-.4	-.4	-.8	-.7	-.5	.9	.7	-.0	-.2		.5	2.1	-.3	-.0
Region 2	1928	-.3	-.5	-.8	-.7	-.4	.3	.3	1.5	1.0	.2	.6	1.7	.4	.0
	1948	-.2	-.7	-.9	-.6	-.5	.6	1.0	2.1	1.7	-.3	1.1	2.0	.8	-.1
	1954	-.5	-.6	-.9	-.5	-.6	.9	.3	1.4	1.0	.4	.8	1.8	.7	.0
	1957	-.5	-.5	-.8	-.5	-.6	.8	.4	1.5	1.4	.3	.8	2.3	.6	-.1
	1959	-.5	-.4	-.8	-.8	-.5	.9	.5	1.2	1.2	.4	.8	1.7	.5	-.1
	1963	-.5	-.6	-.8	-.5	-.6	.9	.7	1.2	.9	.3	.8	1.5	.1	-.1
Switzerland	1928	-.2	-.3	-.5	-.8	-.3	.7	.2	-.3	-.2	1.1	.4		-.1	-.0
	1948	-.7	-.2	-.8	-.6	-.5	.3	.7	2.3	1.1	1.2	1.1		.3	-.1
	1954	-.6	-.2	-.7	-.7	-.4	1.1	.5	.4	-.0	1.9	.8		.3	-.1
	1957	-.4	-.3	-.8	-.8	-.4	.9	.3	.4	.1	1.0	.6		.2	-.0
	1959	-.5	-.3	-.6	-.3	-.4	1.1	.5	.2	.1	1.7	.8		.2	-.1
	1963	-.3	-.3	-.7	-.5	-.3	.9	.6	.0	-.1	1.0	.6		.3	-.3
Region 3	1928	.9	-.5	-.9	-.7	.2	.7	-.4	-.4	-.2	-.5	.1	-.6	5.3	-.6
	1948	.5	-.6	-.9	-.4	-.2	.3	-.1	1.0	1.3	-.1	.4	-.2	3.1	-.3
	1954	.9	-.6	-.9	-.1	-.1	1.0	-.2	.0	.0	-.0	.2	-.3	2.7	-.3
	1957	.7	-.6	-.9	-.3	-.2	.7	-.3	-.1	.0	-.2	.1	-.3	2.3	-.1
	1959	.8	-.5	-.9	-.3	-.1	.9	-.3	-.1	-.1	-.1	.3	-.3	2.9	-.4
	1963	1.0	-.5	-.8	-.3	-.1	.6	.1	-.2	-.0	-.2	.1	-.1	3.9	-.5
Rest of World	1928	.0	.4	-.8	-.8	.0	.1	.2	-.5	-.3	-.1	.0	-.4	-.5	
	1948	.3	.2	-.8	-.4	.1	-.7	.2	-.2	-.3	.0	-.1	-.2	-.2	
	1954	.3	-.1	-.7	-.7	.1	-.1	.4	-.3	-.2	-.1	.0	-.6	-.4	
	1957	.3	.1	-.5	-.5	.1	.0	.4	-.3	-.3	-.1	.0	-.7	-.2	
	1959	.4	.1	-.5	-.4	.1	.0	.3	-.2	-.4	-.1	-.0	-.6	-.3	
	1963	.3	.3	-.5	-.1	.2	-.1	.0	-.3	-.3	.2	-.1	-.8	-.2	

Table 13.4

RATIOS OF FOREIGN TRADE TO NATIONAL INCOME
1913-1963

	1913	1928	1938	1954	1957	1960	1963
Netherlands		77.6	51.7	94.0	95.1	120.0	
Belgium		113.5	68.4	69.5	80.0	94.4	
W. Germany (GFR, 1954-63)	41.6	36.0	14.6	35.4	42.0		38.3
Italy	29.5	30.5	16.6	25.7	31.5	44.2	
France	42.5	46.4	21.3	25.5	26.2		27.8

Sources: 1913-57   Karl W. Deutsch and Alexander Eckstein, "National Industrialization and the Declining Share of the International Economic Sector," World Politics (January 1961), 274-276, Tables 1 and 2, with references.

1960   United Nations, Yearbook of Account Statistics, 1961, pp. 24, 28, 141, 146, 181, 186.

1963   United Nations, Monthly Bulletin of Statistics (April 1965), 107, 167.

declined permanently, suggesting relatively basic changes in French economic and political life.

The *relative* size of the foreign trade sector of a country is a significant indicator of the potential influence and power base of interest groups concerned with foreign trade; and there is some evidence that the attitudes of businessmen closely concerned with foreign trade tend to be significantly less narrowly nationalistic than are the attitudes of businessmen chiefly oriented toward the domestic market.[4] In all these regards, the socioeconomic weight of foreign trade, and of the interests associated with it, had declined substantially in the French economy and body politic.

In earlier sections, it was shown that there was no increase between 1928 and 1963 in the structural integration of French exports, such as they were, to the Six; and that there was only a moderate increase over the same period in the French propensity to accept exports from the Six as imports into France. Since we now find that since 1928 the total weight of all imports and exports in the French national income has declined by more than one-third, it follows that the relative weight within

[4] See Daniel Lerner, "French Business Leaders Look at EDC: A Preliminary Report," *Public Opinion Quarterly* (Spring 1956), 212-221, esp. p. 220.

the French economy of economic links to the Six has suffered a moderate but significant net decline, for the overall share of all French foreign trade among the total of French economic activities has declined by such a substantial amount. This decline precedes the establishment of the Fourth and Fifth French Republic, and the attainment of executive office by General de Gaulle.

In the light of these data, the preference of the French government for a less closely-integrated "Europe of the Fatherlands" and its distant attitude toward British participation in Continental European politics may not be due wholly to the unique personality of General de Gaulle. Rather, these French attitudes may be based in substantial part on the realities of the French economy, polity and social structure, and on the habits and daily behavior of large masses of Frenchmen. To the extent that this is true, many such French attitudes and policies may persist beyond General de Gaulle's tenure of office. They may change slowly over time, but with no certainty that these slow changes will all be in the direction of European integration.

THE PRESENT DISTANCE TO EUROPEAN UNITY: A PROJECTION FROM ECONOMIC DATA

It is possible that the evidence concerning European unity may turn more favorable in future years. Richard L. Merritt's study of the process of integration among the American colonies during the years 1735-1775 shows that the trend of certain quantitative indicators of such integration resembled a learning curve, rising to a temporary peak, then falling back again, but rising still later to new and higher peaks in the course of about two decades.[5] If Western European integration should follow a similar course, a clearly rising trend in relevant mass and elite opinion data, symbols in newspapers, in the RA scores for such intra-European transactions as trade, mail, travel and student exchange should be expected to supervene in the late 1960's or early 1970's. Our present evidence does not exclude this possibility, but it does suggest that no strong increase in the structural integration of Western Europe—that is, in the daily mass behavior of its populations and economies—seems likely to be achieved before the 1960's are ended.

On the level of the aggregate behavior of entire countries and populations, we may consider trade as an indication of integration. A

[5] Richard L. Merritt, *Symbols of American Community, 1735-1775* (New Haven: Yale University Press, 1966).

rough calculation may then permit an appraisal of the distance still to be traversed if the EEC countries were to become as integrated in regard to trade as is a single nation-state of comparable size. Such a nation-state of about 170 million population, and equal to the aggregate of the six EEC countries, *if* it resembled the 73 states for which we have data for the mid-1950's, could be expected to have a foreign trade turn-over (i.e., imports plus exports) of roughly ten per cent of its gross national product (GNP).[6] Since Western Europe is relatively poorer in raw materials and oil, however, than are such large countries as the United States and the Soviet Union, as well as India and Communist China at their present levels of development, it may be more realistic to put the irreducible foreign trade quota of "EEC-land" with the rest of the world at 14 or 15 per cent of GNP, that is, at about twice the corre-sponding quota of the United States which in the 1960's also was import-ing oil, ores and other raw materials from abroad. The remainder of what had been the foreign trade of its formerly sovereign components could then be expected to become internal trade within the larger new unit or federation. In 1957, the total foreign trade of the EEC countries taken together was 34 per cent of their aggregate gross national prod-uct. If they had become one single country, with much the same economic policies as prevailed in other large countries at the time, their residual "foreign" trade with the rest of the world should have shrunk to about ten per cent of their gross national product, and the rest of their former foreign trade, amounting to 24 per cent of their aggregate GNP, should have become part of their domestic trade.

No more integration than this, however, should be expected: Ten or 15 per cent of GNP might be considered almost an irreducible amount of foreign trade in a peacetime private enterprise-cum-welfare economy of 170 million people, and this proportion would thus indicate a limit to the integrative process in regard to trade.[7]

In order to come closer to this limit in their economic behavior, prior to formal political unification, the six EEC countries would have to reach a point where roughly three-fifths of their aggregate foreign trade would remain within the EEC area, leaving only two-fifths of their

---

[6] Cf. The data and regression chart in K. W. Deutsch, Chester Bliss and Alexander Eckstein, "Population, Sovereignty and Trade," *Economic Development and Cultural Change* (July 1962), 353-366 and Figure 1, p. 361.

[7] I am indebted to Professor Robert Triffin for having pointed out to me this line of reasoning. The responsibility for the provisional computations is, of course, my own.—K.W.D.

trade, amounting perhaps to 14 to 15 per cent of their aggregate gross national product, to trading with the rest of the world.

To the extent that the largest member countries of the EEC may be considered smaller but similar versions of the EEC itself, similar proportions should apply to the appraisal of their respective foreign trade as an indicator of European integration. According to this reasoning, Western Germany, for example, if it were as integrated into the EEC area as a district or province is integrated into a national state, might still be expected to have something like 60 or 65 per cent of its foreign trade within the EEC area, and 35 or 40 per cent with the rest of the world. In fact, however, the German Federal Republic in 1957 carried on only about 24 per cent of its foreign trade with other EEC countries, leaving 76 per cent to trade with the rest of the world; and in 1965 the proportions were 37 and 63 per cent respectively—less than two-thirds of the way to the theoretical limits of trade integration indicated earlier. The corresponding figures for France are quite similar: Twenty-eight per cent intra-EEC trade against 72 per cent with the rest of the world in 1928; only 23 and 27 per cent in 1957 and 1959, respectively; and 37 per cent in 1963.[8]

The corresponding figures for all EEC countries, singly and together, and for the middle 1960's, will take more time and effort to compute; and a great deal of research and analysis, as well as studies of relevant historical cases, still remains to be done in this area. The impression at this stage, however, seems clear from this line of investigation: The Western Europe of the EEC countries seems to be less than two-thirds of the way to the level of economic integration normally associated with national states or federations; and it is moving in this direction at a rate that even in 1976 will still leave Western Europe at an appreciable distance from this goal. Any substantially faster rate of progress, on this showing, would require a substantially greater political effort to be made.

THE PACE OF INTEGRATION: TIMETABLES AND CONSTRAINTS

There is still another set of considerations which suggests the need for a larger political effort to lift the social and economic integration

[8] Data from United Nations Statistical Papers, *Directions of International Trade* (1960), pp. 186-190; and Statistical Office of European Communities, *General Statistical Bulletin*, 1966, No. 4, Tables 76-80. We are also indebted to unpublished research by Robert Schaefer, Yale University, 1965-1966.

of Europe out of its recent slowdown.[9] On several matters of European economic policy, firm decisions were reached, with fixed timetables for implementation, notably in regard to tariff reductions and to a common market of the EEC for agricultural products, and particularly for cereals. Some of the early steps in implementing these policies have been carried out, but these early stages demanded far less of a readjustment of existing habits, practices, and interests than the later steps of these same policies are likely to require. Many intra-European tariffs, for example, have been reduced by 60 per cent since 1958, with no major strains resulting, but it seems likely that these tariffs were higher than needed for actual protection.

In view of the rather similar cost conditions for industry in the different EEC countries, it is possible that much of the effective tariff protection for various national industries always rested in the last 20 or 40 per cent of the original tariff rates. Those remaining 20 per cent of the original tariff rates that would have to be eliminated in the next few years under existing European treaties and agreements, together with the informal protection conferred by national consumer preferences and administrative practices, may carry with them most of the effective protection which many national industries thus far have enjoyed, and the actual economic, social and political adjustments to substantial changes in intra-European trade and industry may yet have to be made.

Something similar holds for agriculture. Eventually, the present agreements imply, West German wheat production may have to be substantially reduced and French wheat production expanded, with the added possibility of German imports of United States grain being replaced by French supplies. This would require from West Germany some reduction of her domestic food supply, and perhaps also a loosening of some economic ties with the United States in regard to agricultural imports; and it would sharply increase the German Federal Republic's economic dependence on France, at a time when French political and military ties to NATO and to the United States have been conspicuously loosening. Theoretically and legally, West Germany may have no choice but simply to follow the timetable of the economic agreements that take her in this direction, while French leaders have brought about a drastic change in France's relationship to NATO after 1969, with further changes still to come.

[9] Here again I am indebted to Professor Robert Triffin for valuable suggestions, without wishing to saddle him with responsibility for the results in the present text. —K.W.D.

Some of the fixed and agreed-on timetables of European tariff integration, therefore, may be in serious conflict with the political and military timetables of major European governments, and with the subtler and less readily controllable timetables of the changing social, economic and political aspirations and behavior of the Western European masses and elites.

CHAPTER 14

The Halt in the Growth of Integrative Sentiment: The Evidence of the Elite Press

The impression of a slowdown or halt in the integrative process is confirmed by the evidence of content analysis of "prestige" newspapers. To test changes in French and German elite attention and attitudes between the years 1953 and 1963, and in order to compare them with similar British and American data, four newspapers—*Le Monde*, the *Frankfurter Allgemeine Zeitung*, the London *Times*, and *The New York Times*—were selected as the relatively most representative elite newspapers of France, Germany, Great Britain and the United States, respectively. In these papers, all editorials that appeared in 1953 and in 1963, respectively, and that dealt with intra-European or Atlantic politics were identified, and a sample of 200 such editorials was chosen by random sampling procedures. This sample was then subjected to intensive General Inquirer content analysis by computer.

The procedure of machine content analysis is described in published literature and in a separate report by J. Zvi Namenwirth and Thomas J. Brewer.[1]

THE METHOD OF MACHINE CONTENT ANALYSIS

Lists of about 4000 relevant names, key words, and political symbols were drawn up and grouped into a "dictionary" under 99 themes, such as "European," "Atlantic," "military," "economic," "danger," "positive attitude" (i.e., "sign accept"), "negative attitude" (i.e., "sign reject"). The texts of the sample as well as the dictionary were put on punched cards and then on computer tape. The frequency of each theme was tabulated for each year and paper. The strength and degree of statistical significance of positive or negative association between any clusters of two or more themes were computed, and so was the smallest number of such clusters or "factors" which still account for a substantial variation observed. The changes in each of these factors from paper to paper and from period to period were analyzed, and the significant differences were noted and interpreted in the light of all other information available on the topic.

It turned out that four basic themes, dimensions or factors accounted for 42 per cent of the entire variation observed for all 99 themes, four papers, and both years. The themes, and the share of the total variance accounted for by each, were these:

1. NATO vs. EEC Perspective (16%).
2. Idealized Future vs. Concrete Issues (11%).
3. Supranational Alliance vs. French or German Domestic Politics (8%).
4. United States Pressures for Integration vs. Legal Temporizing (7%).

Comparison among the four papers, and thus indirectly among the four countries whose elites furnish many of their respective readers,

---

[1] See especially J. Zvi Namenwirth and Thomas J. Brewer, "Elite Editorial Comment on the European and Atlantic Communities in Four Countries," in *The General Inquirer: A Computer Approach to Content Analysis*, eds., Philip J. Stone, Dexter C. Dunphy, Marshall S. Smith and Daniel M. Ogilvie (Cambridge: M. I. T. Press, 1966), pp. 401-427. The four newspapers were selected as relatively most representative of elite attention and interest in their respective countries on the basis of our own best knowledge and judgment, and in accordance with the criteria that led to their selection for the earlier study by Ithiel de Sola Pool, with Harold D. Lasswell, Daniel Lerner *et al.*, *The "Prestige Papers": A Survey of Their Editorials* (Stanford, Calif.: Stanford University Press, 1952).

shows that in both 1953 and 1963 expressions of sentiment in favor of general supranational integration of the European countries are strongest in *The New York Times*, whose readers would be least directly involved in carrying out any such policies of integration. It is weaker in the London *Times* and the *Frankfurter Allgemeine Zeitung*, whose readers would be more directly involved; and it is weakest in both 1953 and 1963 in *Le Monde*, many of whose readers are members of the elite of a key country for any serious supranational integration in the West European or North Atlantic area.

The comparison among the four papers also shows that the three European papers resemble each other more in their preferences and distribution of attention, and that they all differ in outlook more strongly from *The New York Times* than they do from each other. In 1963, this difference between the European papers and *The New York Times* was larger than it had been in 1953.

Comparisons between 1953 and 1963 reveal a number of major changes that occurred in the relevant editorials of the elite papers from 1953 to 1963.

THE FOUR MAIN CHANGES IN PRESS ATTENTION AND ATTITUDES, 1953-1963

First, interest in the Atlantic Alliance, with military emphasis and seen against the background of a bipolar world (Dimension I in the factor analysis), has declined markedly in all three European papers during the decade. This decline is moderate but clear in the London *Times*. It is greater in the *Frankfurter Allgemeine Zeitung*; and it is still greater in *Le Monde*. All three European papers have moved toward greater concern with primarily European integration, seen in economic terms and against the background of an increasingly multipolar world. Only *The New York Times* has not shared in this trend. Its editorials alone intensified their Atlantic and military emphasis and their view of the world as a continuing bipolar power system.

Second, there has been a decline in the attention of all four papers to any general political or legal designs for a unified Europe and a corresponding shift to greater concern with concrete difficulties of European integration or cooperation in regard to such matters as agriculture (Dimension II in the factor analysis). In 1963, only *The New York*

Times still maintained a reduced but still marked preponderance of interest in idealized political or legal designs for a unified Europe. The London *Times* and the *Frankfurter Allgemeine Zeitung* dropped their earlier preoccupation with general legal or political schemes for a united Europe and shifted to a clear emphasis on practical day-to-day problems. Finally, *Le Monde*, which had been wary of general European schemes even in 1953, had become considerably more so ten years later.

Third, the concern with domestic French and German controversies, as opposed to any attention given to the requirements and costs of supra-national alliances (Dimension III in the factor analysis), was substantially uniform among all four papers and remained unchanged over the ten-year period. According to some theories of political integration, such concern with domestic controversies should have been expected to decline and the interest in the needs of supranational alliances to increase, if there had been major progress toward supranational integration during that decade. No evidence of such a shift, however, could be found.

Fourth, in all four papers, concern increased from 1953 to 1963 in regard to United States pressure for the extension of the powers of supranational organizations, particularly within an Atlantic framework; and there was a corresponding decline of interest in legal temporizing and in the unchanged maintenance of existing institutions (Dimension IV of the factor analysis). By 1963, supranational integration had become more closely identified with United States initiatives and pressures.

On this issue, the London *Times* and the *Frankfurter Allgemeine Zeitung* shifted from their earlier skepticism toward benevolent neutrality, while *Le Monde* reduced its earlier strong distrust to a more moderate but still marked attitude of skepticism. Only *The New York Times* went very nearly all out from an attitude of moderate but marked concern in 1953 for American initiatives and pressures for European unification. It went so much further in that direction by 1963 that its distance from the European papers on this issue had increased to such an extent that it seemed to be living in a different world from theirs.

The chief form of United States activism, as discussed in these editorials, referred to American efforts to merge military and economic supranational instrumentalities in Europe or in the Atlantic area. Such a linkage between economic and military policies, however, appeared in 1963 as a theme chiefly created by American speakers and writers, with no substantial support in any of the European papers we studied.

THE CONTRAST BETWEEN GROWING EUROPEAN DISTINCTIVENESS AND HALTING EUROPEAN ZEAL

Taking together these different basic themes, or dimensions of editorial discussion, it appears that the three European papers between 1953 and 1963 became somewhat more like each other, albeit at the price of all appearing markedly less zealous in the cause of any general design for European unification or Atlantic Alliance. At the same time, all three European papers became markedly more different in themes and outlook from *The New York Times*. In many respects during the decade, the minds of the European editors and those of the editors of *The New York Times* seem to have been moving in opposite directions.

References to arms control and disarmament were so infrequent in the editorials on European integration and Atlantic politics, as studied in all four papers, that no statistical analysis could be undertaken on them. These problems were largely avoided, in accordance with well-known psychological principles of avoiding painful, frustrating or conflicting themes. Together with the decline in military themes, previously reported, this avoidance might suggest a relatively unstructured European editorial opinion on these matters, with correspondingly greater external freedom of policy choices for the United States. It also suggests perhaps a continuing resistance in the minds of European editors to see Atlantic or European integration as largely or primarily oriented to defense. From the evidence in the press one may speculate whether, ever since the days of the controversy over the abortive European Defense Community (EDC) in 1954, a military or weapons systems emphasis has tended to be a psychological liability rather than an asset to the cause of European integration.[2]

In sum, the evidence of the relevant editorials in *Le Monde* and the *Frankfurter Allgemeine Zeitung* and their comparison with relevant editorials in the London *Times* and *The New York Times* reveal no substantial progress in integrative sentiment, neither in Atlantic nor in European terms, from 1953 to 1963. Rather, Atlantic integrative interest has declined, and the strength of European integrative interest has remained much what it was, with minor modifications.

[2] Cf. Daniel Lerner and Raymond Aron, eds., *France Defeats EDC* (New York: Frederick A. Praeger, Inc., 1957), and contemporary French mass opinion polls reported in *Sondages,* published by Institut Français d'Opinion Publique (IFOP).

CHAPTER 15

A Europe of Nation-States: The Evidence of Mass Opinion

Europe in 1970 and 1975 seems likely to remain predominantly a Europe of nation-states. This is indicated by the expectations of our elite respondents, as well as by mass opinion polls. When elite members were asked: Will Europe be united within the next ten years, only minorities of the articulate respondents—42 per cent in Germany and 19 per cent in France felt it at all possible or were confident that it would be.

THE PERSISTENCE OF NATIONAL THEMES IN MASS OPINION

The answers from mass opinion polls in both countries point the same way, and so does the markedly greater elite and mass attention to national concerns, rather than to European ones. In 14 polls between

245

1951 and 1965, large samples of Germans were asked by German interviewers: "What is the most important question for people in West Germany today to be concerned with?"[1] In January 1965, as many as 47
per cent said "national reunification," and another 4 per cent said
"Berlin," bringing the total percentage giving top priority to these two
national German issues to 51 per cent, while only 3 per cent said "European union." National interests out-polled European interests by more
than fifteen to one for the top spot of attention—and had done much the
same throughout the period. In 1961, after the construction of the Berlin
Wall by the East German Communist regime, when the Germans were
intensely worried about Berlin and badly disappointed in their hopes for
national reunification, sentiment for putting European union in first place
dropped below one half of one per cent, and top preference for the Berlin issue rose to 37 per cent, while the national reunification issue
dropped to about 19 per cent, giving these two national issues a total of
56 per cent of first rankings. Even at this blackest moment of the German hopes for national reunification, national concerns out-polled European concerns by more than twenty to one.

In January 1963, however, after the Cuban crisis of the previous
October, interest in European unification rose to a peak of 12 per cent,
but even then the joint total of the German national issues of reunification (31%) and Berlin (11%) amounted to 42 per cent, and thus still outweighed the peak interest in European unity by more than three to one.

Mass interest in problems of armament, disarmament and nuclear
affairs as a possible first-ranking issue was only slightly higher than it
was in European union; it declined from a high of 15 per cent in January
1955 to 4 per cent in January 1959 and 3 per cent in January 1965,
while interest in the preservation of peace and in an East-West compromise as the most salient issues held at 16 per cent in January 1955 and
1959, but had dropped to 10 per cent by January 1965.

Among the respondents in January 1965, the youngest sub-group—
those 16 to 29 years old—cared slightly more than their elders about
European union (5 per cent), but also about national reunification (50
per cent) and about the Berlin problem (6 per cent) totalling 56 per
cent giving top place to these two national concerns; and they were
somewhat less concerned with questions of disarmament (2 per cent),
peace (3 per cent), and economic questions (20 per cent). Among the

[1] Data on responses to this question are from Institut für Demoskopie, *Pressedienst*,
May 1965.

young, national reunification as the most urgent issue thus still outpulled European union by a ratio of ten to one.

THE GAP BETWEEN FRIENDLINESS AND TRUST

As the nation-state remained the main focus of attention, so it remained the chief repository of trust. Though mutual friendliness between France and Germany increased very markedly between 1952 and 1964 in the mass opinion of the two countries, increases in more definite expressions of trust lagged far behind. General "good" feelings for Germany, reported by French poll respondents, rose spectacularly from 9 per cent in 1954 to 53 per cent in early 1964, while West German "good" feelings about France rose similarly from 12 per cent in 1954 to 46 per cent in early 1963. In February 1964 French "good" feelings toward Germany surpassed for the first time French sympathies for the United States. German "good" feelings toward France, though also much increased, remained confined to a minority of German respondents, and far below the 76 per cent majority holding "very good" or "good" opinions of the United States.

Poll data available for the period 1954-1961 reveal, however, that all answers to specific questions, "Which country would you trust as an ally in case of war?" showed markedly greater trust of France and Germany in Britain, and still much greater trust in the United States, than between those two continental countries. Pessimism between France and Germany about each other's role as an ally was exceeded, however, by pessimism about Italy, as a military ally, which was general.

From 1955 to 1961, the gap between general friendliness and specific trust increased between France and Germany, and between either of these countries and Great Britain; but it did not increase between either France or Germany and the United States. Feelings of mutual friendliness between France and Germany increased further from 1961 to 1964, but few data have become available thus far. The available data to 1961 are summarized in Table 15.1.

If 21 per cent of French respondents in 1961 had indicated trust in Germany, roughly the same proportion—20 per cent—in an early 1965 poll named the German Federal Republic as "the best friend of France," ahead of Great Britain (14%), the United States (12%), Belgium (11%), and the Soviet Union (4%). No other country was named by more than

Table 15.1

FRIENDLINESS AND TRUST IN FRENCH AND WEST GERMAN ATTITUDES TOWARD FOUR COUNTRIES, 1954-1961 *

I = Good feelings
II = Trust in case of war

French Attitudes Toward:	West Germany		Italy		Britain		U.S.	
	I	II	I	II	I	II	I	II
Nov.-Dec. 1955	11	6	—	4	35	30	38	36
Nov. 1956	—	21	—	12	38	47	27	32
Nov. 1957	23	18	—	9	22	19	21	24
June 1961	30	21	32	11	44	32	49	45
Change 1955-1961	+19	+15	—	+7	+9	+2	+11	+9

Trust Gap (II minus I)	West Germany	Italy	Britain	U.S.
Nov.-Dec. 1955	−5	—	−5	−2
Nov. 1956	—	—	+9	+5
Nov. 1957	−5	—	−3	+3
June 1961	−9	−21	−12	−4
Change 1955-1961	−4	—	−7	−2

West German Attitudes Toward:	France		Italy		Britain		U.S.	
	I	II	I	II	I	II	I	II
Dec. 1955	11	5	—	4	35	23	57	49
Nov. 1956	10	9	—	6	14	12	67	51
June 1961	37	20	23	7	53	27	73	65
Change 1955-1961	+26	+15	—	+3	+18	+4	+16	+16

Trust Gap (II minus I)	France	Italy	Britain	U.S.
Dec. 1955	−6	—	−12	−12
Nov. 1956	−1	—	−2	−16
June 1961	−17	−16	−26	−8
Change 1955-1961	−11	—	−14	+4

* Figures given are percentages.

Source: From data in Richard L. Merritt and Donald J. Puchala, eds., *Western European Perspectives on International Affairs: Public Opinion Studies and Evaluations* (New York: Frederick A. Praeger, Inc., 1967).

3 per cent. This scattering of French views compares with the solid 58 per cent of American respondents who named Great Britain as the best friend of their country and with the 56 per cent in Britain who saw their nation's best friend in the United States.[2]

French popular feelings of trust in West Germany had improved moderately from 1955 to 1956, but they did not increase any further from 1956 to 1961, during a period in which more general French feelings of friendliness toward that country had improved so markedly. In June 1961, only 21 per cent of French respondents said that they trusted Germany "a great deal," while slightly more, 23 per cent, declared that they did not trust Germany at all. A majority of Frenchmen in the 1961 poll avoided a decision by saying "up to a point" or "don't know." On the German side, there had been little improvement between 1952 and 1956, but there were small but marked gains from 1956 to 1961. In June 1961, about 20 per cent of German respondents were willing to trust France "a great deal" and only 13 per cent said "not at all." Two-thirds of the German respondents, however, avoided a stand and took refuge in saying "up to a point" or "don't know." So far as the evidence of these polls goes, France and Germany on the mass opinion level continued to trust each other far less than they trusted the United States and Britain.

In evaluating the discrepancy between the substantially increased mutual friendliness in French and German mass opinion, and the absence of any commensurate increase in clear expressions of mutual trust —in contrast to the higher levels of such trust expressed toward Britain and the still higher trust in the United States—one is reminded of the well-known distinction in market research between relatively noncommittal expressions of customers to the effect that a product looks appealing or good to them, and any more firm intention or willingness to buy that product, that is, to commit significant resources to its acquisition and to forego alternative opportunities. The generality of French and German voters, as represented by the samples questioned, seems to have become attracted to the show windows of French-German friendship and European unity, but most of them have not yet formed a firm intention to make a major purchase or definite commitment.

[2] Data from the Institut Français d'Opinion Publique (IFOP), the American Institute of Public Opinion (AIPO), and the British Gallup Institute, reported in EMNID, *Informationen,* No. 12 (22 March 1965), pp. 8-10.

POSSIBILITIES FOR LONG-TERM vs. SHORT-TERM CHANGE

Under the surface of this hesitant development of mass opinion, however, still slower but potentially cumulative changes may be in the making. Factor analysis of French and German opinion poll results between 1954 and 1962 indicates a marked increase in the similarity of underlying images between the two countries, as expressed by the amount of observed opinion variation that could be accounted for by factors common to opinion in both countries.[3]

In particular, there was a marked increase between 1954 and 1962 in the importance of an image of a united Europe in both French and German opinion. Most of this increase occurred between 1957 and 1962.

During the same years, there occurred a marked decline in the perception of any military threat and of the danger of nuclear war. Increased relevance of European unity thus appeared quite compatible with a decreased sense of military danger.

The overall impression from the analysis of the trend of French and German mass opinion data from 1954 to 1962 is that of opinion halting or hesitating at a threshold. There is a consensus that European unity is a good thing, and that some steps should be taken to maintain and strengthen what European unity there is, and to go somewhat further in that direction. There seems to be no clear image in mass opinion as to what these steps should be, or how far they should go, nor is there any sense of urgency about them. German mass views are more clearly favorable on this abstract level, while French views are more reserved, particularly in regard to political integration. In neither country, however, was there a clear image of, or any strong desire for, merging the bulk and substance of national sovereignty in a larger European government or political decision system. While it seemed ready to accept further marginal reductions of national sovereignty in favor of European institutions, both French and German opinion continued to take for granted the national state as the main arena of day-to-day politics and the chief instrumentality of government.

At the same time, the data suggest that mass opinion has been coming to accept the general notion of European unity. There is, thus, now in European mass opinion a latent clash between the continuing

[3] Data on which the findings in this section are based are presented in Donald J. Puchala, "European Political Integration: Progress and Prospects" (New Haven: Yale University, Political Science Research Library mimeographed, 1966).

acceptance of the reality of the nation-state and the newly accepted image of some vague sort of European unity.

The ensemble of the present public moods would not be much help to statesmen who would lead their countries toward a greatly deepened union. Rather, they may facilitate general expressions of good will, combined with policies of temporizing, caution, national consolidation, and only gradual and sectoral advance toward somewhat greater European integration. Bolder steps toward substantially greater European unity would have to be "sold to" mass opinion by the sustained and concerted efforts of leaders and elites—assuming that these elites had the capacity and motivation to do so in preference to other short-run goals.

CHAPTER 16

National States and Limited
Supranational Steps

The results of the elite interviews conducted in the summer of
1964 with 147 French and 173 West German respondents have been incorporated in earlier sections of this book, together with some interpretations and judgments of the authors.[1] Only a few major points will be in-

[1] In preparing the present summary, percentages are given on the basis of all 310
elite members included in the survey, including those who said "don't know," and
also those who for one reason or another did not comment on this particular question,
if this category amounted to no more than five per cent of the total. If a larger
proportion did not touch on a particular question, the percentages given refer only
to the "articulate" respondents, that is, to those who did make any comment, even
if they only professed themselves to be undecided or uninformed. In the cases
where the percentages refer only to the "articulate" respondents—in most cases more
than three-quarters, and practically always more than two-thirds, of the total—the
actual number of articulate respondents has been indicated. Only those statistically
significant findings are reported here. Responses to all questions are given in detail in
Karl W. Deutsch, Lewis J. Edinger, Roy C. Macridis, Richard L. Merritt, and Helga
Voss-Eckermann, *French and German Elite Responses, 1964: Codebook and Data*
(New Haven: Yale University, Political Science Research Library mimeographed,
1966).

The footnotes with the notation "Q.," followed by one or several numbers,
refer to the number of each interview question, as given with a tabulation of responses in Deutsch *et al.*, *French and German Elite Responses,* where further details
can be checked. The punch cards for the study may be obtained at nominal cost
from the Political Science Research Library of Yale University.

dicated here, based both on the frequencies of responses received and on the qualitative aspects which emerged in the context of extended interviews.

PERSISTENT NATIONALISM WITH MAJOR CLEAVAGES: THE DIVIDED ELITES OF FRANCE

French elite responses show the continuing strength of self-assertive nationalism, not only in terms of numbers but also in terms of the more subtle indications of emotional involvement attached to them. At present, this nationalism is not aggressive; it does not appear to be directed toward the conquest or reconquest of colonies or territories. Rather it is centered upon the tenacious and continued assertion of a unique French identity, which must not become submerged or lost in any larger non-French political system. Nearly seven-eighths of elite respondents see the current policies of France as increasingly nationalistic in flavor, and nearly three-quarters see the world as an increasingly multilateral power system, replacing the earlier bipolar pattern of American-Soviet predominance. Three-fifths pronounce themselves definitely in favor of this world trend, and another one-fifth support it with reservations. A special "manifest destiny" for France is asserted by 53 per cent of the respondents, but opposed by a very strong minority of 46 per cent.[2]

The 65 younger members of the French elite—those under 50 years of age—are more strongly united than their elders in perceiving current French policies as increasingly nationalistic (89%) and the world as multipolar (77%), as well as in approving of the world trend they perceived (65%), but only a strong minority (47%) of the articulate young affirms a belief in a manifest destiny for France. The younger members of the French elite thus may be more likely than their elders to back President de Gaulle and his successors in policies designed to fit the idea of an increasingly multipolar world in which the old bipolar American and Soviet leadership in two rival coalitions of West and East is becoming obsolete. They are less likely, however, to back affirmative assertions of a French nationalism or manifest destiny, which only a strong minority among them seems willing to endorse outright.

As far as this evidence goes, any United States policy that seems to

[2] Q. 46; Q. 25; Q. 26; Q. 34. In these and the following chapters, response percentages for subgroups, such as those by age or occupation, are given when they seem to differ significantly from the national elite average.

put pressure on France to conform to American ideas of coalition leadership might thus be resisted not only by avowed Gaullists but by almost three-quarters of French elite members, and by even more among the young. At the same time, a visibly tolerant and accommodating policy toward France—if carried through without an air of condescension—should make it very hard for President de Gaulle or his successor to rally any strong majority support among the young elites for any unprovoked nationalistic initiatives unfriendly to the United States.

Among the occupational groups, a somewhat stronger minority of intellectuals (22%) thinks that current French policies are only in part nationalistic, rather than predominantly so, but the intellectuals as a group show the strongest consensus on the image of a multipolar world (85%). This latter view is also endorsed, however, by more than two-thirds of the businessmen and of the politicians, and by 70 per cent or more of the remaining groups. Thus the most striking impression of French elite nationalism, next to its strength, is its relatively even distribution—particularly in view of the fact that outright Gaullists form less than one-fifth of our sample.

STRENGTHENED NATIONAL CONSENSUS AND GREATER READINESS FOR SUPRANATIONAL STEPS: THE INTEGRATED ELITES OF THE GERMAN FEDERAL REPUBLIC

In striking contrast to France, the strongest impression from the German elite interviews is the high degree of consensus on the domestic regime and on the basic policies of the German Federal Republic. Unlike their French counterparts, nearly three-quarters of the German respondents express themselves definitely as satisfied with the regime, and the addition of those moderately satisfied brings the chorus of approval to 93 per cent. Only 4 per cent admit even moderate dissatisfaction, and no West German respondent at all is recorded as dissatisfied to any more definite extent.[3]

Strong majorities expressing definite approval of the GFR regime are found among German elite respondents at all levels of age and class, and in all groupings of occupation, religion, present political party affiliation and pre-1945 political record. This definite support is strongest among those with no pre-1945 political affiliation (85%), lower middle-class background (81%), Roman Catholic faith (81%) and current CDU/

[3] Q. 1.

CSU ties (77%), but it is also above the 70 per cent level among former Nazis, and among current SPD members, and at or above 65 per cent among Protestants and among members of Germany's small third party, the FDP. It is relatively lowest among former anti-Nazis, but there, too, it comprises a clearcut majority of 55 per cent, with another 33 per cent expressing moderate satisfaction, so as to bring the ensemble of all degrees of approval for the regime to 88 per cent for this group.[4]

Groups most strongly and definitely supporting the regime are the military (93%), the non-business interest groups (85%), the civil servants (81%), and the younger leaders (80%). Even moderate dissatisfaction is negligible in all groups.[5]

If the definitely satisfied are further divided into those "highly satisfied" and those just simply "satisfied," then again Roman Catholics (25%), CDU/CSU adherents (23%), elite members of lower middle-class background (21%), and those with no political affiliations during the Nazi era (21%) emerge with the strongest proportions of pro-regime enthusiasts. The bulk of support for the GFR regime within these groups, however, as in all groups, is solid rather than enthusiastic, with neither accolades nor reservations.[6]

CONTRASTING FRENCH AND GERMAN ELITE PERCEPTIONS OF THEIR OWN INFLUENCE

The contrast between the highly integrated West German elites and the divided and partly alienated elites of France appears strikingly in the respective assessments of the members of each group of their own actual influence over the politics and policies of their own country.

As recorded by the interviewers, 73 per cent of the 131 German respondents about whom we have such data convey a sense of perceiving themselves as having actual influence above the average in regard to the general affairs of their country, as against 13 per cent who see their influence as below average; and 65 per cent of 100 articulate respondents see themselves as wielding more actual influence than the average in regard to foreign policy, as against only 13 per cent who assess their actual influence as below average. Among the 133 articulate French, only 33 per cent see their actual influence as higher than average in regard to

[4] Q. 1, by religion, class and current and former party affiliation.
[5] Q. 1, by age and occupation.
[6] Q. 1, by religion, class and current and past political affiliation.

political affairs in general, with nearly as many—28 per cent—considering their own influence in these matters as below average. In regard to foreign policy, the French balance tips: Only 18 per cent of the 133 articulate respondents think that their actual influence is above average, and twice as many—36 per cent—perceive their own influence on foreign policy as less than average.[7]

Some of these French-German contrasts presumably reflect the actual procedural differences between the committee politics of post-Adenauer Germany and the personal style of leadership of President de Gaulle in France. They probably also reflect, however, a contrast between considerable German elite identification with, and partial French elite divisions about, or alienation from, many of the substantive current policies of their respective countries.[8]

Striking differences between the French and the German elites appear also in the degree of alienation from the politics and institutions of their country, as shown by each respondent during his interview and as noted by the interviewer immediately afterwards. "Alienation," of course, is a somewhat technical term for the well-known feelings of estrangement and distrust, of not belonging, of being excluded from, not caring for and not identifying with some otherwise familiar and supposedly "normal" environment, group or institution. In politics, this feeling is often expressed by many subtle cues, such as by saying "they," instead of "we," when speaking of one's country or one's government. A high degree of alienation thus means a low degree of identification or solidarity. In rating our respondents, on the degree of alienation which each had conveyed in regard to his national political system, our interviewers found that 30 per cent of the French, but only 19 per cent of the Germans, had shown such alienation at least to a "higher than average" extent.[9]

French elite respondents also convey a higher sense of anxiety, and a lower sense of their own efficacy, than do their German colleagues. Among 134 Frenchmen, 38 per cent convey an above-average sense of their efficacy in domestic politics, as against 34 per cent who seem more anxious than the average. Among the corresponding 113

[7] Q. 4b, Latent Attitude, Deck I.
[8] The substance of these findings is not likely to be accounted for by any effects of interviewer bias. The results are stable for both groups of interviewers—four in France and four in Germany—and they are confirmed by the parallel results of an independent elite study in France and Germany by Professor Daniel Lerner of the Massachusetts Institute of Technology and Professor Morton Gorden of the University of Pennsylvania. (Personal communication from Daniel Lerner, 2 February 1966.)
[9] Q. 16, Latent Attitudes.

German elite members for whom ratings are available, only 19 per cent seemed to feel more anxious, and as many as 60 per cent more efficacious, than the average in domestic matters. In regard to foreign policy, 36 per cent of the French elite respondents feel efficacious above the average, but a slightly larger proportion—38 per cent—feel more anxiety than average. Among the 113 German elite members rated on this point, efficacy wins out over anxiety by nearly two to one: Forty-seven per cent stress their sense of efficacy, and only 24 per cent seem to feel more anxious than the average.[10]

Finally, French elite members were rated by interviewers as more toughminded in domestic politics than in regard to foreign affairs; West German leaders, on the contrary, appear more toughminded toward foreigners than toward their own countrymen. "Toughmindedness" can be defined roughly as the perceived psychological readiness and willingness of a respondent to accept some harm to himself and to others, as the price of a policy he desires. Among 136 French respondents who were rated, the proportions of toughminded attitudes are 65 per cent in domestic matters and 59 per cent in regard to foreign policy; the corresponding West German proportions among the 152 and 154 West Germans so rated are 52 per cent in domestic affairs and 63 per cent in foreign policy.[11]

Taking together the ratings on efficacy and anxiety, toughmindedness and alienation reported in the preceding paragraphs of this section, it appears that a significant proportion of French leaders feel toughminded but ineffective and anxious in dealing with their own countrymen and, to a lesser extent, with their international environment. In West Germany, this toughminded but frustrated group is smaller, and its remaining frustrations seem to be less in the domestic than in the foreign field.

DIVIDED FRENCH VIEWS ON SUPRANATIONAL INTEGRATON BUT CONSENSUS ON ALLIANCES

On many issues, hardcore nationalist views command only minority support among French elites, with other minorities taking a more internationalist or integrationist posture. A plurality of nearly one-half denies flatly that Western Europe will be unified within the next ten years, while nearly one-fifth definitely expect this to happen and roughly an-

[10] Q. 10, b-1 and b-2, Latent Attitudes.
[11] Q. 11, b-1 and b-2, Latent Attitudes.

other one-third say, "It depends." As to the preferred form of European integration, if and when such integration should occur, French elite members are almost evenly divided: Forty-nine per cent want supranational institutions to predominate, but 41 per cent want the nation-states to remain dominant, and another 15 per cent prefer "confederation"—an answer which either avoids a decision or carries the somewhat conflicting implications of a confederation of sovereign states and of the possibility of majority rule among them.[12]

More strongly nationalistic views tend to find less support. Only 26 per cent endorse "an independent foreign policy" for France, even conditionally, and 30 per cent name national instrumentalities as the best means for defending the French national interest, whereas 62 per cent prefer a foreign policy of alliances, and 70 per cent choose alliances and other more international arrangements as the best means of national defense.[13] (See also page 259.)

Confidence in European integration within the next ten years is highest among the old. Among respondents under 60 years of age, however, clear majorities say that this will not happen. Pessimism about European integration is strongest among the French military—not one of whom thinks that it will be achieved within ten years—and also among civil servants and businessmen.[14]

Even within an integrated Europe, the nation-states should predominate according to majorities of the military, the businessmen and the intellectuals, whereas a majority of the civil servants would prefer supranational institutions to prevail. National dominance is also preferred by 50 per cent of the Middle Elite—those between 50 and 60 years of age—but supranational dominance appeals to a 49 per cent plurality of the younger leaders.[15] Strong groups among the young thus seem to be both sympathetic to supranationalism and pessimistic about European integration, at least for the next ten years.

National action in foreign policy is not backed by a majority in any age group or occupation, but the strongest nationalist minorities in regard to this issue are found among the Middle Elite age group, the military and the politicians.[16]

There is substantial French consensus in favor of a policy of alli-

[12] Q. 50; Q. 48.
[13] Q. 27 and 28.
[14] Q. 50, by age and occupation.
[15] Q. 48, by age and occupation.
[16] Q. 27, by age and occupation.

ances and of at least some moderate further reductions of national sovereignty. As mentioned earlier, an independent national policy for France is endorsed, at least conditionally, by only 26 per cent of respondents. Its unconditional supporters within that group, however, amount only to 12 per cent, while a much stronger minority, 44 per cent, definitely favors cooperation in alliances, and an additional 18 per cent do so conditionally, bringing the total of those favoring alliances at least somewhat to a majority of 62 per cent. An even larger majority, 83 per cent, is willing, at least conditionally, to favor efforts toward further limitations on national sovereignty; and more than one-half of this support—45 per cent of all respondents—is definite, and only 14 per cent express any degree of opposition—even conditionally—to this supranational trend.

Nonetheless, much of the internationalist or supranationalist feeling in France is limited and qualified. Enthusiasts form only 25 per cent of the French respondents, against 38 per cent who explicitly insist on conditions for their support—in contrast to West Germany, where these proportions are reversed. (A more detailed comparison of French and German elite views on this point is presented in Table 16.1.)

On these matters, the majority consensus among French elite members seems clearly more favorable than the current policies of President de Gaulle in regard to limited steps toward international alliances and increased participation in supranational institutions.[17] It seems tempting to speculate that eventually General de Gaulle himself, or else the regime succeeding him, may well make some limited gestures—and even take some limited actual steps—in such a more international direction.

Definite support for further reductions of national sovereignty is greatest among non-business interest groups, civil servants and the younger leaders. It is weakest among the military, businessmen, the middle-aged leaders and the politicians, but the military, the businessmen and the Mid-Elite are foremost in giving such support conditionally. Together, definite and conditional supporters form a large majority in every group. The strongest minority holding out definitely for undiminished national sovereignty—23 per cent—is found among the politicians.[18]

Although independent national action in foreign policy is supported only by about a quarter of all respondents, even conditionally, it

[17] Q. 47.
[18] Q. 47, by age and occupation.

Table 16.1

FRENCH AND WEST GERMAN VIEWS ON THE SENSIBILITY OF FURTHER LIMITATIONS OF NATIONAL SOVEREIGNTY

QUESTION: *To what extent do you consider efforts in this direction (limiting national sovereignties in favor of international associations) to be sensible?*

	FRANCE		GERMANY	
	Number of Respondents	Percentage	Number of Respondents	Percentage
Enthusiastically in favor of further limitations of sovereignty	29	20%	79	46%
Generally in favor of further limitations of sovereignty (not excited about it)	37	25	43	25
Conditionally in favor of further limitations of sovereignty (if conditions prevail or develop)	56	38	34	20
Indifferent; undecided	3	2	1	1
Conditionally against further limitations of sovereignty	8	5	4	2
Generally opposed	9	6	4	2
Vehemently opposed	4	3	0	0
Not ascertained	1	1	8	5
Total	147	100%	173	101%

is more popular among the military, the politicians and the Mid-Elite. Cooperation in alliances is definitely preferred only by strong pluralities among all respondents and in most occupational and age groups, but it has definite and strong majority support only among the non-business interest groups (which include church organizations, farm groups and labor unions). Nearly half of the young as well as of the Senior Elite definitely favor a policy of alliances, as against hardly more than one-fourth of the Mid-Elite who do so.[19]

[19] Q. 27, by age and occupation.

These foreign alliances, however, are seen by many respondents as just that: alliances between sovereign and equal powers. Even the American alliance, accepted as necessary by a large majority of the French, is not to extinguish or submerge the autonomy of France. And the French acceptance of a rapprochement with Germany is tempered even more strongly with nationalistic reservations.

ALLIANCE AND INTEGRATION: THE WEST GERMAN FOREIGN POLICY CONSENSUS

Again in contrast to the situation in France, the foreign policy of the German Federal Republic is seen as decidedly oriented toward further limitations of national sovereignty by 55 per cent of German elite respondents, and has the definite support of the same proportion, 55 per cent. The addition of moderate supporters then brings the German majority consensus on foreign policy to 74 per cent. A plurality of 31 per cent of the cumulated multiple responses to another question forecasts that "all features" of current West German foreign policy will continue beyond Chancellor Erhard's tenure of office, and another 30 per cent single out the current—and highly cooperative—West German policies toward the United States and toward NATO as likely to continue, so that the definite consensus on the post-Erhard continuity of West Germany's current policy toward the United States and NATO totals 61 per cent.[20]

Continuity for Bonn's current (1964) policies of French-German rapprochement and European integration is explicitly forecast by 17 per cent; together with the 31 per cent who expect "all features" of current West German foreign policies to continue, this amounts to 48 per cent, just short of a majority.[21]

Unconditional support for current West German foreign policy is highest among civil servants (69 per cent) and businessmen (67 per cent). Definite disapproval averages only 14 per cent, but is more than doubled (29%) among university professors. Belief in the post-Erhard continuity of the Federal Republic's policies toward the United States and NATO is strongest among the military (91%), the politicians (69%) and the civil servants (68%); it is weakest among the mass media leaders (37%) and among the non-business interest groups (52%). These

[20] Q. 31; Q. 33.
[21] Q. 33.

last two groups, however, compensate to some extent for their weaker "Atlantic" orientation by leading with stronger explicit expectations of continuity for West Germany's policies toward France and European integration, with 26 and 22 per cent, respectively. Since their expectations for a continuation of "all features" of foreign policy are far below average, however, their total endorsement of continued French-German friendship and European integration also remains somewhat below average.[22]

The West German elite consensus is overwhelming in regard to Germany's need for allies. As many as 93 per cent name alliances and international instrumentalities as the instruments for defending the national interest. No one at all named a national nuclear deterrent; and only seven per cent chose national instrumentalities such as national conventional weapons or national diplomacy. Responding to another question, 79 per cent definitely—in contrast to a mere plurality of 44 per cent in France—favor cooperation in alliances, but only 6 per cent in Germany favor an independent national foreign policy even conditionally, in contrast to a more sizable minority (26%) of Frenchmen. Enduring common interests of Germany with the United States are stressed by 72 per cent of German elite respondents; and 71 per cent endorse policies favoring supranationalism and bringing about further reductions of national sovereignty.

Current West German foreign policy is seen by 55 per cent as clearly directed toward further limitations of national sovereignty, while another 34 per cent think that the trend is mixed, but only 3 per cent see it as increasingly nationalistic.[23]

The support for alliances and international instrumentalities as the best means to defend the national interest is virtually uniform among all groups, but rises to 100 per cent among civil servants and the young.

As a foreign policy, cooperation in alliances (as opposed to any independent national foreign policy) is backed most strongly by the military (93%), the politicians (87%) and, once again, the young (87%), whereas 30 per cent of the businessmen hedged on this issue.[24]

Enduring common interests with the United States are perceived fairly uniformly among all groups. Efforts toward further reductions

[22] Q. 31, by occupation; Q. 33, by occupation.
[23] Q. 28; Q. 27; Q. 35 and 47; Q. 46.
[24] Q. 28, by age and occupation; Q. 27, by age and occupation.

in national sovereignty find most definite favor among university professors (86%), the military (79%), the Middle and Junior Elites (74%) and the politicians, but only bare majority support (52%) among the mass media personnel.[25]

The belief that current West German policies are decidedly directed toward further limitations of national sovereignty is endorsed by majorities in all age groups. It is held most strongly by politicians and civil servants (68 and 63 per cent, respectively), but only by 38 per cent of the mass media personnel. A bare majority of the latter, and of the university professors—52 per cent in each case—considers current GFR policies as mixed, partly nationalistic and partly supranational.[26]

There is less agreement among German leaders as to just how far these internationalist policies will go, or ought to go. A strong plurality (46%) expects European integration to be achieved within the next ten years, while 35 per cent consider this unlikely. A predominantly supranational form of European union—if it should come to pass—is chosen by a bare majority of the respondents, but 46 per cent prefer either "confederation" (25%) or arrangements implying the clearcut predominance of nation-states (21%). In France, only 19 per cent of the cumulated responses expect European union within 10 years, while 49 per cent explicitly do not; and 58 per cent prefer either confederation (15 per cent) or national predominance (43 per cent).[27]

Believers in European integration within ten years form a majority only in two German groups, the military and the politicians (67 and 52 per cent, respectively). Explicit pessimism is weakest among the young (26 per cent), and strongest among businessmen (44%), civil servants (44%), university professors (43%) and the leaders between 50 and 60 years of age (43%).[28]

CHANGED FRENCH AND GERMAN ATTITUDES TO EDC

German internationalism has significantly weakened, however, in regard to the project of a European Defense Community (EDC), which was to merge the conventional forces of France, Germany, Italy and

[25] Q. 35, by age and occupation; Q. 47, by age and occupation.
[26] Q. 46, by age and occupation.
[27] Q. 48 and 50.
[28] Q. 50, by age and occupation.

the Benelux countries, and which in 1954 had been accepted by all these countries except France. In 1964, views about EDC had become divided in Germany as well as in France. Only 35 per cent of the 152 German leaders who gave their views on this matter still clearly favor EDC, but 44 per cent are definitely opposed; and if conditional opponents and supporters are included, German elite members still reject EDC by a plurality of 49 against 46 per cent.

German opposition to EDC is now strongest among the younger leaders (61%), the military (57%), the mass media leaders (55%) and the politicians (55%). It is still relatively most popular with the Middle Elite of 50- to 60-year-olds and with civil servants (both 44%).[29]

This German change in attitude may not be unrelated to the increased military strength of the German Federal Republic, and so may be the corresponding and converse change in France. The French elite members, whose country had rejected EDC in 1954, endorsed EDC ten years later; though only a very small plurality of the 51 French leaders who comment on this topic do so in definite terms, 23 per cent in favor and 18 per cent against. The addition of conditional responses swells this small and possibly unrepresentative French pro-EDC group to a majority of 54 per cent of the articulate respondents, against 30 per cent who are either definitely or at least conditionally opposed.[30] This proportion of at least conditional French support for EDC seems close to the 55 per cent of the French elite respondents who, according to the Lerner-Gorden survey in 1961, favored a revival of EDC, or the 49 per cent who at that time endorsed the integration of "a major part" of the French armed forces into "a permanent supranational army" under either European or NATO command.[31]

The EDC project by 1964 still tended to divide French opinion rather than to unify it, almost as much as it did by then in Germany, and it continued to divide the two countries. The divergent French and German views of the EDC project, however, are only a minor instance of the divergent images which the elite majorities in each of the two countries hold of the world in which they are living.

---

[29] Q. 83, by age and occupation.
[30] Q. 83.
[31] Morton Gorden and Daniel Lerner, "The Setting for European Arms Controls: Political and Strategic Choices of European Elites," *Journal of Conflict Resolution*, 9 (December 1965), pp. 419-33.

CHAPTER 17

Multipolar or Bipolar: French and German Perceptions of World Politics

In contrast to France, two-thirds of the West German leaders continue to see the world as a bipolar power system, dominated by the United States and the Soviet Union, and they believe that it will remain so. Among the French leaders, on the contrary, nearly three-quarters see an increasingly multipolar world around them. Faith in a continuing bipolar world is strongest among West German non-business interest groups (82%) and mass media personnel (76%), but it is shared only by a minority of German civil servants (44%). Explicit belief in a multipolar world is relatively stronger among civil servants (50%), politicians (40%) and the younger leaders (36%).[1]

This continuing bipolar world is accepted as a practical reality by a majority of German leaders: 58 per cent of the 150 articulate respondents on this point are willing to have within NATO a multilateral

[1] Q. 25; Q. 25, by age and occupation.

nuclear force (MLF) commanded only by the United States (56%) or by the United States and Britain (2%), and only 33 per cent demand a command structure in which Germany might be included directly or indirectly.[2]

Nearly one-half of the German leaders indicate some emotional attachment to the image of a bipolar world. Among the 66 per cent of German leaders who think that the world will stay bipolar, or will become even more so, more than three out of five (62%) definitely like the trend they think they see; and only one in ten among them feels clearly dissatisfied with it. By contrast, among the 30 per cent who think that the world is becoming increasingly multipolar, and the era of American-Soviet predominance is waning, only about two out of five welcome this trend as it appears to them; and more than two out of ten definitely express themselves in opposition, bringing the aggregate proportion of those with emotional attachments to the bipolar perspective to 47 per cent of all respondents (as against 22 per cent who would like a multipolar world).[3]

The French-German contrast here is not only one of cognition, but of preference. The relevant German desires may be not only some abstract calculations as to whether German national interests might fare better in a bipolar or a multipolar world, but also perhaps a very human inclination of many West German leaders to justify and protect their past political investments in a set of West German policies, geared to such a bipolar perspective, to which some of these leaders have committed much of their efforts, their reputations, and even aspects of their self-image as patriots and realists. The strength of these German emotional ties to the bipolar perspective, and the anxieties aroused when it appears to be challenged, together with the emotional ties of many French elite members to a multipolar view, may continue for some time to raise difficulties for any closer French-German cooperation in European affairs, and generally in international politics.

In the bipolar world in which many German leaders think they are living, any French assertion of national independence arouses suspicions of unreliability and fears of betrayal of the embattled alliance of the West. In the multipolar world which many French leaders think they see around them, all alliances are likely to be transitory and today's ally is also a potential rival for tomorrow. This difference in national

[2] Q. 58.
[3] Q. 25 and 26, cross-tabulated.

perspectives may well help to retard the development of German trust in the French and of French trust in the Germans.

FRENCH ELITE CAUTION TOWARD GERMANY

Such persistent nationalist feelings clearly seem to play a part in the overwhelming French consensus on great caution toward Germany, or on *not* trusting her beyond a certain point. Even where French respondents do not state their views explicitly, nearly all of them in one way or another convey indications of some distrust. Nearly one-half of the French elite respondents do not state their views on the French interest in German reunification; of those 77 who did speak out, 58 per cent consider it a threat to French security, and only 32 per cent think that it might make France more secure. Consistent with this, only seven per cent of those 109 French leaders who expressed their views on this point flatly favor German reunification, while another 32 per cent do so conditionally, and a majority of 55 per cent opposes it at least conditionally, including 28 per cent of unconditional opposers. As to reliance on West Germany as an ally, almost all Frenchmen—136 out of 147— went on record, but only a handful—nine per cent—of those who gave opinions would rely on her "a great deal," although 85 per cent say they would trust her "up to a point." [4]

Generally, moderate distrust of Germany is much higher among the French elite, and clearcut trust and distrust are much lower, than they are on the level of French mass opinion, as reported in Table 15.1.

Sympathy for German reunification is relatively strongest among French leaders of 60 years and older, among the military, the civil servants and slightly less so among businessmen. Opposition is most pronounced among the young leaders, and nearly as much so among the Middle Elite group between 50 and 60 years of age, that is, the political generation of Gaullism and World War II; and there are even stronger misgivings among intellectuals, non-business interest groups and politicians. Three-fifths of the articulate politicians in our sample declare themselves at least conditionally opposed to German reunification.[5]

Trust or distrust toward Germany as an ally is similarly distributed. The Senior Elite is more than nine-tenths cautious, but none of them

[4] Q. 38; Q. 37; Q. 59.
[5] Q. 37 and 38, by age and occupation.

express acute distrust. Clearcut trust and distrust are expressed by more than one-eighth, respectively, among the Middle Elite, but here, too, 72 per cent cautiously say they trust Germany "to a limited extent." Trust in Germany is professed by minorities of one in six or one in seven among businessmen, civil servants and the military, but the attitude of caution is overwhelming in all French groups.[6]

GERMAN ELITE CAUTION TOWARD FRANCE

If 85 per cent of the French respondents chose the noncommittal middle position "to a limited extent" in answering the question whether France could rely on Germany as an ally, a similar attitude of caution is adopted by only 33 per cent of the 153 German leaders who indicate their degree of trust in France. The rest of the articulate West German leaders is divided: 29 per cent are willing to trust France "a great deal," but a plurality of 39 per cent say "not at all."

In these German views of France, as in the French views of Germany, explicit distrust is much stronger at the elite level than it is in mass opinion. The division of views is sharpest among the 34 members of the German Junior Elite who expressed their views: 32 per cent trust France a great deal, but 41 per cent refuse to trust her at all. Among German occupational groups, the most cautious and noncommittal are the military; most trustful toward France, the civil servants; most distrustful, the university professors, again the civil servants—who seem most strongly divided—and the mass media elite. Every German age or occupational group, however, is strongly divided on this issue of how far to trust France.

DIFFERENCES IN FRENCH AND GERMAN WORLD IMAGES ON THE MASS OPINION LEVEL

The different perception of world politics by the elites of France and Germany is to a considerable extent paralleled, and perhaps reinforced, by contrasting perceptions on the level of mass opinion. A considerable number of French and German public opinion polls from the years 1952-1962 were analyzed, for the purpose of making comparisons between the two countries, as well as comparisons of political attitudes among different groups, and comparisons with a smaller number of com-

[6] Q. 59, by age and occupation.

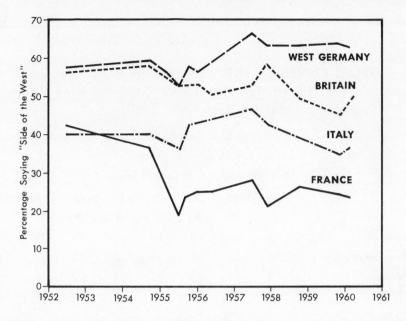

parable polls from Italy and Britain. Methods used included the chart-
ing of trends with the help of graphs, and factor analysis with the aid
of computers. From these analyses several tentative findings emerge.
Throughout the periods 1954-1958 and 1959-1962, the difference between French and German mass opinion on many substantive foreign
policy issues tended to be larger than that between opinion in either
of these countries and that in Italy or Britain, or between British and
Italian attitudes (Figure 17.1).

Conversely, questions about the Western Alliance in peacetime,
and about the same alliance in case of war, reveal very marked decreases between 1954 and 1958 in its support by French respondents
for either case, and by German opinion for the latter and more serious
eventuality, but considerable stability in the British popular commitment
(Table 17.1). French peacetime support for the West, as well as for
the United States in case of war, declined drastically before 1955, and
it does not appear to have recovered much thereafter. President de
Gaulle's cool policy toward the United States followed at least two years
after this shift in French mass opinion. By 1958, this shift was accen-
tuated further by the increase in the proportion of respondents who
said explicitly, "neither side" (rather than merely "don't know"), from
58 per cent in June 1955 to 67 per cent in October 1958. This increase

Table 17.1

SUPPORT EXPRESSED FOR THE WEST IN PEACETIME AND FOR THE UNITED STATES IN CASE OF WAR WITH RUSSIA, 1952-1960*

A—Side with West at present
B—Side with U.S. in case of war

	Sept. 1952		June 1955		Oct. 1958		Feb. 1960	
	A	B	A	B	A	B	A	B
France	42	36	18	19	26	23	23	—
West Germany	58	52	52	41	63	38	62	—
Italy	40	36	37	34	31	30	36	—
Britain	57	58	52	57	49	48	49	—

Gap between support in war and peacetime (B — A)

France	−6	+1	−3	—
West Germany	−6	−11	−25	—
Italy	−4	−3	−1	—
Britain	+1	+5	−1	—

* Figures given are percentages.
    Source: From data in Richard L. Merritt and Donald J. Puchala, eds., *Western European Perspectives on International Affairs: Public Opinion Studies and Evaluations* (New York: Frederick A. Praeger, 1967).

in explicit popular neutralism again preceded most of General de Gaulle's foreign policy moves emphasizing French independence.

German mass opinion data from 1960 and 1963 also permit a comparison between emotional attitudes toward certain countries and relatively rational policy preferences for closer relations with the same countries. The results show the smallest gap in German mass opinion between policy preferences and spontaneous emotions in the case of attitudes toward the United States (Table 17.2). The friendship to the United States and the weaker sympathies for Britain impose little strain on German mass emotions. The dissonance between policy choices and spontaneous emotions was somewhat larger in the case of German mass

Table 17.2

MASS EMOTION AND CURRENT POLICY PREFERENCES IN GERMAN ATTITUDES TOWARD FOUR COUNTRIES 1961-1963*

	1		2	3	
				Emotional Gap: Difference	
			Current Policy	**between Current Policy**	
GERMAN	**Mass Emotional**		**Preference:**	**Preference and Mass**	
ATTITUDES	**Attitude: "Good**		**"Need for Closer**	**Emotional Attitude†**	
TOWARD:	**Feelings"**		**Relations"**	**(Column 2 minus 1)**	
	Percentage		Percentage	Percentage	
	July 1961	Feb. 1963	Sept. 1963	July 1961	Feb. 1963
United States	73	76	90	17	14
Britain	53	49	65	12	16
U.S.S.R.	5	4	27	22	23
France	37	46	71	34	25

* Data in column 1 are from Richard L. Merritt and Donald J. Puchala, eds., *Western European Perspectives on International Affairs: Public Opinion Studies and Evaluations* (New York: Frederick A. Praeger, 1967). Data in column 2 are reported more completely on p. 149, n. 8, with references.
† The figures in column 3 are only approximate, since the polls were taken at different dates within the 2-year period, as indicated. The ranking, however, consistently shows the largest gap in the attitudes to France.

attitudes towards the U.S.S.R., and largest in the case of German mass attitudes towards France.

The strongest difference between French and German mass opinion in the analysis of these particular surveys is found in the area of international politics. Germans had a clearly favorable image of the Western Alliance and a clearly unfavorable one of the Soviet Union, while the French attitude toward symbols of Western unity or a "Western camp" was negative in 1962, and their anti-Russian posture was conditional and reserved. French popular opinion became increasingly pessimistic about NATO from 1957 to 1961, and in the confrontation of 1962 it continued to blame the United States for world insecurity, while being divided in blaming the Russians for recklessness. German mass opinion in the same situation, however, saw United States policy as directed toward world security and saw the Russians as acting recklessly. Generally, German mass opinion was markedly pro-American, while a French majority was so only with reservations, and a sizable French minority gave outright anti-American responses.

Generally, the increased similarity of French and German mass perceptions in 1962, as compared to 1957 and 1954, was not matched by any net increase in the similarity of French and German political values. Although Frenchmen and Germans had come to agree to an increased extent on what they saw in the world around them, they continued to disagree on what they liked. Whether continued disagreement on political values in a common perceptual world will make for more or for less political contention between the two nations, or whether it will make for a prolonged period of cross-pressures and relative immobility, remains to be seen.

CONTRASTING FRENCH AND GERMAN ELITE VIEWS OF FUTURE CHANGES

In regard to domestic politics, a majority of French elite members seems impressed with the persistence of the old French political forces and structures as they had existed before de Gaulle; and they expect that after de Gaulle many of these will reassert themselves at least to a significant extent. Many French respondents expect therefore that many of the changes initiated by the de Gaulle regime may not last, or may be counteracted by new and opposite changes after de Gaulle's departure from politics. French expectations thus tend toward only superficial short-run changes after de Gaulle, with relatively little net change in French society as the ultimate result. Thus, as reported earlier, 48 per cent think that the Fifth Republic is very likely to survive de Gaulle, and another 24 per cent give it some chance, making a total majority of 72 per cent of those willing to bet at least cautiously on its survival.[7]

At the same time, however, 70 per cent feel that the old political parties are not dead; 49 per cent also think that they will become stronger after de Gaulle, and another 24 per cent think that the parties will retain their present strength. While 57 per cent of the 113 elite respondents who made a forecast on this point do not expect a revival of the old "popular front" alliance of Communists, Socialists, and Radicals familiar from the 1930's, and while 50 per cent of our entire sample definitely oppose such a revival as undesirable, 48 per cent insist that the old conflict between the political Right and Left still remains im-

[7] Q. 14.

portant, as against 46 per cent who claim that this no longer is the case.[8] These expectations of French elite members in 1964 must be evaluated in the light of the 1965 presidential election, in which President de Gaulle won a 53 per cent majority only in the second round, and in which a "popular front" candidate, François Mitterand, received 32 per cent of the popular vote—a proportion corresponding very roughly to the traditional share of the main "popular front" parties, the Communists and Socialists, with a part of the Radicals added.

The overall impression from all these expressions of attitudes, and from the comments that went with them, is that Gaullism has not remade the persistent patterns of French politics, but rather that these patterns have influenced much of Gaullism, and that much of Gaullism, since it is responsive to many of these perennial patterns and psychic needs of French politics, is likely to endure with these core patterns much as they have endured, despite so many surface changes.

German expectations of change are quite different. Many German respondents consider the politics of the Nazi era and even of the Weimar Republic far more thoroughly buried, and they expect the institutions of the Bonn Republic to continue, including the processes of change which had been hopefully initiated during the 1950's. Consequently, they expect few or no important short-run changes in either domestic or foreign policies after Erhard's departure, but they show much greater confidence than the French that long-run changes have occurred, and that their consequences will continue to work out well.[9]

Thus, of the 152 German elite respondents who expressed their views, 87 per cent consider Nazism dead—63 per cent say so definitely, and another 24 per cent say so more cautiously "to all intents and purposes." Definite assertions of the death of Nazism are most often made by civil servants (86%), businessmen (75%) and leaders between 50 and 60 (72%); and they are least frequent among university professors (45%), non-business interest groups (48%) and the Junior Elite (53%).[10]

The possibility of a Nazi revival was discussed by 154 elite members. Of these, 6 per cent see a moderate possibility of such a revival, and another 46 per cent are willing to concede a minimal possibility

[8] Q. 8 and 15; Q. 5, 9 and 10.
[9] Q. 7, 32 and 33.
[10] Since only 152 German leaders commented on this point, all group percentages as given here were recomputed as percentages of the actual respondents in each group. Alternative computations on the basis of the entire sample, including the 21 nonrespondents, give much the same picture; Q. 11; Q. 12, by age and occupation.

for it, or for a possible revival in some modified form, but nearly one-half of the respondents—48 per cent—flatly deny all possibilities whatever of such a Nazi resurrection. These denials are most frequent among former Nazis (65%), and also among FDP members, civil servants, businessmen and elite members of lower middle-class backgrounds, while such confidence was weakest, and latent fears of a possible Nazi revival were strongest, among former anti-Nazis (67%), SPD members, university professors, non-business interest groups, upper class respondents, and, to a very slight extent, the young.[11]

Some possibility of an SPD government within the next 10 years is seen by 73 per cent of 159 articulate respondents; and 40 per cent consider it likely. A majority agrees, however, that there are only minor differences between the SPD and the major non-Socialist parties, and that an SPD government would make little difference to German foreign or domestic policies, except at most for such matters as some domestic economic policies, and the recruitment of political personnel. The Junior Elite sees most chances for an SPD government (55 per cent against only 24 per cent who think it unlikely), and more than three-fifths of this younger group also expect such an SPD government to produce some changes. Other groups with somewhat greater expectation of change from an SPD government are politicians, university professors and members of the SPD.[12]

At the same time, nearly one-half of 154 articulate respondents believe that the present governing party, the Christian Democratic Union (CDU/CSU), will remain at least as cohesive as it is now, and only 37 per cent expect it to become somewhat more divided by factional strife. The prospects presented by all these responses seem to be for stability, party compromises and continuing consensus.[13]

FRENCH-GERMAN DIVISIONS ON GERMAN REUNIFICATION AND EUROPEAN UNITY

French and German elite expectations differ strongly in regard to German reunification, as well as to European union. Of the 173 Ger-

[11] Q. 12; Q. 12, by age, occupation, class and current and past political affiliation. These elite views should be evaluated against the persistence of an extreme right-wing and pro-Nazi fringe of 5 to 10 per cent in German mass opinion polls, and the 8 per cent of votes cast for the neo-Nazi National Democratic Party in the 1966 state elections in Hessen and Bavaria.
[12] Q. 19; Q. 13 and 20; Q. 19 and 20, by age; Q. 20, by occupation and political affiliation.
[13] Q. 18.

man leaders in our sample, only 9 did not comment on this point, while over one-third of the French did not. Among the 164 articulate German respondents, 20 per cent definitely expect reunification to take place within the next 25 years, but only 2 per cent among the 92 articulate French do so. Another 38 per cent of the Germans have at least conditional hopes for reunification within the next quarter century, but only 11 per cent of the French agree with them; and 83 per cent of the Frenchmen commenting consider German reunification as at least unlikely within that period.[14]

The cleavage is strongest between the administrative elites of the two countries, followed by the politicians. German civil servants and politicians are the strongest supporters of reunification (87 and 84 per cent, respectively), and they show the largest shares of definite believers that it will be achieved within the next 25 years (33 and 22 per cent, respectively). Among French civil servants and politicians, a near-unanimous 93 and 94 per cent insist that German reunification will not come to pass within the next quarter century; some add "probably never."[15]

As to European unification, a strong plurality (46%) of the 158 German elite respondents who expressed their views gives it at least a moderate chance of succeeding—or making substantial progress— within the next 10 years, while 35 per cent feel that it probably or definitely will not succeed within that time. Among the corresponding French group of 141 articulate respondents to this question, only 19 per cent see even a moderate chance of success or at least substantial progress for European integration within a decade, and nearly one-half (49%) say that it probably will not be achieved or make much progress within that period.[16]

Among French age groups, Junior and Middle Elites are agreed in their pessimism about European integration within the next 10 years. Among French occupational groups, not a single military man expects that Europe will be united within the next 10 years, and 71 per cent of the military say that it will not.[17]

[14] See also pp. 267-268; Q. 39.
[15] Q. 37 and 39, by occupation.
[16] Q. 50.
[17] Q. 50, by age and occupation.

CHAPTER 18

Reliance on the United States and Britain, Divided Views on NATO: French and German Linkages and Clashes

French and German elites share a clearcut consensus on their basic dependence on the Atlantic Alliance for their military protection. They also share a confidence that the United States will not abandon Europe and that their own countries will continue to share common interests with the United States for a long time to come. In their views on these points, French elite members match more closely the views of their German counterparts, and less the mood in which President de Gaulle has sometimes attempted to reduce the importance of Atlantic ties.

CONTINUING STRATEGIC DEPENDENCE ON THE UNITED STATES

Large majorities of all elite respondents—90 per cent in Germany and 72 per cent in France—agree that their countries depend for their ultimate military security "completely" or "in large measure" upon the deterrent force of the United States. If one counts only the views of those 159 German and 137 French respondents who commented on this point, the percentages rise to 98 and 77, respectively. Here Frenchmen and Germans differ only in shades of emphasis: Most of the articulate Germans (76%), said "completely," while most of the articulate French (60%) preferred the term "in large measure." The overwhelming German consensus on this point becomes still stronger in view of the fact that in most of the German interviews the phrase "even in the presence of a national deterrent" was added to the question.[1]

Among the articulate French, the sense of dependence on the American deterrent predominates at all age levels but seems to decrease for the younger groups. Among the French Senior Elite, 85 per cent feel "completely" or "in large measure" dependent upon the United States in this respect; among the Middle Elite, 76 per cent, and among the Junior Elite, only 74 per cent do so. Among the West German elite, by contrast, age seems to make no difference.[2]

As regards occupations, the military in both countries agree—100 per cent in France, 93 per cent in West Germany—on their dependence, complete or in large measure, on the American deterrent. In France the average minority of 23 per cent of the entire articulate elite, who explicitly deny such ultimate dependence upon the United States, rises to 33 per cent among the businessmen and to 30 per cent among the civil servants. In West Germany, where no more than 2 per cent of all articulate elite respondents deny their ultimate dependence upon American nuclear protection, the only meaningful difference is between the great majority who believe this dependence to be complete (76%), and the somewhat more reserved minority who feel dependent only "in large measure" (22%). The majority of those who consider their ultimate dependence "complete" is highest among the West German military and the mass media leaders (93 and 91 per cent, respectively), and lowest among university professors and businessmen (56 and 66 per cent, respectively)—one of the rare cases where those last two groups see eye to eye.

Among the 102 French and 158 German respondents who expressed their views on the matter, large majorities—79 per cent in Germany and 65 per cent in France—feel sure that the United States is unlikely to

[1] Q. 75.
[2] Q. 75, by age.

abandon its commitments for the defense of Western Europe. Only 11 per cent of the French and 15 per cent of the Germans think this even conditionally probable. Here both French and German elite consensus differ specifically from the views of President de Gaulle, who has cast doubts on the reliability of the American commitment, but nearly one-third of the French leaders avoided giving an opinion on this point.[3]

Faith that the United States is unlikely to abandon its commitments to defend Europe is strongest in France among the politicians, the non-business interest groups, and the leaders over 60 years of age (74 per cent in each case). It is weakest among French Middle Elite (52%), the civil servants (53%) and the military (57%); and the overall 10 per cent minority who thinks the United States might abandon its commitments under some conditions rises to 29 per cent among the military and 23 per cent among the businessmen. Nonetheless, trust in American protection is expressed by clear majorities of the articulate French respondents in every group of age or occupation.

In West Germany, trust in the durability of the United States commitment to defend Europe is still higher, with an average of 79 per cent. It is strongest among the German military (93%), civil servants (87%), businessmen (83%) and the Senior Elite (83%), and weakest among university professors (60%) and the Junior Elite (67%). These last two groups also furnish the strongest minorities who think an American abandonment of European defense likely under some conditions (30 and 28 per cent, respectively, against 15 per cent for all articulate West German respondents). Here again, however, trust in the United States very much predominates in all groups.[4]

These feelings of trust are reinforced in both countries by the perception of long-run common interests, linking their own country and the United States, which are referred to by 88 per cent of the French leaders and by 72 per cent of the Germans, and which are rather uniformly strong in all groups of age and occupation in both countries.[5]

There is also agreement among 65 per cent of the German and 62 per cent of the French elite respondents that NATO can be relied on completely or to a considerable extent, with most Germans choosing the stronger and most Frenchmen the more cautious formulation. Opponents of NATO are in the minority: Eighteen per cent of the German and 30

[3] Q. 78.
[4] Q. 78, by age and occupation.
[5] Q. 35, by age and occupation.

per cent of the French leaders prefer to rely on NATO only "to a limited extent" or not at all.[6]

In Germany, such trust in NATO is strongest among the military (85%) and weakest among politicians (48%); it is also slightly above the average among the Junior Elite (69%) and slightly below among the Middle Elite (59%). In France, differences among occupational elites are smaller, but NATO is trusted most by the leaders of the non-business interest groups and the military (78 and 71 per cent, respectively), and least—but still substantially—by the intellectuals (56%). Differences among age groups are insignificant.[7]

A COMMON DESIRE FOR CLOSER TIES TO BRITAIN

Large majorities—68 per cent in Germany and 63 per cent in France—also agree that Britain ought to be included in an integrated Europe; this elite consensus again differs markedly from the policies favored by President de Gaulle. The French President's minor gestures of friendliness toward Britain in 1965 and 1966 may, in part, have been responsive to this mood. Common long-term interests with Britain are stressed by a majority of 52 per cent in France, but only by 28 per cent in Germany. The latter proportion is the same as that of German respondents perceiving common long-term interests with France, while 37 per cent of the French respondents see such long-term common interests with Germany. Common interests with the six EEC countries, including Germany and France, are perceived, however, by 35 per cent of the German and 88 per cent of the French elite members.[8]

In France, long-run common interests with Britain are rather evenly perceived in all age groups but are mentioned most often by members of non-business interest groups (63%), civil servants (62%) and politicians (61%), and least often by the military and the businessmen (29 and 32 per cent, respectively). In Germany, long-term common interest ties to Britain are relatively most popular among politicians and the Middle Elite age group (37% each), and least popular among the Senior Elite (15%), the civil servants (19%) and the businessmen (19%).[9]

[6] Q. 53.
[7] Q. 53, by age and occupation.
[8] Q. 35.
[9] The percentages given here are of total respondents, not of mentions, since most respondents mentioned more than one country; Q. 35, by age and occupation.

The same elite proportion of 28 per cent in Germany stresses common long-term interests with France, and 37 per cent in that country feel they share such common long-run interests with Germany. In addition, common interests with the other five EEC members, including Germany and France, respectively, are emphasized by 88 per cent of the French and 35 per cent of the German elite members.[10]

Long-term common interests with Germany are most strongly perceived by the French military and businessmen and most weakly by members of non-business interest groups. Age seems to make no difference; and common interests with the EEC countries are seen fairly evenly in all groups. In Germany, common interests with France are mentioned most often by the mass media leaders (38%), the businessmen (33%), the leaders of non-business interest groups (33%) and the Junior Elite (33%), but least often by the military and the Middle Elite (21 and 25 per cent, respectively).[11]

The result is somewhat paradoxical but fits in well with other evidence. In terms of political and military interests, as perceived by their own elites, France and Germany are linked together by their common ties to the United States, and to a lesser extent to Britain, more strongly than they are linked to one another directly or through the European Common Market. If this is so, then any weakening by either country of its ties to the United States might well have the result of enfeebling the weaker ties that now link France and Western Germany. In contrast to some pronouncements by President de Gaulle, the majority of French elite respondents prefers to keep France linked strongly to the United States and Britain—if this can be done on terms nearer to political equality.

DIVIDED VIEWS ON NATO

French aspirations to equality or near-equality in the status of a great power are involved in many of the cleavages between French and German views on NATO, and in the French preference for European arrangements. A reform of NATO, in the direction of greater equality and a greater European—and hence French and German—influence in the making of NATO policy, is endorsed by 78 per cent of the 117

[10] Q. 35.
[11] Q. 35, by age and occupation; percentages are of respondents, not of mentions.

French elite respondents who commented on this topic, as against only 47 per cent of the corresponding German group of 140 articulate respondents; and this smaller German pro-reform vote is partly offset by another substantial German minority of 38 per cent who say that NATO needs no reform—a complacent view shared by only 2 per cent of articulate French elite members.[12]

When asked to choose between a policy of strengthening mainly NATO or instrumentalities of European unity, such as EEC, 40 per cent of the 124 articulate French respondents to this question prefer EEC, against only 4 per cent who choose NATO. On the German side, only 14 per cent of the 141 respondents commenting on this topic pick EEC, while 11 per cent give priority to NATO, and a 72 per cent majority replies firmly "both"—a middle way that is also endorsed by a French plurality of 49 per cent. Any attempts by President de Gaulle, or by any successor, to force a choice between European and Atlantic commitments thus seems likely to be opposed from the outset by nearly three-quarters of the German and nearly one-half of the French leaders. Since no choice is likely to please both of the opposing minorities in each country that would be willing to make a choice, this means that any course toward pitting "Europeanism" against "Atlanticism" seems likely to be opposed by a majority of elite members in France and by a large elite majority in Western Germany.[13]

Occupational and age groups deviate only moderately from the average trend in their respective countries, but they do so in opposite directions. In France, belief in the compromise policy of strengthening both NATO and EEC declines among the younger leaders, from 63 per cent among the Senior Elite to 53 per cent for the Middle Elite and to a mere plurality of 47 per cent among the Junior Elite. The small minority of negative responses, rejecting both NATO and EEC, increases with youth, from no answers among the Senior Elite to 7 and 8 per cent among the Middle Elite and Junior Elite, respectively. Similarly, no one among the French Senior Elite prefers NATO, but 7 per cent of the Middle Elite and 6 per cent of the Junior Elite do so. In West Germany, belief in the compromise of strengthening both NATO and EEC is relatively weakest among the Senior Elite (53%), and strongest among the Middle Elite and the Junior Elite (65 and 64 per cent, respectively), but

---

[12] Since the data given here are summaries of 24 more detailed alternatives given by the respondents, no breakdown by age or occupation has been attempted; Q. 54.
[13] Q. 55.

preference for NATO is least popular among the Junior Elite, where no more than 3 per cent endorse it. In both countries, however, the young are slightly more oriented toward Europe: Forty per cent of the Junior Elite in France and 13 per cent of the Junior Elite in West Germany prefer to strengthen EEC—an attitude which makes each the relatively most "pro-European" of the three age groups in its country.[14]

As to occupational elites, none of the French military express preference for NATO; and in all groups such preferred support for NATO is minuscule. The compromise policy of strengthening both NATO and EEC finds most favor among businessmen and civil servants (56 and 52 per cent, respectively), who are the only French groups to give it majority support; and strengthening EEC is preferred most strongly among leaders of non-business interest groups (46%). In West Germany, by contrast, preference for NATO is relatively most popular among the military (20%) and the university professors (18%)—a somewhat uncommon combination, which may testify to the success of past United States policies aimed at each of these groups. Preference for NATO is least favored by West German businessmen (7%), mass media leaders (7%) and civil servants (8%). Strengthening Europe first is relatively most often supported by German civil servants and leaders of non-business interest groups (25 and 19 per cent, respectively). The compromise policy of strengthening both NATO and EEC is backed most strongly among West German politicians (by a majority of 75 per cent), in contrast to their French counterparts who do so only by a plurality of 40 per cent, the exact average level for all elites of their country.[15]

These divergent alignments of the age and interest groups of the elites of the two countries suggest that it would be almost no less difficult to bring France and Germany rapidly together on any common European or Atlantic policy than it would be to get them clearly and conspicuously apart. The elites of the two countries appear now to be enmeshed in a web of crosspressures, crosspurposes and divergent expectations, which would make any early major step toward either unity or separation of their policies quite difficult.

At the same time, the French elites' estrangement from NATO is spectacular, and seems to go far beyond any personal influence of President de Gaulle. So long as the French cannot come closer to NATO, and the German elites cannot compromise their commitment to both NATO

[14] Q. 55, by age.
[15] Q. 55, by occupation.

and EEC and to the rapprochement with France, the German Federal Republic's political and emotional relations to NATO are likely to be subject to strain.

Despite the reluctance of French, and even more of German, leaders to choose between Atlantic and European alignments, the ensemble of their replies to the various questions conveys a more subtle impression of a change which may not be demonstrable but may still be real. There seems to have been a shift in the attention and imagination of French and German leaders. Their reason, and their perceptions of military necessities, still tie them to the Atlantic. But their hearts, their vision, and imagination seem increasingly preoccupied either with Europe or with their own nation-state. The vision of a rich, multidimensioned and growing Atlantic community has faded.

CHAPTER 19

Differentiated French and German Views of Cold War Problems and International Relaxation

French and German elite members strongly agree in seeing in Communist states and activities the greatest threat to the security of their countries, and in opposing definitely the elimination of nuclear weapons from Central Europe solely, or the withdrawal of troops from that area alone. On these three topics, the majorities of articulate elite respondents are 76, 63 and 61 per cent for France and 70, 65 and 72 per cent for Germany, respectively.[1]

[1] Data for Q. 62 are percentages of all respondents. On Q. 91 and 93, articulate respondents numbered 65 and 87 for France, and 161 and 165 for Germany, respectively.

284

THE COMMON PERCEPTION OF A COMMUNIST THREAT

In both countries, the perception of a Communist threat is strongest among the 50- to 60-year-old leaders, but whereas the difference is large in France (91% against 70% and 69% for the Senior and Junior elites, respectively), it is only slight in West Germany (57%, against 53% and 54%, respectively, for the Senior and Junior elites).[2]

French fears of the Communist countries are strongest among politicians (87%) and the military (86%), and relatively weakest among the leaders of the non-business interest groups (59%). No Frenchman named Germany as a threat to France; but 5 per cent named the United States, and this minority rises to 15 per cent among the French intellectuals—a minority that once again suggests a possibly significant difference between the current attitudes of French and German intellectuals toward the United States, and perhaps also a difference in earlier United States policies toward the intellectuals of those two countries.

In West Germany, a threat from the Communist countries is perceived most strongly by the military (93%), the civil servants (88%) and the businessmen (78%), and least strongly by the university professors (43%) and the politicians (66%). Only one single German—a businessman—named the United States as a threat, but a minority of 8 per cent of all respondents says that the greatest threat to German security is Germany itself—either "West Germany" (5%) or "divided Germany" (3%); and the fear of West Germany itself as a threat rises to 29 per cent among the German university professors.[3]

Despite the perception of a Communist threat, European integration is seen as primarily nonmilitary in purpose. The Communist threat is perceived as chiefly military in nature in 59 per cent of the French responses, but only by 46 per cent of the 134 German elite members who give their views on this matter. Strengthening the West against Communism, however, is seen as the "primary value" of European integration only in 19 per cent of the French and 10 per cent of the German responses to this question, as against 45 per cent French and 67 per cent German responses emphasizing economic and cultural purposes of European integration, and another 35 per cent French and 22 per cent Ger-

[2] Q. 62, by age.
[3] Q. 62, by occupation.

man views which stress the purpose of enhancing Europe's political and diplomatic bargaining power.[4]

The nature of the chief threat to their country—which meant a Communist threat to 76 per cent of all French and 70 per cent of all German respondents, is defined as "military" by a 67 per cent majority of the 132 French leaders who comment on this question (and 20 of whom name two threats apiece); but their view is shared only by a plurality of 46 per cent of the 134 articulate Germans (who were recorded as naming only one threat each). Another 40 per cent of German answers refer to nonmilitary Communist threats of a political, ideological or social nature—a fear echoed in a negligible 3 per cent of the French answers. French and German leaders thus in part seem to see themselves as facing two different kinds of Communist threat. They agree, however, on one point: Not a single German, and only two Frenchmen, express any fear of Communist economic competition.[5]

Fear of a Communist military threat is stronger in both France and Germany among the Middle Elite than among either the younger or the older leaders. A minority of 16 per cent of the answers given by the French Junior Elite denies that there is any threat of any kind at all, but not a single German leader of any age appears to share this optimism. In France, the businessmen (78%) and the military (75%) are most insistent on seeing the Communist threat in military terms, but their view is shared by lesser but still substantial majorities among the politicians (69%) and the civil servants (59%); and only among non-business groups (38%) and intellectuals (46%) does it remain a minority view. In West Germany, by contrast, majorities of the military (54%) and the businessmen (52%) emphasize the nonmilitary versions of the Communist threat; and only among the mass media personnel (67%) and the civil servants (60%) does the image of a Communist military challenge find majority support, while remaining least popular among the university professors (21%) and the politicians (40%).[6]

The appeal of anti-Communism as a primary purpose for European integration declines in France among the younger leaders: it is endorsed by 27 per cent of the Senior Elite, but by only 18 per cent of the Middle

---

[4] On the latter question in Germany, 168 articulate respondents were recorded as naming one purpose each; in France, 144 such respondents named 357 purposes. Percentages are of responses in each case.

[5] Q. 62; Q. 63.

[6] Q. 63, by age; Q. 63, by occupation.

Elite and 16 per cent of the Junior Elite. In West Germany, anti-Communism as a primary European goal is least unpopular among the Middle Elite, 11 per cent of whom back it, but it is limited to no more than 5 per cent among both the Senior and Junior Elites.[7]

Among occupational elites, the military in both Germany and France furnish strong minority support for anti-Communism as a primary European task (29% in each country), but in France they are outdone in this respect by the political elite (35%). Economic and cultural tasks for European integration draw most support from German businessmen (79%) and university professors (76%); in France, these goals appeal most to civil servants and non-business interest groups (53% each). Strengthening the political power of Europe is not a very popular goal in either country, but seems relatively most attractive to French intellectuals (43%) and to the German military (29%).[8]

COMMON EXPECTATIONS OF GREATER FRIENDLINESS WITH EASTERN EUROPE

There is an overwhelming consensus among both French and German elite members that in the next few years relations between their nations and the countries of Eastern Europe will become more cordial. Of the 118 French respondents who state their views on this point, 99 per cent expect this, and they are joined in this by 83 per cent of the 162 German elite members who respond to the same question. These majorities are close to constituting a record in elite opinion surveys on topics of this kind, and particularly so in the case of France. A plurality of French respondents (48%) foresees more cordial cultural relations, whereas a German plurality (38%) expects more cordiality in politics.[9]

In France, the 99 per cent majority swamps all differences of age and occupation. In West Germany, more cordial relations with the countries of Eastern Europe are expected most widely among the non-business interest groups (93%)—that is, churches, farm groups and labor unions—and, interestingly enough, among the military (92%), followed by the politicians (89%) and the Junior Elite (86%).

[7] See also footnote 4 on p. 286; Q. 52, by age.
[8] See also footnote 4 concerning the meaning of percentages on this question; Q. 52, by occupation.
[9] Q. 45.

The relatively least optimistic group are the German mass media leaders, among whom only 70 per cent expect more cordiality with Eastern Europe during the next years.[10]

MISGIVINGS ABOUT PROPOSALS FOR GERMAN CONCESSIONS TO THE EAST

In regard to the boundaries and unity of Germany, however, the usual proposals for the relaxation of tensions are viewed with much less favor. A bare majority—52 per cent—of the 155 articulate German respondents to this question says that German recognition of the Oder-Neisse boundary with Poland would ease tensions in Central Europe, but they are backed by only a plurality of 42 per cent among the 52 French elite members who comment on the matter. A plurality of 41 per cent among the 153 German leaders who express their views also thinks that recognition of the Oder-Neisse Line might help German reunification, but they are supported by no more than 16 per cent of the 50 Frenchmen who give their views. Proposals for the recognition of East Germany are viewed as still less promising: Only 25 per cent of 153 articulate Germans, and 18 per cent of 55 articulate French leaders, think that it might ease international tensions.[11]

The German Junior Elite is still less optimistic than the older groups about the possible effects of a West German recognition of the East German regime: Only 18 per cent of the younger leaders—against 37 and 30 per cent among the Middle Elite and Senior Elite, respectively—think that it might at least somewhat aid German reunification. The members of the Junior Elite are more optimistic than their elders, however, about the possible effects of a recognition of the Oder-Neisse Line: Forty-seven per cent among them think that this might be at least some help to German reunification (against only 39 and 40 per cent, respectively, at the Middle and Senior age levels); and a 53 per cent majority of the Junior Elite—just as of the Middle Elite—think that recognizing the Oder-Neisse Line might do at least some good toward easing tensions in Central Europe (against only 49 per cent among the Senior Elite who think so).[12]

Among the French, this picture is reversed: Their Junior Elite expects far less from any recognition of the Oder-Neisse Line than do

[10] Q. 45, by age and occupation.
[11] Q. 44; Q. 43; Q. 42.
[12] Q. 42, by age.

the older groups. Only 29 per cent among the French Junior Elite favor recognition of the Oder-Neisse boundary, against 36 per cent among the Middle Elite and a majority of 54 per cent among French leaders over 60 years. Only 8 per cent of the French Senior Elite see any use in recognizing East Germany, as against 23 per cent among the Middle Elite and 16 per cent among the younger leaders. The younger French and German leaders may find it even harder to reach agreement on some of these matters than does the older generation.[13]

In Germany, the most hopeful occupational groups in regard to easing tensions in Central Europe through recognizing the Oder-Neisse Line are the university professors (86%) and the businessmen (59%). Most opposed to this policy, as useless or as likely to increase tensions, are the politicians (58%), the civil servants (53%), the military (50%) and the non-business interest groups (50%). In France, optimism about the benefits of an Oder-Neisse recognition is greatest among the non-business interest groups (55%) and the intellectuals (50%). Pessimism and opposition are strongest among the French military (80%) and the politicians (63%).[14]

The Communist-dominated regime of East Germany is viewed with far more misgivings than the Oder-Neisse boundary. In France, three-quarters of the 55 articulate respondents oppose East German recognition as unhelpful or dangerous. This opposition is strong in all groups but rises to 100 per cent among the military, 92 per cent among the politicians and 80 per cent of the businessmen. In West Germany, the average opposition of 61 per cent against recognizing the East German regime rises to 82 per cent among the politicians, 75 per cent among the military and 71 per cent of the civil servants. The optimistic minorities who hold that such recognition would ease international tensions are relatively strongest among the West German university professors (43%), media leaders (42%) and businessmen (30%).[15]

OPPOSITION TO ARMS REDUCTION
FOR CENTRAL EUROPE ONLY

The unpopularity among French and German elites of plans for regional relaxation or arms reduction in Central Europe alone appears

[13] Q. 42, 43 and 44, by age.
[14] Q. 44, by occupation.
[15] Q. 42, by occupation.

clearly in their attitudes toward the proposed denuclearization of Central Europe, which is backed by only 25 per cent of the 65 articulate French and 29 per cent of the 161 articulate German respondents. In Germany, this proposal finds majority support among the university professors (52%) and substantial minority support among the mass media personnel (43%) and the Junior Elite (31%). It is rejected as useless or worse by majorities in all groups except the university professors, and most emphatically so by the military (93%) and the civil servants (76%). Even among the 34 Social Democrats in our sample, only 5 (15%) favor the complete neutralization of Central Europe and 7 (21%) favor it conditionally, but 21 (62%) wholeheartedly oppose the idea.[16]

DIVERGENT FRENCH AND GERMAN LONG-TERM EXPECTATIONS

French and German elite groups produce parallel majorities in six of ten questions relating to the cold war complex, as just summarized. But even where their overt views agree, there are strong differences in saliency, and perhaps also in underlying expectations. On the one hand, a majority of German respondents endorses here a partial continuation of the "hard line" policy of Bonn in the hope that it will lead to a desirable shift in the power balance in a bipolar world, and eventually to German reunification. Many of the French respondents, on the other hand, who endorse the same "hard line" policy, expect it to produce no particular changes, but rather to preserve in an increasingly multipolar world the present German status quo.[17]

[16] Q. 91, by age, occupation and party.
[17] Q. 42-45, 52, 62-63 and 91-93.

CHAPTER 20

French-German Elite and Mass Agreement on Arms Control and Disarmament

French and German press, elite and mass opinion on disarmament and arms control will be reported elsewhere in greater detail.[1] Here it must suffice to indicate only some of the main findings.

THE RISING INTEREST IN ARMS CONTROL AND THE GROWING FRENCH-WEST GERMAN CONTRAST, 1946-1963: THE ATTITUDES OF THE EUROPEAN PRESS [2]

The machine content analysis of 1953 and 1963 editorials, reported in a preceding section, was limited to four elite papers and to editorials

[1] See Karl W. Deutsch, "Integration and Arms Control in the European Political Environment," *American Political Science Review*, 60 (June 1966), 354-365 and Karl W. Deutsch, *Arms Control and the Atlantic Alliance* (New York: John Wiley & Sons, 1967).

[2] Data in this section are from Richard L. Merritt and Ellen B. Pirro, "Press Attitudes to Arms Control in Four Countries, 1946-1963" (New Haven: Yale University, Political Science Research Library, mimeographed, 1966).

dealing with European or Atlantic integration. To supplement it, another content analysis operation was carried out on a larger number of newspapers and periodicals, from the same four countries, but focusing this time upon editorial responses to specific proposals or events relevant to disarmament or arms control. For this purpose, a list was compiled of ten such major proposals or events, with the first five items spanning the years from the Baruch Plan of 1946 to the Rapacki Plan of 1957, and the second five items, the years from Khrushchev's speech in 1959 to the nuclear test-ban in 1963. For editorial comments on these ten events, 97 newspapers and periodicals were searched, 35 from the United States, 29 British, 16 French and 17 German. A total of 655 issues were consulted for the relevant periods, and 370 editorials were found and analyzed.[3]

Within the selected periods, following major disarmament-related proposals or events, the general issue of disarmament and arms control was perceived as fairly salient. Over the entire period 1946-1963, editorial responses were found in an average of 58 per cent of the journal issues examined for the four countries. The general attitude toward efforts at disarmament or arms control was overwhelmingly friendly, with 63 per cent of all mentions favorable.

Over time, interest in arms control and disarmament rose substantially in all four countries, from an average of 43 per cent during 1946-57 to 70 per cent for the years 1959-63.

Specific arms control proposals were treated most often as serious and sincere, despite a minority current of comments labeling many of them as unrealistic or as propaganda. The emotional attitudes toward specific proposals, however, were fairly evenly divided; they were almost as likely to be negative as positive or neutral.

Among the four countries, most attention to arms control problems was paid by the press of the German Federal Republic (77%) and of France (61%), followed by that of the United Kingdom (48%) and the United States (45%). To the extent that these differences reflect reader interest, rather than the accidents of our very crude sample selection, they may indicate the existence of a significant reservoir of public interest in disarmament and arms control in Germany and France.

As targets of attention, Russia, the United States and France were the countries whose names and comments received most attention over the period as a whole, accounting for about two-thirds of all national

[3] See *ibid.* for lists of the events and publications.

comments reported. They were followed by Britain, Red China (and other Asian Communist countries) and West Germany, and further, at a considerable distance, by scattered references to other European nations, other West European nations, the East Asian allies of the United States and the members of three other Asian and African regional groupings.

Emotional attitudes toward nations varied. Toward the United States they were about 30 per cent friendly and 60 per cent neutral. Toward the Soviet Union they were most often negative (56%), or else neutral (34%). Toward Great Britain they were almost as often friendly (41%) as they were neutral (44%). Toward France and Germany they were predominantly neutral. Countries perceived as allies tended to get somewhat less attention than those seen as adversaries, such as Russia or Communist China. The attention-getting power of the United States, however, constituted a partial exception.

There was a frequent tendency in the press of the United States, France and Great Britain, respectively, to pay most attention to the proposals of its own government, and less attention to the proposals or moves of other countries. Although there were some exceptions to this— the German press paid a great deal of worried attention to many moves by other countries—the evidence confirms the familiar picture of the national press of each country conducting often a kind of national monologue rather than genuine cross-national communication within the Western Alliance. The attitudes and attention patterns of the French and German press were not markedly more similar between these two countries than they were between any one of them and either Great Britain or the United States.

THE DECLINE OF SPECIFIC PROPOSALS FOR ARMS CONTROL IN EUROPE, 1960-1964: THE EVIDENCE OF A SURVEY OF PROPOSALS FROM SIX MAJOR COUNTRIES, 1947-1964 [4]

A survey of 64 proposals, made between 1947 and 1964 from the United States, the Soviet Union, Britain, France, West Germany and Poland, for arms control or disarmament in Europe, included both official proposals and major public suggestions made by political leaders,

[4] Data in this section are from Bruce M. Russett and Carolyn C. Cooper, "Major Proposals for Arms Control in Europe: A Review" (New Haven: Yale University, Political Science Research Library, mimeographed, 1966).

parties or respected writers. Its findings are subject to the limitations that only proposals specifically focused on Europe were considered, that repetitions or minor variations of old proposals were excluded, and that some proposals may have been overlooked, but it seems likely that all salient Europe-centered proposals were included. The survey shows:

> French interest in arms control has been much lower than that of any other major country. During the 18 years covered, there were only 4 French proposals, two of which were made in 1959 by political leaders, who were out of office, Pierre Mendès-France and Jules Moch. No official French proposals were found after 1956, and no significant French proposals from any source after 1959.
>
> In rank order of frequency, proposals came most often from the Soviet Union (18), and the United States (14), followed by Britain (11), the German Federal Republic (10) and Poland (7), and, at a considerable distance, France (4).
>
> Over three-fifths of the proposals for Europe, made by government spokesmen of some kind, and nearly nine-tenths of the proposals from opposition leaders or private persons, fell into the five-year period from 1955 to 1959. During this peak period, official West and East bloc proposals were equally frequent. From 1960 onward, official proposals from the United States for European arms control diminished; Britain and Western Germany made no such official proposals at all, and by criteria of relevance for this report they contributed only one unofficial proposal apiece, and France contributed nothing at all. The East bloc countries, however—that is, the U.S.S.R. and Poland, continued in 1961-1964 to make proposals for Europe at nearly the same rate as in 1955-59, with a somewhat larger share of proposals coming from Poland.

This undiminished East bloc activity might have the possible effect of preempting some of the role of champions of European disarmament for the East bloc countries, but also of associating to some extent in the minds of West European elite members the entire topic of arms control with East bloc propaganda, so as to reinforce the partial withdrawal of West European elite interest from this topic. If Europe-centered United States proposals should again become salient and frequent, Western European elite interest might again increase.

The shift, however, in United States interest to more nearly world-wide approaches to arms control and disarmament, such as the 1963 Nuclear Test-Ban Treaty, accords well with the preferences of the French and German elite members, most of whom favor further world-wide arms control arrangements of this kind, but many of whom express misgivings about narrowly regional arms control arrangements for Central Europe alone, which they fear might leave the area unprotected in a world of military pressures.

SUPPORT FOR DISARMAMENT AND ARMS CONTROL

There are clear indications of anti-Communism, and of tough-mindedness in regard to disarmament, among majorities of both French and German elite respondents. Inspection arrangements are demanded or are desired as a safeguard in any East-West arms control agreement by 78 per cent of the articulate German elite members, but only by 38 per cent of the corresponding group in France.

Among the French and German elites, support for arms control and disarmament produces a striking number of strong and parallel majorities. Efforts to stop the proliferation of nuclear weapons "to countries that do not now possess them" are supported by articulate majorities of 78 per cent in France and 90 per cent in Germany. Discussions of disarmament are favored by 69 per cent of the articulate French respondents and 76 per cent of their German counterparts; 20 per cent among the French supporters of disarmament discussions say, however, that the idea is utopian but worth discussing anyway. Some plan for arms control is endorsed by 66 per cent of French and 61 per cent of German responses, and only 17 and 30 per cent, respectively, do not favor any plans. The 1963 American-British-Soviet Nuclear Test-Ban Treaty—which France has not joined—is endorsed by a French plurality of only 46 per cent, but by a strong majority of 84 per cent in Germany.

Further arms control and disarmament agreements are definitely backed by 52 per cent of the 134 French and again by 84 per cent of the 165 German respondents who comment on the matter. Even if their own countries should not be consulted about future arms control agreements, 55 per cent of the 129 articulate French respondents and 65 per cent of the corresponding 152 Germans still are willing to support them. German mass opinion in mid-1964 took the same view by a majority of 71% of all those with definite opinions on this point.[5]

[5] Survey by Institut für angewandte Sozialwissenshaft (ifas), Bad Godesberg, Summer 1964 ($N = 1,833$). Further U.S.-Soviet arms control agreements were backed by 80 per cent of respondents in the mass opinion poll. When asked about such agreements being readied without consultation with the West German government, many German voters appeared undecided. Thus, 24 per cent could not envisage such a possibility; and among the 76 per cent who could envisage it, 31 per cent had no opinion or did not know. Among the remaining 45 per cent who did have opinions, however, 31 per cent favored such agreements, with 13 per cent in opposition.

THE LACK OF POPULAR SUPPORT FOR NATIONAL NUCLEAR DETERRENTS AND MLF PROPOSALS

The idea of a national nuclear deterrent is unpopular among the elites in France, where it is official government policy, and still more unpopular among the elites of Germany, where it sometimes has been described—by outside observers—as a possible latent aspiration. In fact, it seems to be not even that. A national nuclear deterrent is rejected as unnecessary for national prestige or national independence, and as not credible to the nation's enemies, by majorities ranging between 54 and 63 per cent in France, and 64 and 94 per cent in Germany.

France's current national *force de frappe* is not expected to survive President de Gaulle. Only 22 per cent of all French respondents expect it to be kept and strengthened, while 49 per cent expect it to be turned into a European institution, and another 6 per cent expect it to be abandoned.

Although clear majorities reject the main arguments in favor of a national nuclear deterrent, French respondents are exactly divided between 46 per cent who feel that such a deterrent still is worth its cost, and the same proportion who feel that it is not.

There is no such division in West Germany where the thrifty rejection of a national nuclear deterrent as not worth its cost is backed by a landslide majority of 96 per cent of the 163 German respondents to this point. This German majority is so large as to swamp all differences among age or interest groups.

These massive German elite data tend to disconfirm the notion of a supposedly strong German desire for national nuclear weapons—a desire which would have to be bought off or headed off by offering the German Federal Republic some share in a supranational nuclear weapons system. So far as our evidence goes there is no such German desire for national nuclear weapons at this time.

A multilateral nuclear force (MLF) under NATO is clearly favored by only 18 per cent, and clearly opposed by 27 per cent of the 100 French respondents who comment on this proposal. In Germany, where practically all respondents comment, the same proposal divides the elites exactly, with 34 per cent clearly in favor and an equal 34 per cent definitely opposed. This last division contrasts sharply with the usual propensity for strong elite consensus in the Bonn Republic.

A European multilateral nuclear force, independent of NATO,

would be somewhat more popular among elites in France, where a plurality of 40 per cent of 134 respondents clearly favors it, with only 12 per cent clearly opposed, but it would be much less popular in Germany, where no more than 6 per cent of 168 respondents back the project, while a solid 80 per cent express their clearcut opposition.

If a multilateral nuclear force within NATO should come into existence, only 16 per cent of the 102 French respondents to this question would definitely wish their country to participate, but another 43 per cent might agree to such a course under certain conditions. Among the 160 German respondents to the same question these proportions are reversed: Fifty-eight per cent clearly favor participation in such a NATO development, with another 13 per cent supporting it conditionally; and only 17 per cent definitely oppose it.

The proportions of the various responses to these and related questions confirm an impression from our interviews: There is no substantial German pressure for an MLF, but rather a willingness to go along with such a scheme, if Germany's ally, the United States, should insist on it.

The pattern of responses to this entire complex of questions suggests that neither French nor German elites are pressing strongly at this time for nuclear weapons, either national or collective. Rather, the issues of the national deterrent and the MLF tend to evoke opposition or division. This contrasts with the high majorities in both countries in favor of arms control.

The evidence of the elite survey, as far as it goes, accords well with the data from mass opinion polls and the other types of evidence examined in this study. All of this evidence is limited and incomplete, and must be appraised with judgment. At the same time it should be borne in mind that none of the evidence we have found, in terms of differences among age groups or of trends over time, points to the likelihood of any drastic changes in the next few years. If such drastic changes in French or West German attitudes or policies should occur during the next decade, they are likely to come as a result of drastic changes in the arena of world politics rather than of any autonomously developing changes in the French or West German political system.

In terms of these limitations and considerations, several conclusions can be drawn from our study, and it is in these terms that they should be evaluated.

CHAPTER 21

Conclusions

The lines of evidence pursued in our inquiry tend to converge. Although there are minor differences, the weight of evidence brings out several major points.

THE STRENGTH OF NATIONALISM

The movement toward structural European unification since 1957 has been largely halted or very much slowed down. The next decade of European politics is likely to be dominated by the politics of nation-states, and not by any supranational European institutions. In this regard and for this period, the views of President de Gaulle, that only nation-states will be obeyed and supported by the population, and the view of Raymond Aron, that there will be no European federation—even for the next twenty years—seem to be borne out by the great preponderance of all the data that we have examined.

Within France, and within Germany, the various elite groups generally are closer in their attitudes to each other, and to the mass opinion of their own country, than they are to the opinion of their counterparts in the other country. Nationality continues to be a far stronger determinant—or indicator—of political attitudes than are class, age, occupation, religion, party affiliation and, even for most respondents, ideology. At present, it appears that the nation-states are continuing their hold on the minds of both leaders and masses in Western Europe; and they are likely to continue to do so for the next decade.

A provisional factor analysis of our elite survey data confirms this finding.[1] Its results suggest that nationality seems to be between two and ten times as powerful as any one cross-national factor, such as religion, occupation, socialist party affiliation, etc., in accounting for the distribution of responses.

To restore in the mid-1960's to the movement toward European unification once again the vigor and the momentum of the years 1947-1955 would require much larger efforts on the part of Europeans and of the United States than seem to be contemplated now in any quarter of authority. In terms of economics, it might require an input of a scale as large as that which Marshall Plan aid was in relation to the shrunken European economies of 1948, and hence it might have to be correspondingly larger in the 1960's. In politics, it would require a visible increase in the share of American attention fixed on Europe rather than on Asia. It would need a broadening of emphasis beyond predominantly defense-oriented and military concerns to more inclusive economic, cultural and social patterns of integration; and it would also require a reorientation of the priorities of attention and policy of the French and West German elites and governments. No indication of the likelihood of any of these changes is currently in sight. There is not now enough

---

[1] The provisional data are given in Helga Voss-Eckermann, "French and German Elite Interviews, 1964: A Factor Analysis" (New Haven: Yale University, Political Science Research Library, mimeographed, 1965). This report includes three analyses: 1. France (45 questions); 2. West Germany (43 questions); and 3. France and West Germany, treated as a single country (37 identical questions asked in both).

These findings were further confirmed by a comparison of so-called "Tau Alpha" and "Tau Beta" coefficients for a large number of our questions. These coefficients indicate the extent to which such background conditions as age, occupation and nationality seem to account for the distribution of answers given by our respondents. The results of this computation suggest again that among our respondents the influence of country or nationality tends to be several times stronger than that of such cross-national conditions as age or occupation. See the rank-order data on Tau coefficients on file at Yale University, Political Science Research Library.

general consensus between France and Western Germany to sustain a major common policy, and even less a common body politic, either at the level of mass opinion or at the level of the elites. The development of such a basic consensus is likely to require far more than ten years, even under favorable conditions.

THE DESIRE FOR ALLIANCES AND NEAR-EQUALITY

Alliances, particularly with the United States, and limited steps toward additional supranational arrangements and institutions are popular among elites and acceptable to mass opinion. National isolationism is being rejected, but increasing national equality—or perhaps a share in great power privilege—is being demanded, particularly by the elites of France.

THE DESIRE FOR WIDER ARMS CONTROL AND DISARMAMENT

There is a striking consensus in France and Germany on the desirability of arms control and disarmament on a more than local or regional scale, and including further direct agreements between the United States and the Soviet Union. There is a particularly strong consensus on the desirability of halting the spread of nuclear weapons to nations which do not now possess them.

THE LACK OF ANY STRONG GERMAN DEMAND FOR NUCLEAR WEAPONS

There is at present strong opposition in Germany against the acquisition of national nuclear weapons, and there is no strong positive desire for any German share in a nuclear weapons system through some multilateral arrangement, such as the MLF project; and there is overwhelming and deep-rooted French hostility to any idea of a German national nuclear weapon, or to a substantial German share in a multilateral nuclear weapons system.

300

THE POSSIBLE EUROPEAN SUPPORT FOR A NUCLEAR NON-PROLIFERATION TREATY

Under these conditions of European politics, the most nearly acceptable approach to arms control and disarmament might be an international agreement limiting the possession of nuclear weapons to those five powers now possessing them: the United States, Britain, France, the Soviet Union and Communist China.

These five are the governments in control of the five countries whose special importance is recognized in the United Nations Charter by giving them the status of Permanent Members of the United Nations Security Council. The legal status of Communist China is currently blocked in this respect, but her acquisition of a nuclear device has been tacitly tolerated by all other nuclear powers; and an explicit or tacit nuclear *modus vivendi* with Communist China does not seem unacceptable to European leaders.

Even without an agreement with China, an anti-proliferation agreement and extended nuclear test-ban among the "Big Four"—the United States, the United Kingdom, France and the Soviet Union—might prove feasible, and might pave the way to further steps to arms control. Such an approach might meet some of the French desire for a full and genuine share in international leadership; and our data suggest that such an accommodation of French desires on the part of the United States and Britain would be acceptable to the majority of the West German leaders.

The picture emerging from this study is complex but not without hope. At moments of crisis, when the chips are down, the main ties of Western unity will be to Washington rather than among the European countries. For the next decade at least, national political issues will predominate over supranational ones in both France and Western Germany. Viable alliances during this period will have to be concluded on specific matters, among sovereign powers, and on a footing of equality, particularly in regard to France. Greater unity of action, as well as deeper emotional ties in Western Europe, are growing very slowly. In terms of European unification, we may expect after 1975 a possible resumption of the advances of the 1950's, but not much earlier. Until then we can expect to hold the present plateau and improve it slightly.

Western Europeans on the whole, if French and German leaders are representative of their opinions, now favor worldwide measures of arms control. They favor particularly the relaxation of tensions between the great powers, extensions of the ban on nuclear testing, and measures against the proliferation of nuclear weapons to any countries not now possessing them. They favor all these policies, however, only provided that they can keep the American alliance and the American nuclear shield. Within this very wide range of policies acceptable to Europeans, the United States at this time has a remarkably wide range of discretion and perhaps an unparalleled opportunity for leadership.

This American opportunity would diminish, one may judge, to the extent that Europeans should come to feel that the United States was so preoccupied in Asia, or so inclined to put its own national judgment in important foreign policy matters ahead of and above the judgments of its European partners, that basic European interests in an essential measure of equality and security would seem to them endangered. The increased American involvement in 1965 and early 1966 in the Vietnam war did evoke or enhance concerns of this kind in some European circles, particularly in France. Since there is also in some European quarters a limited degree of verbal and press support for the Asian policy of the United States, the total effect of greater American involvement in Asia is likely to increase the divisions of opinion within and among the European countries and to decrease their responsiveness to American initiatives. To the extent that the continuing evolution of American policy should succeed in containing or abating such European fears and divisions, or that American involvement in Asia should remain visibly limited, the American opportunities for leadership in Europe in regard to arms control, security and the wider concerns of the Western Alliance would remain open.

Appendix

EUROPEAN ELITE INTERVIEW QUESTIONNAIRE
(Summer 1964)

This questionnaire takes the form of an "open-ended" interview schedule. The interview is to cover four major areas of inquiry: *Domestic Affairs, Foreign Policy and International Relations, European Alliances and Integration,* and *Arms, Arms Control and Disarmament.*

Although this interview is to be open-ended, there are, concerning each area of inquiry, a number of salient points or issues. Interviewers should probe for attitudes concerning these salient points in their follow-ups to the main questions phrased below. A list of salient points precedes each set of questions.

I. DOMESTIC AFFAIRS

Salient Points

a. Respondent's evaluation of the current regime in his country; his feelings concerning the permanency of the current form of government and its institutions; personnel changes that he thinks either likely or unlikely.

b. Respondent's evaluation of the structure of the political system in his country; who has the power; has the distribution of political influence among social groups changed since World War II; is it likely to change again in coming years?

c. Respondent's impression of the political process in his country; where are the great domestic cleavages?

d. Respondent's evaluation of the cohesiveness of his society.

Questions

1. Are you content with the present governmental system in (France) (Germany)?

2. What are the positive features of the present form of government?

3. What are the most important cleavages and conflicts in (French) (German) politics today?

FRANCE	GERMANY
a. Do you believe that the conflict between left and right is as important today as before World War II? What do you think constitutes the major difference between the principal parties today?	**a.** What do you think constitutes the major differences between the principal parties today?
b. Do you believe that any specific social group or groups have gained political power in recent years? For instance, do you think that the army, the civil service bureaucracy, or financial interests have gained in political influence recently? What about the scientists and technicians?	**b.** Do you believe that any specific social group or groups have gained political power in recent years? For instance, do you think that the civil service bureaucracy, or economic interest groups, or the clergy have gained or lost political influence recently? What about the press, professors, and informal groups?

c. (Ask in both countries) To what extent and in what ways do you see the governmental system affected by the changing political power of the groups we have talked about?

d. Are the "old parties" dead? Do you expect to see a revival of the popular front? Would you favor such a revival?	**d.** Is Nazism dead? Do you foresee any possibility of a Nazi revival?

4. What would be likely developments in (French) (German) domestic politics over the next ten years?

FRANCE	GERMANY
a. Do you expect the Fifth Republic or any of its features to continue to exist after General de Gaulle leaves the political scene?	**a.** Do you expect the Chancellor, the Bundestag, or the Länder to become of greater or lesser importance over the next several years, or will the balance of the past continue about the same?
b. What role will the parties play after de Gaulle leaves the political scene?	**b.** What about the CDU; is it likely to become more cohesive, less cohesive, or remain about the same over the next several years?
	c. Do you see prospects for an SPD government? If so, do you think that an SPD rise to power would mean a significant change in the political system of Germany?

5. How will (French) (German) society react to a major upheaval in the world?

II. FOREIGN POLICY AND INTERNATIONAL RELATIONS

Salient Points

a. Respondent's perception of the structure of international politics; is it increasingly bipolar or decreasingly bipolar; what is respondent's evaluation of changes in the international system?

b. Respondent's definition of his nation's national interest; how may it be best pursued and protected?

c. Respondent's evaluation of the foreign policy of the current regime; what changes in foreign policy are likely; what features of the current foreign policy are likely to continue over time?

d. Respondent's feelings about German and East European questions and respondent's suggestions for ways to ease tension in Central Europe.

e. Respondent's own position and evaluation of the following foreign policy orientations: Nationalist, (in France) Gaullist, Atlanticism.

Questions

6. Some people say that the domination of world politics by America and Russia is disappearing. They say that in the future, as in the past, many nations will again be masters of their own independent foreign policies.

   a. Do you agree with this observation?

   b. Would you favor such a trend in world affairs?

7. Some people say that an independent foreign policy for a nation with the resources of (France) (Germany) is outmoded. Others say that in spite of all this talk about cooperation between various countries in alliance, when a nation's vital interests are at stake, it has to act according to those interests and disregard everything else.

   a. How do you feel about these questions?

   b. What, in your estimation, is the best way for this country to defend its national interests at the present time?

   c. Do you think that such policies will continue to be feasible in the future?

8. Do you in general approve or disapprove of (de Gaulle's) (the German government's) actions in international politics?

   a. What in your opinion are the most significant features of (de Gaulle's) (Germany's) foreign policy?

   b. What developments in (French) (German) domestic politics are most likely to bring about a change in (French) (German) foreign policy?

   c. Do you believe that any features of (de Gaulle's) (Erhard's) foreign policy will be continued after he leaves the political scene? Which ones?

   d. (Ask in France only) In speaking to leaders in other countries of Europe we gained the impression that nothing seems to puzzle them more than de Gaulle's reference to a "manifest destiny" for France—this country's obligation to be great. Do you agree that France has such a destiny? How do you define it?

9. With which of the following countries, in your opinion, will (France) (Germany) continue to share common interests for a long period?

   > Great Britain
   > (Germany)
   > (France)
   > United States
   > Russia
   > The countries of the Common Market

   a. (Ask in France only) What do you see as the major source of friction between France and the United States at the present time?

   b. (Ask in Germany only) What do you see as the possible major sources of friction that might arise or are arising between the United States and Germany?

10. Many people consider the reunification of Germany one of the world's most critical unsolved international problems. How do you feel about the whole question of German reunification?

    a. (Ask in France only) What do you think is the French interest in the reunification of Germany?

b. Do you expect Germany to regain her unity in the next twenty-five years?

c. Do you believe that the status of Berlin will be changed? What would you consider an acceptable and what an unacceptable change of the present situation in Berlin?

d. Do you think that the recognition of East Germany (the D.D.R.) will substantially ease international tensions?

e. What do you think would be the effect of a recognition of the Oder-Neisse Line on German reunification?

f. Do you think that recognition of the Oder-Neisse Line will substantially ease tension in Central Europe?

g. Do you foresee any substantial change in this country's relations with the nations of Eastern Europe in the next several years?

III. EUROPEAN ALLIANCES AND INTEGRATION

Salient Points

a. Respondent's impression of the desirability of European union and his feelings about the feasibility of such a union at present and in the next several years.

b. Respondent's impression of the possible nature and extent of European union; does he think Europe will take the form of a confederation, a federation, etc.; which countries does he feel should and would be included in this European union?

c. Respondent's evaluation of the purpose and importance of European union.

d. Respondent's feelings about his country's membership in NATO and other regional and international organizations.

e. (For Germany) Presumed effects on chances of reunification; possible conflict between European union and opportunity for German reunification.

Questions

11. Most people agree that since World War II the general trend in Western Europe has been toward limiting national sovereignties in favor of international associations.

    a. How strongly is the (French) (German) policy oriented toward further limitations of national sovereignty?

    b. To what extent do you favor policies in this direction?

12. There is much discussion nowadays about European integration. Suggestions have been made concerning different forms of European unity

ranging all the way from simple cooperation among sovereign states to the merging of all states into one centralized European state. What form of union most nearly describes an integrated Europe as you usually think of it?

a. What countries do you think should be included in this European union?

b. How likely is it that such integration will be achieved in the next several years?

c. Is it more likely that some different form of European union will be achieved?

d. What do you think the map of Europe will look like in 1975?

13. What, in your thinking, would be the primary value of a united Europe? That is, what do you think is the purpose of European integration?

14. At the present time to what extent can (France) (Germany) rely upon NATO to protect her security?

a. (If "can't rely upon NATO") In what ways do you think the structure of the NATO alliance should be changed so that (France) (Germany) can rely upon NATO to protect its security?

b. Do you think (France) (Germany) should work primarily to strengthen NATO, to strengthen European unity, or do you feel that the two are compatible and that to strengthen one is also to strengthen the other?

c. There has been talk of an internationally controlled nuclear force for NATO. What do you think of this attempt?

d. If such a force came about, should (France) (Germany) be a part of it?

e. Do you think all members of the alliance should have equal voice in deciding when and whether nuclear weapons should be used? Who should control the nuclear force?

f. To what degree could (Western Germany) (France) rely on (France) (Western Germany) to protect her security?

g. (Ask in Germany only) How would that be affected by the demise of de Gaulle?

IV. ARMS, ARMS CONTROL AND DISARMAMENT

Salient Points

a. Does respondent feel his security threatened; what is the nature of the threat; what defense may be taken against the threat?

b. Does respondent see any purpose in a national nuclear deterrent for any country that does not now possess nuclear weapons, that is, what are his views on the question of nuclear proliferation?

c. What form of arms control or disarmament arrangement does the respondent think will be most effective in reducing the threat of war; what form of arms control or disarmament arrangement does respondent feel might be feasible to both East and West at the present time and ultimately?

d. Is arms control a military or a political question in the respondent's mind; is the substance of the agreement most crucial (i.e. "reach the agreement in any way as long as the military threat is reduced") or is the procedure by which the agreement is reached most crucial (i.e. "we will respect an agreement reached only if our country has been consulted in the negotiation and given its approval")?

Questions

15. What is the greatest threat to (French) (German) security at the present time? How long do you think the threat will continue?

    a. Is there a military threat?

    b. What form does it take?

    c. What do you think would be the best defense against this threat? That is, what kind of forces, and what kind of weapons? (Probe: for views on multilateral vs. unilateral forces, etc.)

    d. How likely is it that a war will break out between European countries?

16. What do you think is (would be) the purpose of a national nuclear deterrent?

    a. Do you feel that having a national deterrent is a necessary condition for (French) (German) independence?

    b. Do you feel a national deterrent is necessary for (French) (German) prestige in the world?

    c. Do you think that a nuclear deterrent for this country is (would be) worth the cost?

    d. Do you think this nation's national deterrent is (would be) credible to the nation's enemies?

    e. (Ask in France only) If de Gaulle were to disappear from the political scene, what, in your judgment, is likely to happen to the *force de frappe?*

    f. (Ask in Germany only) If de Gaulle and his *force de frappe* were to disappear, what would be the effect of the situation on Germany?

    g. In spite of (this country's national deterrent) (talk in this country about building a national deterrent), is it not true that (French) (German) military security depends ultimately upon America's nuclear striking force?

h. How likely is it that America will ever use its striking force to protect the security of a European ally? Under what circumstances do you think the United States would use its striking force?

i. How likely is it that the United States would abandon its commitment to defend Western Europe? What would be your feelings if the United States did adopt a "fortress America" policy?

17. Do you think that efforts should be made to halt the proliferation of nuclear weapons to countries that do not now possess such weapons? In your view which countries should possess nuclear weapons and which countries should not?

    a. What would be your judgment if East Germany or another Eastern European country were to acquire nuclear weapons?

18. Would you prefer the creation of a European atomic striking force independent of NATO? How do you feel about the creation of a European army conventionally armed? Would you favor the EDC today?

19. The USA and USSR recently concluded a bilateral agreement banning nuclear testing in the atmosphere. Do you approve of this East/West agreement?

    a. How do you feel about the fact that (France) (Germany) was not consulted during the negotiation of this agreement between the USA and the USSR?

    b. Would you favor further arms control and reduction agreements between the USA and the USSR?

    c. Do you think (France) (Germany) should be consulted in the negotiation of these further agreements?

    d. Would you prefer further arms control agreements even if this nation were not consulted?

20. For many years statesmen and negotiators from both the East and the West have been offering alternative schemes for arms control and disarmament, some of them dealing with problems of arms control in Europe and others more universal in scope. Are you familiar with any of these arms control schemes? Do you favor any of them more than others?

    a. Do you think that the prohibition of nuclear weapons in Central Europe would ease the threat of military conflict in that area?

    b. How do you feel about the complete neutralization of Central Europe?

    c. Should foreign troops be withdrawn from Western and Eastern European countries? Would such a troop withdrawal substantially ease international tensions?

    d. Do you think an arms reduction agreement between East and West should be enforced by inspection? What do you think would be the most feasible form of inspection?

e. Do you see any chance that an arms control agreement would result in some danger to the security of West Berlin? If disarmament and arms control can only be had at the expense of reducing the security of West Berlin, would you still be in favor?

f. Do you think progress toward reducing international tension through disarmament is possible, or is the whole question of arms control and disarmament a figment of "wishful thinking"? Can you foresee conditions that will make international arms control more possible?

Table A.1

SELECTION OF FRENCH RESPONDENTS

	Contacted	Positive Answers		Interviewed		
		Number	as % of Contacted	Number	as % of Contacted	as % of Positive Answers
Political Leaders	141	71	50	32	22.6	45
MRP	9	4	44	2	22.2	50
Gaullists	45	19	42	12	26.7	63
Communists	10	0	0	0	0	0
Radicals	16	8	50	6	37.5	75
Socialists	14	9	64	8	57.1	89
Independents and Conservatives	22	11	50	4	18.2	36
Local Officials—Mayors, etc.	25	20	80	0	0	0
Military	19	7	37	7	36.8	100
Intellectuals, Mass Media	72	41	57	30	41.7	73
Civil Service	113	62	55	32	28.3	52
Trade Unions and Prof. Assoc.*	54	35	65	27	50.0	77
Business	42	20	48	19	45.2	95
Total	441	236	54	147	33.3	62

* Includes two members of the Communist Party.

Table A.2

SELECTION OF WEST GERMAN RESPONDENTS

	Contacted	Positive Answers		Interviewed		
		Number	as % of Contacted	Number	as % of Contacted	as % of Positive Answers
Political Parties	133	93	70	38	29	41
CDU/CSU	72	48	67	17	24	34
Federal Ministers	17	9	53	5	29	56
Federal Legislators	35	24	69	8	23	33
Länder Ministers	11	8	73	2	18	25
Others	9	7	78	2	22	29
SPD	41	30	73	15	37	50
Federal Legislators	21	15	71	9	43	60
Länder Ministers	11	9	82	5	45	56
Others	9	6	67	1	11	17
FDP	20	15	75	6	30	40
Federal Ministers	4	2	50	2	50	100
Federal Legislators	12	9	75	3	25	33
Länder Ministers	3	3	100	1	33	33
Others	1	1	100	0	0	0
Administration	134	100	75	30	22	30
Civil Service	94	68	72	16	17	24
General	83	58	70	12	14	21
Judiciary	11	10	91	4	36	40
Military	40	32	80	14	35	44

Table A.2
(continued)

	Contacted	Positive Answers		Interviewed		
		Number	as % of Contacted	Number	as % of Contacted	as % of Positive Answers
Business	136	96	71	36	26	38
Industry and Commerce	120	85	71	31	26	36
Banking	16	11	69	5	31	45
Non-Business Interest Associations	91	71	78	27	30	38
Trade Unions	14	12	86	7	50	58
Churches	19	13	68	4	21	31
Roman Catholic	9	6	67	2	22	33
Protestant	7	5	71	2	29	40
Other	3	2	67	0	0	0
Others	58	46	79	16	28	35
Communications	156	121	78	42	27	35
Mass Media	114	87	76	21	18	24
Press	69	54	78	15	22	28
Radio-TV	37	30	81	4	11	13
Other	8	3	38	2	25	67
Universities	42	34	81	21	50	62
Social Sciences, History, Law	34	27	79	16	47	59
Natural Sciences	8	7	88	5	63	71
Total	650	481	74	173	27	36

Index